PRICKLY PEAR

THE SOCIAL HISTORY
OF A PLANT IN THE EASTERN CAPE

Nowinile Ngcengele picking prickly pear fruit (Opuntia ficus-indica),
near Grahamstown (see Chapter 1)

PRICKLY PEAR

THE SOCIAL HISTORY
OF A PLANT IN THE EASTERN CAPE

WILLIAM BEINART

and

LUVUYO WOTSHELA

WITS UNIVERSITY PRESS

Wits University Press
1 Jan Smuts Avenue
Johannesburg
South Africa
www.witspress.co.za

William Beinart is Rhodes Professor of Race Relations, African Studies Centre,
University of Oxford, United Kingdom.
Luvuyo Wotshela is a researcher, University of Fort Hare History Project, South Africa.

First published 2011

ISBN 978 1 86814 530 0

Edited by Lara Jacob
Proofread by Julie Miller
Cover design by René de Wet
Layout and design by René de Wet
Printed and bound by Paarl Media

CONTENTS

PREFACE

We have aimed to write this book on the prickly pear for a general audience. About half the book (especially Chapters 2-5) is largely based on documentary sources, and the other half (Chapters 1 and 6-9) largely on interviews and observation. We have tried to cross-reference throughout. We did some interviews separately and some jointly. We have decided not to identify the specific interviewers on each occasion. Broadly speaking, we did the interviews and observations in Fort Beaufort township, and on some farms, together. Luvuyo Wotshela did the great bulk of interviewing in the former Ciskei while William Beinart (sometimes assisted by Troth Wells, who also took a number of the photographs) did most of the interviews with experts.

The original archival research was mostly done in the 1990s as part of a larger project funded by a British Academy grant. Interviews and subsequent research were funded by a grant from the Nuffield Foundation, UK, by the Rhodes Chair of Race Relations, University of Oxford, and by the Govan Mbeki Research Office, Travel and Subsistence Fund, University of Fort Hare. The Oppenheimer Fund at the University of Oxford made it possible for Luvuyo Wotshela to visit Oxford for a spell of joint writing. The Nuffield Foundation grant was held jointly with Dr Karen Middleton, with whom William Beinart co-authored some preliminary comparative papers, and who has published on the history of opuntia in Madagascar. Thanks are due to all of these institutions for their financial assistance.

William Beinart is Rhodes Professor of Race Relations, African Studies Centre, University of Oxford, United Kingdom.

Lovuyo Wotshela is a researcher, University of Fort Hare History Project, South Africa.

ACKNOWLEDGEMENTS

Sincere thanks are owed to many people who spoke to us about prickly pear and related themes, as well as those who assisted in our quest for documentary material. They are mentioned in the footnotes. In particular we would like to thank Nowinile Ngcengele and her associates in Fort Beaufort, for her patience and enthusiasm through a sequence of interviews. Troth Wells and Ntsiki Wotshela gave us every kind of assistance and hospitality when Luvuyo Wotshela was in Oxford and William Beinart in Fort Beaufort. Neither of us was able to spend long sequences of time on this book, but the research and writing, in short and concentrated spells, was particularly enjoyable. We would also like to thank Julie Miller of Wits University Press for her patience and encouragement in taking this book through to print.

GLOSSARY OF SCIENTIFIC AND COMMON NAMES FOR PRICKLY PEAR

Note that in scientific literature, the binomial Latin name for species is often shortened to the initial for the first word. For example, *Opuntia ficus-indica* would be written *O. ficus-indica* after the first mention. Please also note that italics is used for scientific names and words not in English. Doornblad, kaalblad and rondeblaar are not treated as non-English words but as common names, so are not in italics.

Cactus pear. See spineless cactus.

Doornblad. Old Cape name for the spiny *Opuntia ficus-indica*.

Kaalblad. Old Cape name for the spineless *Opuntia ficus-indica*. This may have been the original variety of prickly pear introduced into South Africa.

Opuntia. A genus of about 160 different species of cactus native to the Americas, mostly from Mexico, the southern United States and central America, including the Caribbean. Most have oval or paddle-shaped, flat cladodes – as their leaves are called in scientific literature. Perhaps 10 to 12 species established themselves in the wild in South Africa and to different degrees became invasive. There are many other genuses of cactus, some of which also reached South Africa.

Opuntia aurantiaca. The jointed cactus. Smaller species than *Opuntia ficus-indica*, with smaller, more cylindrical cladodes. Introduced as a garden or rockery plant, it was not useful but became invasive and was particularly difficult to control. Called *katjie* (or *litjieskaktus*) in Afrikaans and *ukatyi* in Xhosa (after a cat, because its spines are like cat's claws).

Opuntia ficus-indica. The most common prickly pear with the best edible fruit and the origins of most spineless cactus. Called *turksvy* in Afrikaans and *itolofiya yasendle emhlope* or *itolofiya yasendle* in Xhosa (wild, white prickly pear of the veld).

Opuntia lindheimeri. Smaller plant than *Opuntia ficus-indica* with rounder cladodes and reddish-purple fruit. Called *rondeblaar* in Afrikaans, fruit called *suurtjies* and *ebomvu* or *isiqhamo esibomvu* or *ugazini* in Xhosa (meaning red-fruited). *Opuntia spinulifera* is a larger *rondeblaar*, with a distinctively round cladode, but was not common in South Africa.

Opuntia stricta. Similar to *Opuntia lindheimeri* with a cladode that is less rounded but also has a reddish-purple fruit to which the term *suurtjie* also seems to be applied.

Prickly pear. The common English name for a wide variety of Opuntia species. The term probably originated in the Caribbean or North America and spread through the anglophone world from the late eighteenth century. In South Africa it included about ten different introduced species but usually refers to the most common *Opuntia ficus-indica*.

Rondeblaar. See *Opuntia lindheimeri*.

Spineless cactus. These are cultivated varieties of opuntia with few, if any, spines on their cladodes. They are now generally called cactus pear in the scientific literature and are largely derived from *Opuntia ficus-indica*. Early varieties were cultivated in Mexico, the Mediterranean and elsewhere, one or more of which probably came to South Africa in the eighteenth century. The term now usually refers to varieties from the Mediterranean, and especially those bred by Luther Burbank in California in the early twentieth century. There are many cultivars in South Africa with different growth habits and fruit colours. Called *doringlose turksvy* in Afrikaans and in Xhosa *itolofiya engenameva* (without spines) or occasionally *itolofiya yabelungu* (white people's). They are sometimes named in Xhosa by the colour of the fruit, for example, *itolofiya emthubi* (yellow-fruited).

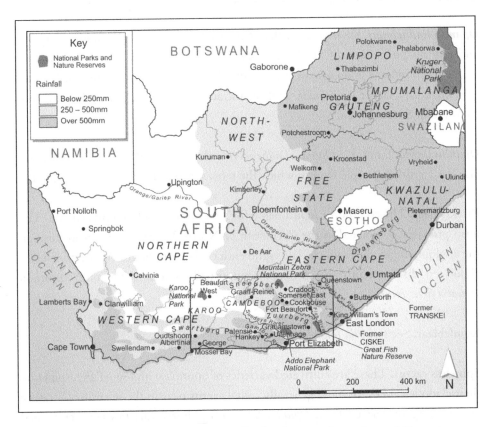

South Africa: Box indicates areas of midland and eastern Cape where prickly pear

became best established

INTRODUCTION

I f you drive along the roads of South Africa's Eastern Cape in the summer months from January to March, you cannot fail to notice African women selling fruit. Most have tin dishes, buckets or plastic bags piled high with *itolofiya* or prickly pear – small fruits with yellowish skins. Our attention was first drawn to prickly pear by the roadside sellers, prompting memories of buying this cheap delicacy in summers long past. We soon discovered that this fruit, and the plant from which it comes, has a rich and fascinating past in South Africa. Both of us have researched on the Eastern Cape for many years. Exploring history from the vantage point of human relations with a plant has opened new avenues and revealed many interesting social as well as ecological issues.

Prickly pear is the common English name for a number of cactus species that originate largely from Mexico and neighbouring parts of Central America. These plants have crossed spatial and racial boundaries. Following their lead, our history explores diverse South

Sketch of Opuntia ficus-indica *showing spines on cladodes and position of glochids on immature fruit*

A mature opuntia plant near Queenstown, 2008, showing hard stem, cladodes,
flowers and immature fruit

African communities and bridges environmental, social and political themes. A study of the prickly pear introduces readers to hidden aspects of the rural and small-town past in South Africa that have echoes in other parts of the world.

These plants are members of the genus opuntia, which includes about 160 species.[1] Opuntias come in many different shapes and sizes. Those called prickly pear generally have oval, flattish, green pads or leaves, called cladodes in scientific literature, which grow out of each other to form a tree-like structure. Some look more like paddles and they vary from about 10 to 50 cm in length. Amongst the cacti, they are distinguished from the tall, cylindrical plants that are celebrated in American Western movies, and those with smaller, barrel-like, or globular shapes.

Hard spines grow out of the sides of the cladodes. Flowers and fruit also sprout directly from the cladodes, usually on their edges. The flowers – yellow to dark orange and shades of red – are large, open and attractive. The fruits are studded with tiny, short, needle-like spicules or glochids, which easily detach when they are approaching ripeness and can penetrate the skin. Anyone who has handled a prickly pear fruit, worse still put it to their mouths without carefully removing the glochids or peeling it, is unlikely to forget the experience. The glochids can remain

---

PRICKLY PEAR'S BIOLOGICAL CHARACTERISTICS

Cacti are remarkable plants, specialised for survival in semi-arid zones and deserts. They can make do with very little rainfall and are highly efficient at taking up moisture through their shallow root systems. They are very largely composed of water. Prickly pear has more than 90 per cent. They lose very little water too. All plants have to transpire, but prickly pear, as with other cacti, generally takes up carbon dioxide at night when temperatures are low. During the day, their stomates, the small pores in the outer surface of the cladodes, remain closed. This strategy conserves water, making prickly pears highly drought-resistant. In fact, they can survive in a wide range of climates and habitats, from deserts with less than 250 mm of rainfall, to more humid zones with over 750 mm. In the Americas, opuntia species are found from Argentina to southern Canada, west to the Galapagos and east to the Caribbean. Some species can survive near the coast where there are no frosts and some at great heights, such as the South African Karoo and highveld, where frosts are frequent. But the species transferred to South Africa do best in the middle range of this rainfall and climate spectrum. Prickly pear can hybridise and adapt their root systems to cope with less arid land.

---

uncomfortably embedded for some days, unless they are patiently extracted with tweezers.

While there are many studies of the global influence of crops and plants, this is perhaps the first social history based around a plant in South Africa. Plants are not quite historical actors in their own right, but their properties and potential help to shape human history. In turn, the trail of prickly pear in South Africa has been profoundly affected by the plant's biological characteristics. Plants such as prickly pear tend to be invisible to those who do not use them, or at least are only on the peripheries of people's consciousness. We will explain why they were not peripheral to many people in the Eastern Cape, and why a wild and sometimes invasive plant from Mexico remained important to African women, such as Nowinile Ngcengele (seen on page 14), in shacks and small towns.

USEFUL PLANT OR DANGEROUS INVADER?

The central tension at the heart of our history concerns different and sometimes conflicting views of prickly pear. Some accepted or enjoyed its presence while others wished to eradicate it. The plant, as we will illustrate, became a scourge to commercial livestock farmers, but for impoverished, rural and small-town communities of the

Eastern Cape it was a godsend. In many places it still provides a significant income for poor black families and especially for women (Chapters 1 and 6). Debates about opuntia have played out in unexpected ways over the last century and more.

Prickly pear species were amongst the earliest plants brought back to Europe by the Spanish conquerors of the Americas. Europeans found them interesting; they soon learned that they were edible and that opuntia nurtured the cochineal insects from which Native Americans made a rich, red dye. Established in the Mediterranean and the Canary Islands during the sixteenth century, the plants spread globally.[2] One species at least was probably brought to the Cape in the seventeenth century. One, almost certainly the *Opuntia ficus-indica*, South Africa's most common prickly pear, was taken to the midland and eastern districts with the earliest Afrikaner frontier farmers in the eighteenth century. Travellers around Graaff-Reinet reported it in the 1770s and these specimens were probably the progenitors of wild, Eastern Cape prickly pear. It is called *turksvy* (Turkish fig) in Afrikaans, and the Xhosa name, *itolofiya*, is an adaptation of this.[3] We do not know when this word was adopted into Xhosa, but it was used in written sources in the late nineteenth century and is recorded in Kropf's classic Xhosa dictionary of 1899 as a word loaned from Afrikaans.

Prickly pear was taken around the world partly because it was a useful plant. While climate and environmental factors shaped its range, human agency played a major role. In South Africa opuntia species have been, at some time in the past, valuable to many communities as multi-purpose fruit, fodder and hedging plants. Trekboers, white commercial farmers, poor whites, African and coloured farm workers, African peasants in the communal lands, as well as black, urban communities, all used it. The fruit was picked and eaten, or purchased by those who could afford it. Both white and black people in the rural areas used it for jam, syrup, chutney and other preserves. It was the base for a beer (*iqhilika*) which was, alongside *mqombothi* or *utywala* (made of sorghum and maize grain), the main, rural, alcoholic drink amongst African and coloured communities in some Eastern Cape districts for over a century. Afrikaners distilled a potent spirit (*witblits*, or white lightning) from the fruit on the farms. The cladodes provided livestock fodder in droughts and were an ingredient for homemade soap. Africans produced a laxative medicine and blood purifier from them. Over time, prickly pear became deeply embedded in the culture and daily life of the Eastern Cape.

While prickly pear was planted initially by people, it then spread like wildfire in ecologically suitable parts of South Africa (Chapter 2). Local animals, such as crows and baboons, absorbed the fruit into their diet and scattered the seeds. By the first few decades of the twentieth century, it covered vast swathes of the midland and eastern Cape, and was invading parts of KwaZulu/Natal and Mpumalanga. Some older thickets of the cactus, guarded by tree-like plants over six metres high, were so dense that they could scarcely be penetrated. Along the Kat River, north of Fort Beaufort for example, 'the prickly pear form[ed] a jungle ... reaching as much as twenty-five feet'.[4] At its height in the 1930s, the plant was estimated to cover 900,000 hectares (over 2 million acres) densely and wild plants penetrated a much greater area.

Prickly pear is now less common than it used to be, although scattered plants can be seen in many parts of South Africa. Thickets are still found in coastal municipalities such as Uitenhage and Albany (now in Cacadu), Hankey, Peddie and parts of Fort Beaufort (in Amathole). There are also plantations of a cultivated variety called spineless cactus (Chapter 3), on farms throughout the drier areas of South Africa. Travellers often notice these strange fields of cactus, their asymmetrical shapes towering over the low Karoo veld.

The scale and range of prickly pear has diminished because the wild spiny plants have been systematically eradicated. During the late nineteenth and early twentieth centuries some wealthier, white, livestock farmers tried to clear it from their own land and called on the state to exercise more general control.[5] They wanted to be rid of it because spiny cladodes could be a danger to livestock. The glochids on the fruits damaged animals' mouths. Prickly pear also spread along the river valleys on land that was valuable for crops. Some farms were so heavily invaded that they were abandoned. Agricultural officials came to regard wild, spiny prickly pear as a pest that infested the land and threatened agriculture and livestock farming. The state initiated a biological control programme in the 1930s, using insects introduced from the Americas (Chapter 5). Cactoblastis moths and cochineal bugs became powerful actors in South Africa's ecological history. Within a few decades, by the 1950s, perhaps 80 per cent of the wild opuntia was destroyed.[6]

In this book, we discuss in detail the benefits of the plant, as well as its economic and environmental costs in successive eras. We explore the way that prickly pear spread in the nineteenth and early twentieth centuries, the growing crescendo of opinion against it and the eradication campaign of the 1930s and 1940s. We then illustrate that the century-old dilemmas about prickly pear have not disappeared. Various opuntia species were declared weeds and this status was confirmed under the Conservation of Agricultural Resources Act of 1983. It is now illegal to nurture wild prickly pear in South Africa, although this legislation is not enforced. Yet once the major threat passed, we will argue, a few scientists – who had once put their energies into eradication – rekindled their interest in the value of opuntia (Chapter 7). Some felt that the cactoblastis and cochineal insects, which continued to reproduce on the surviving plants, kept them more or less under control.[7] These scientists became protagonists for the cactus and connected with a global network of experts that see huge potential in these species. The threat of global warming only adds to the allure of plants that can survive heat and drought. We also illustrate how African usage has continued (Chapter 6) and how Afrikaners have begun to celebrate prickly pear's cultural significance (Chapter 8).

BIO-INVASIONS AND PLANT TRANSFERS

Our study, focussed on one group of plants, has implications for some major environmental debates. Recent scientific writing suggests that invasive plants and animals, or bio-invasions, are now the second most important cause of biodiversity loss (after direct destruction of habitat for settlement, agriculture and extraction) on a global scale. South African scientific literature on bio-invasions emphasises these ecological costs. Two key commentators, Richardson and van Wilgen argue:

> Human communities and natural ecosystems worldwide are under siege from a growing number of destructive invasive alien species (including disease organisms, agricultural weeds, and insect pests). These species erode natural capital, compromise ecosystem stability, and threaten economic productivity. The problem is growing in severity and geographic extent as global trade and travel accelerate.[8]

The view of exotic or alien plants in much recent South African literature is negative and generally pro-eradication. However, it is valuable to think about the global movement of plants in a broader context. Plant transfers have been central to world history. They have been fundamental in demographic growth, great agrarian complexes and in the expansion of empires and settlement – not least the European empires of the last 500 years. In many contexts, introduced plants have been naturalised and adopted into the culinary repertoire and culture of their host societies. In Africa, for example, maize, an American domesticate, has become a staple food. African agriculture and diets are heavily dependent on plants from the Americas: cassava, sweet potato, tomatoes, potatoes, chilli and peppers as well as key export crops such as cocoa and tobacco. It is impossible to imagine the contemporary world without an understanding of the scale and significance of plant transfers.

Transferred plants are often roughly categorised into useful crops, which are controlled in fields or gardens, and invasive weeds. These are culturally constructed categories, refined in scientific studies, but still widely deployed in everyday language and still influential in policy debates.[9] We suggest that the picture can be more complex. It is true that most crops do not become invasive. Maize, by chance, has a heavy cob and seeds which do not spread easily. The seeds are generally ground and cooked before being eaten, and even if eaten whole and raw, their reproductive capacity is destroyed by human and animal consumption. By contrast, hard prickly pear seeds benefit from passing through digestive tracts as this process sometimes enhances their capacity to germinate. Seeds of some of the most invasive species in South Africa are distributed widely through a range of different strategies and vectors. The environmental impact of maize would have been far greater if it had been a self-spreader.

While maize can be controlled, it is not only invasiveness that can cause ecological damage. Maize cultivation has surely been one of the major causes of environmental change in Africa over the last century, and also a threat to biodiversity.[10] But any environmental critique must be tempered by recognition that it is the most important and preferred food source in many African countries. Most African people do not see maize as an alien or exotic, and indeed it is a quintessential feature of Africa's cultural and physical landscape. In other cases, introduced plants, such as the vines of the Western Cape, have become intrinsic elements in the cultural landscape as well as indispensible in the agrarian economy. Vines, however, have displaced large areas of indigenous, fynbos vegetation.

Crops are one category of transferred plant. By contrast there are many exotic or alien plants which are considered to be weeds and seem to have no benefits, only costs, both ecological and economic. South Africa is teeming with them. Examples of these unwanted species include burr-weed (*Xanthium spinosum*), which sticks in sheep's wool and was the first plant to be declared 'noxious' in the Cape in the nineteenth century. Recently the red water fern (*Azolla filiculoides*), which clogs up water systems, has become an expensive nuisance. Both are from the Americas, which is South Africa's main source of invasive weeds – although Australian plants, especially acacia or wattle trees, have also proved particularly troublesome. Attitudes to these plants can change.[11] American jacarandas (*Jacaranda mimosifolia*) were widely introduced to beautify suburban streets in a number of South African cities and now they are cited as invaders. It is possible that a few weeds will reveal as yet undiscovered or forgotten genetic properties – and in fact a number of alien plants are used in the Eastern Cape for medicinal purposes.[12] But by and large these plants are viewed with hostility, many are illegal and attempts at eradication are entirely justifiable.

The designation of some transferred plants as weeds can, however, be slippery. Some alien species lie between the two poles of useful, non-invasive crop and useless, invasive weed. The black wattle tree (*Acacia mearnsii*) is one good example. It was introduced to KwaZulu/Natal from Australia for tanning and timber in the nineteenth century. It was, and still is, grown in plantations and planted by Africans around their homesteads as a quick-growing source of wood and fuel in higher rainfall districts between the Drakensberg and the east coast. While black wattle has massive value for some poor rural communities in these areas, it has become invasive, and environmentalists see it as a particularly thirsty tree that sucks up valuable water.[13] As a result, it has been a major target of eradication in South Africa's national Working for Water Programme. Yet, its benefits have been significant, especially where it has been controlled in plantations and homestead gardens.[14]

Prickly pear is another important example of a plant that is not easily placed in the category of crop or weed. It is a good plant with which to think about these categories because it has slipped across boundaries and attracted such diverse human responses.[15] Wild *O. ficus-indica* was planted and encouraged, or at least tolerated, by many communities. Some species, especially the *O. ficus-indica*, were bred to produce spineless, cultivated varieties. However, a number of wild species certainly became invasive, shouldered aside indigenous vegetation and were seen as damaging weeds. The jointed cactus, *ukatyi* in Xhosa (*O. aurantiaca*), introduced as a rockery plant in the 1860s, had no value and was troublesome to all livestock owners when it escaped into the veld. It remains a scourge and has not been as successfully controlled as prickly pear.

Our argument is that wild *O. ficus-indica* and cultivated spineless cactus remain significant in parts of South Africa. By chance rather than intention, the biological campaign – while it greatly diminished prickly pear – did not entirely eradicate it. The dangers of rampant invasion seem to be over. Our view concurs with that of a few key scientists, such as Helmuth Zimmermann, who argue that it should no longer be considered a weed.[16] Rather, a central problem identified in our interviews concerns access by poor people to the plant and its fruits (Chapters 1 and 9). The history of prickly pear in South Africa, over the long term, should be seen as part of a history of plant transfer, of the history of agrarian systems, rural social life and livelihoods, rather than simply as a case of bio-invasion.

PRICKLY PEAR, PLANTS AND KNOWLEDGE

The history of prickly pear is particularly interesting because it opens doors to unusual aspects of both local and scientific knowledge in South Africa. Native Americans used cactus plants, in their original home terrain, intensively.[17] They harvested and ate the fresh fruit and flowers, dried the seeds for oils and ate the young cladodes as vegetables. They made anti-diabetic medicines and laxatives. Some species of cochineal insects, which fed on opuntia, converted its juice into a reddish liquid. The Aztecs dried and ground them to make a deep, red dye. This was developed into an export industry under the Spanish in Mexico and was one of Europe's major early imports from the Americas.[18]

Although some very general knowledge of opuntia's value was probably transferred with the plants, many of its uses in South Africa were reinvented by white and black rural communities. The technique used for brewing with the fruit was undoubtedly a local one, derived from the Khoisan recipe for honey beer. The dark syrup or *turksvystroop* favoured for many decades on the farms was apparently unique to South Africa. Prickly pear enables us to see something of the diversity of non-agricultural domestic activities and the flowering of local home industries. The plant was valuable to people with little access to manufactured products who used their environment to forage, survive and create tasty food supplements. It was especially important to poor people, and its use provides a window on hidden aspects of Eastern Cape poverty and the imagination used in forging livelihoods.

We should not underestimate the importance of everyday interaction with plants amongst pre-industrial societies, or rural and small-town communities more generally.[19] There were no supermarkets or spaza shops from which to purchase food, nor chemists to supply medicine. People had to make their own. Trading stores did not generally stock fresh produce and cash was in short supply. While this knowledge of and relationship with plants has been quite widely recorded in South Africa, especially in connection with medicinal uses, it remains marginal in the writing of rural history. Discussion of an exotic, introduced plant such as prickly pear reveals that local knowledge was not simply handed down by custom. It was adaptable, innovative and experimental. Nor has it disappeared. The women who we interviewed had little formal education, but they were confidently articulate about their understanding of plants.

Equally, a history of prickly pear reveals some intriguing aspects of the history of science in South Africa. For a few decades in the early twentieth century, the fledgling scientific service within the Department of Agriculture conducted some interesting experiments on the potential of prickly pear for fodder. More importantly, the insects introduced to kill opuntia in South Africa's first major biological eradication campaign were the subject of sustained study and experimentation. For some decades, entomologists in the Department of Agriculture were absorbed by the eradication campaign. Second to vets, they were one of the largest groups of government scientific officers. Some of the country's leading entomologists cut their teeth, metaphorically speaking, on the cochineal. They also needed to get to grips with the interactions between insects and plants. The complex ecological problems thrown up by the spread, control and use of prickly pear produced some fascinating scientific debates through the twentieth century as a whole. Scientists differed on strategy and policy and in recent years, some have questioned the need to eradicate at all. Natural history and natural sciences have been comparatively strong areas for research in South Africa – a vital element in the country's intellectual life. Our history touches on the ideas, conflicts and imaginations of a few of the prickly pear people.

OUR RESEARCH

Our chapters are based on a wide range of sources: formal interviews, chance conversations, participant observation, as well as archival and printed records. The interviews took us to unusual and varied places for historians. Some were conducted on roadsides, a number in townships, especially Fort Beaufort's Bhofolo, and in African villages in the former Ciskei, especially around Hewu. We visited farms to interview white landowners as well as African workers – from the secluded valley of Patensie to Graaff-Reinet, Fort Beaufort and the old Border area around Stutterheim and Queenstown. We found scientists and officials everywhere from Pretoria, Bloemfontein and Middelburg to Bhisho, Fort Hare and Grahamstown. We had instructive conversations at the Uitenhage prickly pear festival. The research in itself, staggered over more than a decade when we were both largely busy on other projects, prompted many revealing and fascinating journeys. It enabled us to see the countryside with new eyes – looking for prickly pear and other plants in hedges and gardens, on farms and in the veld.

The sources and interviews were in three languages. We came across many words and terms that we needed to translate for all of them. In our final bout of writing together in Oxford, we had frequent recourse to Kropf and Godfrey's Xhosa dictionary (1915), as well as an English–Afrikaans woordeboek. Researching prickly pear made us think across cultures and languages in South Africa, and in order to capture how people talked about the plant, we have decided to leave a number of Xhosa and Afrikaans words in the text (with translations).

We found, in the course of our interviewing, that almost everyone from the Eastern Cape has a story to tell about prickly pear. Some just remember being constipated by overconsumption of the luscious fresh fruit. One doctor who worked in the former Ciskei graphically recalled that she had no option but to spoon out the clogged anal passages presented to her during fruiting season. Many people reminisced about their enjoyment of collecting fruit, shared with us their memories of processing it or related their adventures with glochids. Others talked about the ecological, cultural and social aspects of the plant. Perhaps our most important and intriguing interviews were with a group of women beer brewers in Fort Beaufort, for whom *itolofiya* was a significant part of their life and work. It is to them that we now turn in the first chapter of this book.

Prickly pear street sales in Fort Beaufort, 2005

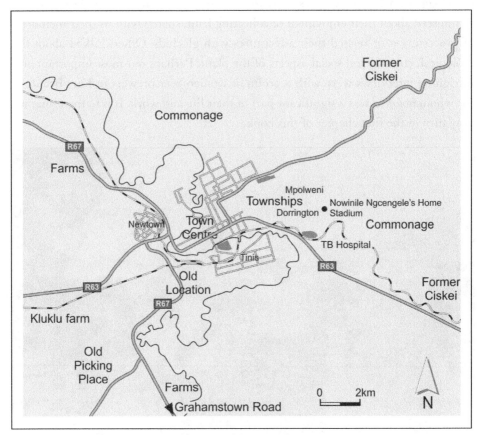

Fort Beaufort and vicinity

PRICKLY PEAR

BREWING AND LOCAL KNOWLEDGE
IN THE EASTERN CAPE, 2000-2006

O ur history starts in the recent past, in Nowinile Ngcengele's shack near Fort Beaufort's dusty football stadium. Despite her obvious poverty, her shack was neat inside with sitting room furniture and a glass-fronted display cupboard. The road alongside her plot is tarred but cattle and goats sometimes roam the verges and stray into the stadium. Nowinile had access to water from a standpipe in her yard. A prickly pear bush stood at the front of the plot. When we first visited in 2004 she was waiting for an RDP house which was built in 2006. Thousands of these structures have spread over the hills around the town.

As it is difficult to find deep historical material on the everyday use of prickly pear, we explore this through contemporary eyes by describing fruit sales and brewing in the eastern Cape in the early years of the twenty-first century. Our core arguments in this chapter are, firstly, that although the population has increasingly moved away from rural areas and agricultural pursuits, knowledge about opuntia is widespread in the Eastern Cape. Old rural skills have been adapted to new urban contexts and local strategies built around such skills and knowledge remain inventive. This spiny plant is a good coloniser and survivor, but it requires careful handling. Secondly, although prickly pear is no longer very important in the area, it remains a significant source of fruit for many people, and provides an income for poor African women.

Fort Beaufort is a town of about 70,000 people in the heart of the province.[1] Its population is overwhelmingly African and most people live in the large township called Bhofolo by the locals (the Xhosa name for Fort Beaufort), which lies on its eastern outskirts. The town and its commonage are surrounded by white-owned farms and by a portion of the former Ciskei.

Nowinile Ngcengele and Nositile Lungisa with the authors outside the former's shack in Fort Beaufort, 2004

In March 2005 we accompanied one group of women through all phases of picking fruit and processing it into beer. Nowinile Ngcengele was our main contact. She was a lively and confident woman in her late seventies, who was happy to talk to us for hours about her life and prickly pear.[2] She also organised demonstrations of prickly pear usage for us. She and the others pronounced *itolofiya,* the Xhosa word for both the plant and its fruit, as *'trofia'*, sometimes suppressing the 'a', a closer fit to the Afrikaans original.

A BRIEF HISTORY OF *IQHILIKA* BREWING

African people brewed beer using a range of techniques from honey, indigenous fruit and grains for millennia. The Xhosa term *iqhilika*, and Afrikaans *karee*, was used for honey beer, a drink and a word that both Africans and Afrikaners adopted from the Khoikhoi *!kharib* or *!xari*. (It is sometimes written or pronounced as *kirrie*, *kerrie*, *t'kiri* or *kili*.) It was then applied to beer brewed from the fruit of prickly pear. We do not know when such brewing began. Sparrman, the entertaining and alert Swedish traveller, was told in the 1770s that alcohol was made from a 'cactus of considerable size' in the Camdeboo, near Graaff-Reinet.[3] He was probably referring to distilling by settlers rather than beer-making by Africans, but brewing seems to have been established in Graaff-Reinet's location by the 1870s.[4] In the 1890s, farm owners and employers complained that:

> the native servants make use of the fruits in the manufacture of pernicious intoxicants which they consume in large quantities, totally unfitting them for their ordinary duties, and in all parts of the country where these liquors are prepared, the assembling of natives during the night for drunken orgies is carried on to such an extent that the matter is becoming really serious.[5]

Prickly pear featured in evidence from farmers to the 1894 Labour Commission in the Cape Colony. As the Member of the Legislative Assembly for Graaff-Reinet noted, 'our difficulty commences directly [as] the prickly pear gets ripe. Then the natives make beer and cause us annoyance'.[6] In Somerset East, a witness said 'in the summer time, the men brew beer and karee with prickly pears. I have seen all the farm hands drunk in the morning with this'.[7] While their view of the beer's impact was clouded by a haze of colonial prejudice, the scale of brewing may not have been exaggerated.

Charles Juritz, the Cape government chemist, was sent samples of beer for analysis of alcoholic content in legal cases arising from prosecutions under the Liquor Law of 1898.[8] This gave landowners the right to control brewing and possession of beer on their private land – and the issue arose as to the strength of 'intoxicating liquor' that fell under the Act. In 1906 Juritz produced an informative survey from the material sent by magistrates. African beer was produced everywhere but he heard specifically of prickly pear beer in New Brighton, Port Elizabeth and in Stockenstrom, Steytlerville and the Midlands more generally. The techniques of brewing, briefly recorded, differed little from those we saw a century later. Residents of New Brighton used a similar method for beer called *idanti* made from hops and sugar – this could also contain prickly pear. Kropf and Godfrey (1915) define it as 'a kind of very intoxicating beer, made from prickly pear and other ingredients'.[9] A version was also made in Ndabeni, Cape Town. The alcoholic content of all these variations was generally low from less than one per cent alcohol by volume to about seven per cent.

Nowinile Ngcengele was born and lived much of her life on white-owned farms in districts surrounding Fort Beaufort. Many people in Bhofolo township come from the farms. It was there that she learnt to handle prickly pear. She was born near the Fish River, around 1927, and then lived on the farm Grenoble in Bedford district. She remembers eating prickly pear fruit of three kinds as a child, white, yellow and sweet red. The fruit was used for brewing on the farms in her youth. She recalls that old men mainly made *iqhilika* in those days, while women brewed *mgqombothi* from sorghum (*amazimba* or *amabele*). Men also made honey beer, which used a similar process to prickly pear beer. Nowinile explained men's involvement as a result of the dangers of brewing at that time. Farm owners and police attempted to prevent brewing and old men were more prepared to take chances. They would hide the beer in *iikani* – big tins used for milk – at some distance from their homesteads. Farmers, she remembered, would pour away (*chitha*) any beer that they found. They thought that *iqhilika* was more intoxicating than *mqombothi* – that it would make people 'wild' and steal sheep. Beer was nevertheless widely brewed although not generally sold on the farms. When it was ready they announced 'we have mixed it' (*sidubile*) and everyone could come to drink.[10]

Nowinile clearly lived on a farm where suppression was the rule and some others confirmed her recollections. Nevertheless, prohibition was very uneven. In 1932, Monica Wilson, the anthropologist, conducted interviews on a number of farms in Bedford and the neighbouring districts of Adelaide and Albany during her research for *Reaction to Conquest*.[11] At four farms, no brewing was allowed at all, although one of these landowners told her that 'a good deal' of honey beer was made. On one farm the workers were Christian and claimed not to be interested in beer. Two landowners allowed brewing once a month, and another two weekly. At one farm brewing was reputed to take place two or three times a week and it was regarded as a centre for sheep theft. This may have been the farm in a 'prickly pear area' where the owner, unusually, allowed Africans to remain as labour tenants rather than labourers: 'in return for building plots and grazing rights [they] cleared a patch of prickly pear each year for the farmer on whose land they lived. No cash passed between them and the farmer.'[12] Thus according to Hunter's records, brewing was permitted on at least half the farms she investigated. Twenty-five years later Margaret Roberts, surveying farm labour in the eastern Cape, also noted that farmers varied in their determination to suppress brewing and very few could enforce this: 'it is generally recognised that workers on most farms brew very much more beer than they are allowed'.[13]

Prickly pear was also widespread for many years on Fort Beaufort commonage and around the two old locations called Tini's and Drayini or Apiesdraai. The latter was on the south-western side of town, to the west of the old Grahamstown road. It was destroyed under the Group Areas Act in the 1960s and the new road built through part of it. Currently, some of this land is occupied by the Winterberg High School, originally for whites but now desegregated. Nothobile Ludziya was born there and she recalled that in the 1940s 'we grew up with *itolofiya* around us' (*sikulele kuyo*).[14] Neither this old township nor the prickly pear that surrounded it is there any longer.

PICKING AND SELLING

Nowinile and most of the women involved in brewing pick the fruit themselves and also sell some of it. She and her group estimated that there were about 50 brewers operating in the town. Others pick and sell fruit but do not brew. Their fruit of choice is the wild *O. ficus-indica*. In Xhosa this is called *itolofiya yasendle emhlope* – the white-fruited prickly pear of the veld. The fruit comes into season during the summer, from early January to mid-March. (This is a summer rainfall area.) While there is a large commonage adjacent to Bhofolo, hardly any of the appropriate prickly pear plants grow there any longer. Many of the women used to pick on white-owned farms surrounding the town, but in recent years access has largely been denied.

Nowinile and her group remember one farm in particular close to Fort Beaufort as a favoured spot for picking. They called it Mandreya's and it clearly had rich stocks. None of the women we interviewed knew the English name of the farm owner, but Nowinile took us to the farm which is a few kilometres south-west of town. We later discovered that the farm was owned by Andre Danckwerts, and the Xhosa version of the farm's name was an adaptation of his first name. They also called this farm KwaMinoli, but its registered name is Kluklu (after the river Xuxuwa).[15] The farmer used to charge nothing for access to his land by pickers. His foreman recorded their names and identity numbers. Some township women were actually employed on the farm to help clear jointed cactus (*ukatyi*, see Chapter 2) and by picking large quantities of fruit, the women helped to protect livestock from damaging themselves by eating it after it had fallen.

Mandreya's was closed to picking around the year 2000. We heard explanations both from the women and from the farmers; they largely concur as to the reasons although they do not share the same opinions about such restrictions. Nothobile Ludziya recalled that 'some people messed up (*bamosha*)' their relationship with Mandreya.[16] She added:

On one occasion, around the year 2000, sheep were stolen and some
were discovered still alive in a shack in the township. From that day
on they closed entry. There was no warning. Mandreya said that the
bakkies were moving in and men came with them. Even though the
sheep were discovered, no one was ever caught, because the owner
of the shack was already in prison (*etrongweni*).

Others thought that 'Mandreya stopped it because a group of hunters went on
the rampage, entered the farm and hunted kudu (*amaqude*).'[17] Farmers said that
when they gave women access to pick on their land, intruders came with them, and
they suffered from the perennial problems of livestock theft, veld fires, hunting and
honey collection: 'fences cut, gates left open, cattle scattered, and vandalism so they
closed ranks and said that's it'.[18]

Danckwerts, who was well-informed about these issues, lives in a lovely, old,
nineteenth-century farmhouse along the Adelaide road. He concurred that there was
a 'criminal element', that 'caused so much trouble', and even threatened his family. In
his eyes, a limited number of women pickers was manageable but 'if you let in one
person, 500 people will come in tomorrow'. He noted that there was competition for
fruit between the outside pickers and his farm workers; so he also 'stopped [outsiders]
from picking because they chased his staff away and that caused fights'.[19] Danckwerts,
ironically, was sure that the wild prickly pear on his farm, and around Fort Beaufort,
was better than the Grahamstown product because it grew on gravel soils in a hotter
climate, which produced sweeter, tastier fruit with an excellent texture. He joked that
when friends came from Johannesburg and loved the fruit they said he was sitting
on a gold mine. Nevertheless, he had converted most of his land into a wildlife farm,
ran an upmarket hunting business (Stormberg Elangeni Safaris) with strong links to
Texas and was keen to clear the prickly pear (Chapter 8).

Rob Sparks, who farmed south of the town, mentioned that he tried to prevent
access because people came with the pickers to hunt warthogs. Warthogs have
spilled over from the Great Fish River Conservation Area. There are few predators
on the farms which can control them naturally.[20] The warthogs are a problem in that
they are strong enough to break through fences and they compete with livestock
for grass. But even so, he preferred not to let outside hunters come onto his land,
because he believed that they would steal livestock and also take other species such
as tortoises. Sparks relied on his own resources; about 600 warthogs had been shot
on his farm in the previous two years and 12 in one weekend.[21]

In the post-apartheid context, farmers are especially nervous about their land rights and their capacity to deal with informal settlers and intruders. If people were allowed to pick annually, one mentioned, then they may get a right of access onto the farms. Many white landowners are trying to reduce the number of black workers resident on their farms. To our knowledge, all the farms immediately around Fort Beaufort were closed to pickers based in the township when we interviewed between 2004 and 2006.

The restrictions on local picking introduced major logistical problems for the brewers in Fort Beaufort. Whereas some used to be able to make the journey to the prickly pear clumps on foot, all of the Fort Beaufort brewers were now dependent on bakkie transport to supplies further afield. In order to do so, they organised themselves into groups of about five to seven members each, and negotiated for transport with African bakkie owners. They had to act collectively in order to afford the costs of hire. In 2005, the bakkie owners charged from R35 to R40 per return trip for each woman. They in turn needed to fill their vans in order to make it worthwhile financially. A few women hitchhiked, for which they were charged about R10 each way, but this depended on passing traffic and could make for a very long day.

The bakkie that Ngcengele's group usually hired had broken down so we drove her and two others, Nositile Lungisa and Julia Khamande, to their currently favoured spot for picking, nearly 70 km south of Fort Beaufort, just north of Grahamstown. They called this area Ngquthu.[22] Nowinile said that they had been picking there for some years.[23] The Makana (formerly Grahamstown) municipality had purchased two farms there for possible extension of township settlements. They have been neglected and the main farmhouse was a ruin. Prickly pear has been allowed to reproduce freely and large thickets covered this land. Clearly the remnant cochineal insects, which keep prickly pear under control in many districts, were less effective here, although we did see some on the plants. Cochineal is weaker in wetter years and wetter areas: it does not – in local language – 'grip' so well (Chapter 5).[24] This helps to explain why the thickets near Grahamstown thrive. Nowinile's group had to pay R10 each to a caretaker to gain access to the fruit. She said that despite the distance involved there were compensating factors in making the trip to Grahamstown: the thickets are dense so that picking times are shorter. This area, which is lower and wetter than Fort Beaufort, had a slightly longer fruiting season.

As our trip was quite late in the season (early March), there was very little fruit left near the road. We walked about half a kilometre through the abandoned farm to the heavily laden plants which were two to three metres high. They picked less ripe, green-yellow fruits, which are better for sale, as well as riper fruits which were turning orange and are better for brewing. The glochids on ripe fruit dislodge easily when disturbed. The women don't like to pick on very windy days as the glochids blow into their eyes. Nowinile warned us when we were picking with them to stand upwind and 'beware of thorns' (*lumkela ameva*).[25] Glochids stick easily into the skin. All of the women wore protective gloves to minimise this risk. One of them showed us the pinprick scars that regular pickers can sustain when the glochids penetrate the skin. The women used homemade wire hooks (*amagwegwe*), about a metre long, to reach the higher fruits. The biggest and juiciest are often on the upmost cladodes. *Amagwegwe* are carefully shaped at the top to catch and hold the fruit so that these do not fall to the ground. Prickly pear bruises easily and damaged fruit is not saleable.

Nowinile and her fellow workers put the fruit into plastic buckets which took 30 to 45 minutes to fill and held about 20 kg of fruit. Generally they would each try to pick two 50 kg sacks (*ingxowa*) on a day's outing so that they would be picking for 3 to 5 hours. Sometimes they also pick cladodes: 'we peel them and boil them to make a drink that acts as a laxative' (see Chapter 5).[26] Cladodes are called *amagqabi* in Xhosa, which is the general name for large leaves; *iblayi*, from the Afrikaans blaar or blad is also used. After cleaning (see page 21), the bakkies come into the fields so that the women can load up directly. One major advantage of using bakkie transport is that they can pick far more than they would be able to if they had to carry the load on their heads. They are also delivered back to their respective homes.

Immediately on return to their homes, the women put the fruits into water. Soaked overnight, the remaining glochids dislodge or can be wiped off; this makes *itolofiya* more saleable and easier to handle for processing. The next morning the fruit is sorted and carried to stalls all around Fort Beaufort. Nowinile sometimes goes to Alice to sell. The favoured sites are at crossroads with heavy pedestrian and car traffic, hiking and taxi spots on the outskirts of town or near the TB hospital, taxi ranks, bus stations and garages. Some women also sell door to door to white and black households. The group we interviewed did not sell to shops. Nositile Lungisa clarified that 'spaces are not owned by a person. Sometimes it depends who arrives first. People identify their own places and return regularly but they won't worry if someone else is there.'[27] During the season, most women are able to sell a substantial amount and there is prickly pear for sale every day of the week: 'at the month end, the sales go very quickly, in a few hours, but in the middle of the month, they are

PICKING AND PACKING THE FRUIT

Nowinile Ngcengele and associates picking prickly pear with a wire hook and gloves on municipally-owned land near Grahamstown.

After picking, the fruits were spread out on the ground and the women searched out a low, heather-like bush with small hard leaves (*amahlamvu*) in order to clean them.[28] When the ripe fruits are brushed, many of the glochids fall off. After this operation, they used their bare hands to handle the fruits and transfer them into a 50 kg, recycled rice bag.

slow'.[29] Most days they are able to sell as much as they have. Some purchasers, those with fridges, buy in bulk – up to 20 litres at a time.

In 2005, Nowinile's group sold fruit at R7 for a 5-litre container. This is about 30 fruits, which makes prickly pear comparatively cheap and a very good deal for purchasers. The women of this and other groups discussed a price between them when picking. They were selling at R6 for the 5-litre container in 2004 and agreed that they would raise the price. They also sell in larger and smaller quantities. They can earn as much as R140, even more, from two bags if they sell most of them.[30] Riper fruits, damaged fruits and those not sold are used for brewing or as fodder for animals – especially pigs, goats and chickens. These figures were confirmed in other interviews.[31]

PREPARATIONS FOR BREWING

Prickly pear fruit has to be used quite quickly; it has a high sugar and yeast content and begins to rot within a few days. The next afternoon, the three pickers brewed together with Julia Khamande's sister, Nosakela Mbovane, at whose house they gathered. They all lived within a couple of blocks of the football stadium. Unlike Nowinile's shack, the Mbovanes owned a standard brick house with a substantial extension built from the housing subsidy under the RDP programme. They had a standpipe in the yard and electricity.

Nosakela's husband, William Mbovane, started a fire using acacia wood (*umnga*). The preparations were an occasion for sociability and a few onlookers gathered. An old man walked past and Julia shouted 'we are going to braai here'.[32] They brought out a large (20 litre), black, cast iron, three-legged pot (*imbiza yesiXhosa*). The women preferred to cook prickly pear fruits in this classic receptacle over a fire rather than in enamel or stainless steel pots on a primus stove or electric cooker (which they had). They boiled up about five litres of water.

A gregarious party peeled and cut the fruits in half.[33] Each has numerous small, dark seeds which were not removed. The peel is used for pig fodder. Nowinile put about 10 litres of fruit into the boiling water. (They did not work with fixed measurements and can vary the amounts.) Nothing else went into the three-legged pot. The mixture simmered for an hour or so, stirred occasionally with a wooden stick, but was not mashed or pulped. When the liquid turned a light yellow, it was ready to be filtered into a clean plastic container. After cooling about five litres of liquid remained. The brewers said that if they used unfiltered liquid, containing cooked fruits or seeds, then it would not ferment; they wanted a liquid 'without a single pip'. They tested the clear liquid for sweetness. When it was lukewarm, they added one kilogram of brown sugar. This can be varied according to taste. Then they added the mula.

MULA

The techniques of brewing with mula for honey and prickly pear beer are different from those for *mqombothi* (*utywala*). The latter is made from sorghum and maize with sprouted sorghum traditionally used for fermentation. Grain beers such as this were a product of agriculture, introduced to South Africa by black African people about 1,500 years ago. Honey beer fermented by roots probably long predated this.

MULA

Mula is a moist, light brown substance kept in a cotton bag which is used for fermentation. It is made from a mix of the dregs of beer and the dried, shredded root of a mesembryanthemum (vygie or little fig) plant of the genus *Trichodiadema*.[34] Nowinile said that this was not available locally on the commonage, but was dug from the neighbouring farms. The plant is quite widespread in parts of the Midlands and Eastern Cape; other roots can serve a similar function. Knowledge of the properties of mula long pre-dates the introduction of prickly pear. Khoisan

people used it for brewing honey beer. Not only Africans but Afrikaners adopted the technique, naming the substance *moer* (yeast or dregs) or *kareemoer*. The Xhosa word 'mula' is probably derived from Dutch. Kropf and Godfrey (1915) translate it as the dregs of coffee. However, Juritz noted in 1906 that it was already widely used to mean the fermentation agent for beers made with honey, prickly pear and brown sugar which he recorded as 'iqilika no busi', 'iqilika ye tolofiya' and 'iqilika ye swekile'.[35]

Cut prickly pear and wet mula, Fort Beaufort, 2005

African women in the early twenty-first century were using a technique that was adapted from the Khoisan and may be thousands of years old.[36] We do not know when this technique was transferred from Khoisan to Xhosa, but there is a very long history of interaction between these societies.[37] The women said that mula was used only for brewing with honey and prickly pear; adaptations of this process included using brown sugar and condensed milk. They said it would not work with other locally grown fruit. In Grahamstown, we were told that similar techniques can be used with pineapple and also a mix of oranges and brown sugar, sometimes with manufactured yeast added.[38]

Mula is derived from the dried mesembryanthemum root – peeled, shredded and ground to produce a rough powder (*umgubo*). The brewers did not actually add the powder. The mula they used was the recycled dregs from the previous brew, partly dried in a white cotton bag. The dregs of the previous brewing session are made up of a combination of the damp mula with the remaining solids of prickly pear. Recycled in this way, and constantly renewed, it lasts for months and it can be used with brown sugar alone. Fresh dried shreds are added when necessary. 'We mix old, thick mula liquid with the new powder to strengthen and freshen it every now and again. I know that others prefer to do this every year, especially during the prickly pear fruiting and harvest season.'[39] Mula does not have a strong taste.

The supply of mula creates a parallel, informal marketing system. Primary sales of mula are conducted by farm workers. Nosakela Mbovane's daughter is married to an employee on Bath farm, about 5 km away. Her husband digs the mula and she sells it in town. Brewers in Fort Beaufort also purchase some of their mula from Merino farm, about 10 km south of Fort Beaufort, owned by the Sparks family. They have prickly pear on their farm, and allow brewing by their farm workers for consumption but not for sale. Nolast Mkhontwana and her husband often dig with a pick-axe for mula on this farm.[40] It grows especially on higher ground and the root can reach about 15 cm if the plant is healthy.

On another occasion Nowinile took us to a farm near Adelaide, where one of her children still lives, to dig mula.[41] The farm workers knew the location of the plants but because it had not rained, it took a few minutes to find them. Mula in the veld is a small creeping succulent. They called this variety, with white flowers, Bosman's or Bushman's mula. Interviews suggest that farmworkers sell mula all year round, but especially in summer during rainy seasons when the root swells. Mbovane explained: 'Just like grass mula is always growing, but after any hard rain it flourishes. For instance three days sunshine or more after a heavy rain makes a huge difference.

After any rain mula would grow faster and the root (*ingcambu*) will look healthier.'[42]

Jikela Ndikila gave one of our most fascinating interviews about mula.[43] He is a fencer who worked on the farms for Andre Danckwerts and others. His job led him across country most days and he was in an excellent position to find and pick the plant as his fences snaked through the veld. He identified four different mula species. A common variety is *Gambushe* – a shrub with light-pink flowers and long, thick roots, 'just like a big carrot'. It does especially well in rainy seasons. *Nontsingana* has short, green leaves and short roots the length of a finger. It has white flowers. *Intshwa* has multiple short roots and short green leaves that grow close to the earth's surface. This is the most common type and the most resilient as it can grow in dry seasons. The fourth variety, which he refered to as *Bosmans*, is not so common. This has green leaves with reddish edges which overlap in their growth like aloes. They have about four, thin, short roots that are easy to dig out. He said that the variety did not matter much to the brewers; he preferred to pick Gambushe because the root size is larger and processing is easier. He peeled and processed the roots before grinding and selling them.

In 2006, Ndikila sold a cup of dry shreds for R20. We heard of lower prices in 2004 to 2005 of around R10 to R15 for a cup.[44] Mula was also sold as a damp, more liquid mix, the dregs of brewing, at about R30 for 2 litres. Some brewers sell mula to others when they have excess dregs left over. Farm workers supplied mula and other ingredients, such as wild honey, to brewers in return for *iqhilika* as well as cash. Nolast, on Merino, mentioned widespread brewing on farms near Fort Beaufort. Farm workers used honey when prickly pear was not in season. Most of the sales of mula are by women, and as it is light, no special transport is required. Farm workers around Fort Beaufort also sell to neighbouring towns such as Adelaide and Alice. Grahamstown has its own supply.[45]

BACK TO THE BREWING

Nowinile and her group added about one kilogram of damp mula to the prickly pear liquid, now lukewarm, as well as some more water. The mula sank to the bottom of the container and the mixture was then left to ferment indoors, covered by a net cloth to keep out flies. The following morning after fermenting for about 18 hours, the prickly pear liquid was visibly bubbling with a pleasant yeasty smell. The brewers filtered the mixture again to produce a clear, yellow-brown, honey-coloured liquid. It was ready to drink less than two days after picking, unlike sorghum beer, which takes longer to prepare – usually three to four days.

MULA AND OTHER FERMENTATION AGENTS

Juritz, the Cape government chemist, heard of a number of plant substances used for brewing in different districts of the Cape and tried to test some of them. One of the plants sent from Port Elizabeth was identified for him as 'mesembrianthemum stellatum', which is now called Trichodiadema stellatum and is still an ingredient for brewing. He also received 'linum capense' from Stockenstrom (species not known) and Anacampseros ustulata from Kenhardt and Steytlerville. The latter is now known as Avonia ustulata and commonly referred to as moerplantjie. Other avonia species were also used, one reputedly containing psychoactive substances. Juritz tested the various roots with different solutions and came to the conclusion that it was not the ground root itself, but moulds or fungi that grew on it as part of the mula – the moist dregs of brewing – which acted as fermentation agents. This led him to surmise that a number of different roots could potentially provide the active yeasty ingredient. In fact, other plants were used in South Africa. Khadi root, also a mesembryanthemum species, gave its name to a brew that was well-known in the early years of the Witwatersrand mining industry. The roots of Peucedenum sulcatum and the fruit of Rhus lancea (commonly called karee) are other examples.[46] Some ingredients were included for flavour, or because their chemical composition added effect to the brew. Juritz concluded that umkwenkwe bark (Pittisporum viridiflorum – cheesewood) played this role in beer. It is also a medicinal plant for people and animals.

A number of people began to congregate at the Mbovane's house. *Iqhilika* was ready for sale at 50 cents for a beaker of about 275 or 300 millilitres. A few old men shared plastic containers of about 1.5 litres purchased for R2. The brewers said that the price had not gone up for a few years. They had no organisation and if they put the price up they might lose their clientele. This is the cheapest form of alcohol for sale in the township and in certain cases the brewers sell on credit, and collect on pay or pension days. There is also the attraction of free *ivanya* or second brew. The women added water to the mula left from the first brew, left it for about half an hour, and refiltered it. This was then served free of charge to the customers. 'It does not taste so good', Nowinile noted, 'and the first is stronger'.[47] The dregs of the mula mix were then scooped into a cotton cloth and hung up to dry. In earlier days it would have been hidden in the thatch of huts.

Iqhilika has a distinctive taste – sweet-sour like most African beers and slightly caramel. Some customers, especially those from the farms where it has been a drink (*isiselo*) of choice for many decades, favour it above any other beer. Brewers see it as a 'gentle drink', which does not make people aggressive, but it is also the drink of the poor in the township. Most of the African middle-class avoid *iqhilika* as it is associated with poverty. People say it drains the body. They say that if you are tired or groggy, you must be drinking too much *iqhilika*. Zintombi Zabo, a brewer in Grahamstown, told us: 'undertakers say that the corpses of those who drink *iqhilika* give a bad smell in their fridges'.[48] Brewers sell throughout the day, as long as they have a supply.

The beer produced was not highly alcoholic, similar in strength to a manufactured lager, although it can be made stronger. As the fencer Jikela said, 'the stronger the mula mixture, and the longer the fermentation, the stronger the drink'.[49] Honey beer or mead (*iqhilika yobusi*), tends to be made with a higher alcoholic content but in his view *itolofiya* brew was the tastiest.

Proceedings were informal and individuals of all ages moved in and out of the large room where the beer was sold. It was not a ritualised event – and it is intriguing that Juritz reported, over 100 years ago, that 'no religious customs or festivities' were connected with *iqhilika*. Women were clearly in control of the proceedings, dispensing

Iqhilika *after cooking and filtering*   *Sharing of* Iqhilika

drink and collecting money. There is no systematic advertising of beer for sale, in part because the legality is still uncertain. People drop in from the street, family members and friends pass the word around. The brewing groups are well known. In some rural districts, flags are erected to signal beer is available but this does not seem to be done in the township. Clearly the process of brewing and drinking *iqhilika* underpins neighbourhood sociability. Brewers did not directly compete with licensed taverns in Fort Beaufort, as they tended neither to hold parties late into the night nor to have music or food. This group usually brewed about 100 litres, and they also had two 200-litre plastic drums that they would use for big events. An average session would bring in about R150 but they could make up to R600.

At the height of the season, Nowinile's group tried to go picking three times a week and would spend the next day selling fruit and brewing. During the season, prickly pear beer is available in the township continuously. In some districts such as Hankey, brewers also used another species of wild prickly pear fruit, reddish in colour, called *ebomvu* or *suurtjies* (probably *O. lindheimeri* or *O. stricta*). It is too sour for most people to eat as a fresh fruit. This ripens later and is available up to April. Moreover, because the mula can be used to make beer with honey or brown sugar, the brewing season extends well beyond the prickly pear season.[50] 'We can use the mula again,' Nowinile explained, 'throughout the year'.[51] *Iqhilika* made with brown sugar alone is less tasty than with *itolofiya*, so the latter is generally preferred when it is available.

In some towns, such as Grahamstown, honey beer is probably more popular.[52] Honey is also sometimes used to strengthen the mula – it reacts better with the mula than prickly pear and makes it stronger.[53] They cannot, however, use any shop-bought honey. It has to contain the comb (*blaai* or *amatyumza*) with a little syrup, but not too much. The brewers in Fort Beaufort find it difficult to get hold of this, although some was available from Mxhelo village, between Fort Beaufort and Alice/Fort Hare. Clearly, mula interacts best with specific fructose sugars that are found in comb-honey and a few fruits.

Sometimes the mula mix which has been saved and recycled for a couple of months starts to taste sour. The brewers then use another indigenous plant to resuscitate it. William Mbovane went to collect a sample for us nearby the house. It is a widely available, green-white lichen called *umtafatafa*, which grows on rocks or acacia trees. This is then cooked with water and the sour mula is added so that they ferment together. The process is similar to brewing but the result is not drunk – they throw the liquid out. The process is used to improve the mula. The dregs of *umtafatafa* are left with those of the mula to dry out and this is used in subsequent brewing. The women call it improving or cleansing (*ukucoca*) the mula. Some lichens are known to contain antibiotics and are widely used for medicinal purposes, including in ointments.[54]

Most brewers in Fort Beaufort are women but activities are not restricted to them. Honey beer has long been brewed by men and perhaps the largest scale operator in the township in 2006 was a young man in his thirties in the Tini's section.[55] His house was close to the old police barracks and in the past he was arrested on a number of occasions but was prepared to pay the fines. He sometimes brewed up to six, 200-litre drums in a week, largely using mula, brown sugar and honey so that he could operate throughout the year. He used some prickly pear in season, but did not pick himself; rather he commissioned women to pick for him. He sold on credit to pensioners, municipal road workers and to workers in the citrus industry, collecting money on pension and pay days. We were told that 'he can be tough in collecting from defaulters', but he operates cautiously in order to keep the police off his back.

POLICING

Brewing was difficult in the apartheid era. It was permitted for personal consumption, but frowned on by township administrators, police and farmers. Sale was policed on farms, in the locations and in the former Ciskei. In earlier years, as noted, farmers were concerned to restrict brewing because the prickly pear season coincided with a period of high demand for agricultural labour. This was no longer a significant concern.

Jikela Ndikila, the fencer, told us that he had been arrested five times for brewing *iqhilika* in the 1980s. On the first occasion, he was released with a warning. From the second to fourth arrests he was fined from R200 to R400 and on the fifth occasion he was detained in prison for a week. At that point he stopped brewing for sale and restricted himself to the mula trade. Alice Ningiza, a hawker and brewer at Fort Beaufort, recalled that 'during toyi-toyi' (the insurrectionary period of the 1980s) arrests declined significantly.[56] Ironically, however, she recalled that 'the toyi-toying youth were harsh on *iqhilika* brewers as they saw them, like shebeen owners, as responsible for diminishing people's commitment to . . . marches, demonstrations and street committee meetings'. So shebeen keepers and brewers were raided by some of the youth, rather than police, during this period. In parts of the Eastern Cape, comrades punished people found drunk by forcing them to imbibe a solution of Omo washing powder.

The police at Fort Beaufort recognised that brewing has long been widespread and in the post-apartheid era regulation became more relaxed.[57] But up to 2003, the Crime Prevention Unit at Fort Beaufort Police Station still made regular arrests.[58] Sergeant Khanyisa Memani told us that she started working at the station in 1994 and moved to the unit in the late nineties to work under Captain Ferreira. He had a network of informers and at times trapped brewers by sending bogus customers to purchase *iqhilika*. When he had sufficient evidence, he raided brewers' houses and arrested them. Magistrates generally imposed fines related to the number of previous offences and to the quantity of *iqhilika* produced. Samples were kept as court exhibits and the alcohol content was sometimes analysed. Another reason for keeping samples arose when adulterated *iqhilika* resulted in illness. There was a fatality in Goma Goma section of Bhofolo in 2001 from impure *iqhilika*, probably containing battery acid.

After 2003 when Ferreira left, Memani thought there was 'a general lack of will on the part of the police to pursue *iqhilika* cases'.[59] They occasionally arrested people for public drunkenness, but these tended to be consumers of retail alcohol (*utywala obuthengweyo*). *Iqhilika* drinking largely takes place in private houses rather than in the streets. There has been a national debate about the legal framework for home brewing and the Liquor Act of 2005 relaxed the controls over marketing. It enabled individuals to apply for short-term permits to sell different types of alcohol. While the Fort Beaufort brewers did not do so, our interviews suggest that overall, neither the police nor the ANC local authorities see *iqhilika* brewing as a significant problem.

The police are well aware of the three main areas of the township where brewers are concentrated and Memani thought that there were well over 50 brewers in these sections alone. Brewing increased in the prickly pear season and around holiday periods when workers returned home and there was more money in circulation. Farm workers also came into town in greater numbers. At one time the police also tried to control the digging of mula, in cooperation with farmers, but they have given this up. Memani added 'we used to joke that *iqhilika* is a thing of the farms' (*iqhilika yinto yasezifama*).

In Grahamstown, there are probably more than 60 brewers and one of them, who also sells alcoholic ginger beer (made of ginger powder, dry yeast and sugar), uses green bottles to disguise the contents.[60] Brewing by coloured people in Hankey, where the product is called *karrie* or *karee* continued through the last few decades despite hostility from farmers and police raids. The fruit brewing season is longer there because the reddish *suurtjies* can be harvested later. Informants in Kamastone, near Queenstown, suggested that brewing was no longer so common, and that the strong Christian communities around the Methodist church had avoided *iqhilika*; it was also 'ruled as an illegal substance' by the Ciskeian authorities. Amongst other places, Middledrift, regarded as 'the home of prickly pear' (*ikhaya letolofiya*), and Peddie, both in the former Ciskei, were, and remain, major centres of brewing.

COSTS AND PROFITS

It is difficult to calculate the exact turnover and profits from any single trip or season, because the picking and brewing group is rather fluid, costs are difficult to calculate and income over a period of time is uncertain. The women that we interviewed did not keep written records. Interviews suggest that although the women club together to hire bakkies, they pick and generally sell fresh fruit as individuals. They tend to brew as small groups – not necessarily including everyone who went together to pick. Not every member of the group brews after every trip. Prices also vary at different times of the season. They could sometimes charge more for fruit when it became scarcer, for example in 2005 prices increased from about R7 for 5 litres at the height of supply to R10 at its end. Individuals could earn anything between R50 to R180 a day from selling. They could then earn about R150 amongst three, or about R50 each, from an average session of brewing.

The costs of transport are R35 to R40 per trip and there are additional small costs such as sugar and sometimes firewood. With three trips a week, say 12 a month, the women in Nowinile's group could earn up to R1,000 a month each. A couple of them mentioned this amount, but it is by no means guaranteed. A few major brews at the height of the season can bring in more but when the harvest season is over, and brewing continues with sugar, the amount is less. The figure of around R1,000 a month during the season was also mentioned by some pickers that we interviewed who lived in rural villages in the former Ciskei. A survey of Grahamstown prickly pear fruit sellers in 2005 found highly variable incomes, with an average of R833 per season. One seller grossed R3,773 in a season.[61] These figures do not include income from brewing; most of the sellers surveyed in this study do not appear to have brewed.

Even if the Fort Beaufort women make less than R1,000 a month each, this was substantially more than the pension payment (R780 in 2005), which is widely acknowledged as a major source of income for the rural and small-town poor in South Africa. The amount was comparable with and generally better than wages for domestic servants, cleaners or similar manual workers. It was higher than the minimum wage. The older women involved in brewing also received pensions. At the end of the prickly pear season, during the winter months from April to September, some of Nowinile's group worked as harvesters, graders and packers of citrus fruit for wages. Fort Beaufort is located in the Kat River Valley which supports a number of citrus farms. Seasonal employment is available for about six months during the naartjie harvest (April to June), navel orange harvest (June to September) and to process valenicias and lemons at the end of the season. Some women also sell these fruits informally but this is a competitive market as local famers sell in bulk. Members of Nowinile's group said that they only sold citrus fruits once in a while when they could get free ungraded oranges from the farmers. Some farmers sell third grade fruit to women hawkers for about R100 per half ton.[62] They repackage the fruit and sell it on at a profit in smaller quantities.

We do not have figures for the proportion of household income generated by prickly pear around 2005. The survey in Grahamstown indicated that fruit selling contributed significantly to the income of poorer households and 95 per cent said that it was an important supplement.[63] Sellers there also ate about 1.5 litres of fruit per person per day. Our picture is similar. As the vast literature on livelihoods amongst poor families indicates, they are often involved in a range of different activities, including informal sector trading and casual labour.

When all of the women brewers and pickers in Fort Beaufort are put together, they clearly generate a turnover of hundreds of thousands of rand annually from prickly pear and brewing. Fort Beaufort is a noted centre for brewing and fruit selling but similar activities take place in many towns and on farms throughout the region from the Kei River Valley in the east to a line north of Mossel Bay and Oudtshoorn in the west. Prickly pear is most likely the basis for a marketed turnover of millions of rand, and substantial quantities of fruit, beer and other products are used for home consumption (Chapter 6).

BAKKIE OWNERS AND TRANSPORT COSTS

As we have mentioned, Nowinile's group was dependent on hiring transport. There are about seven bakkie owners in the old township of Fort Beaufort alone who transport different groups of women to picking grounds. There are also others in the new location and Newtown, formerly the coloured township. Bakkie owners do not specialise in transporting pickers. Some are general dealers, spaza shop or tavern owners and use their bakkies largely for transporting goods. In 2005, they could make R245 to R280 a day transporting women before paying for the costs of petrol, and generally had to wait at the farm for the women. One owner whom we interviewed found that the costs of petrol, at R120 for the Grahamstown farm run, necessitated staying at the picking site if he was to make a profit.[64] For bakkie owners, this is not usually a major part of their business and they are not necessarily dependent on prickly pear pickers or citrus hawkers 'but it is undeniable that at the peak of harvests and sales, both fruits keep bakkie owners or drivers very busy indeed'.[65]

Mncedisi Tsotsa, one of the bakkie owners, lived in a basic RDP low-income house in a new section of the township.[66] His bakkie was very old and not always operating. He drove for Nowinile's group, and others as well, sometimes up to five times a week if his vehicle was in working condition. He could take a maximum of seven at a time and each woman was allowed to bring back two full bags.

Given these transport costs, denial of access to farms surrounding Fort Beaufort is a major handicap for the women. When the local farms were available for picking, the bakkie owners could drop the women off and do other things while they picked – and they charged much less. It is true that even if the women were to pick locally, most would still hire bakkies because they can pick more. There are some advantages in the Grahamstown farms: they have abundant prickly pear, which some felt (unlike Danckwerts) was better quality than could be found around Fort Beaufort. Nevertheless, the women could in theory make an additional R20 per trip, and save time, if they picked locally – even if they hired bakkies. At the best of times this represented perhaps R200 more a month.

Township-based women were also facing competition from those on the farms. Some farmers allowed their own farm workers to pick and sell fruit as a perk. One mentioned that he sometimes gave lifts to women farm workers to sell prickly pear in Fort Beaufort.[67] Nolast Mkontwane, who lived on Merino, noted that 'they are allowed to harvest freely as much fruit as is available on the farm'.[68] She sold 5 litre containers at R6 in 2005 and probably undercut township sellers: farm workers also sold along the road from Fort Beaufort to Grahamstown especially near Sparkington stall. At Leeufontein farm, south of Fort Beaufort, for example, the prickly pear plants are close to the workers' houses as well as the road so they have a significant advantage. Sellers in the townships incurred significantly more costs. Farm workers also brewed, and younger people drink *iqhilika* at *tshotsha* dance gatherings. The farmers had 'stopped bothering as long as people don't fight and keep working'.[69] Some farmers see an added advantage in encouraging the workers to pick fruit in order to minimise damage to livestock. While a number of farmers try to eradicate the remaining prickly pear, this is expensive and difficult.

THE BENEFITS OF PRICKLY PEAR

Prickly pear clearly retains a widespread and distinctive local consumer market amongst both white and especially black people in the Eastern Cape. It is the cheapest fruit available, although ungraded citrus fruits can also be bought very cheaply later in the year. It has cultural value for a surprising range of people. We were told many humorous stories from the days when the plant was used more intensively (Chapter 6). Amongst whites fruit picking is often associated with the carefree days of youth. It was clearly of central importance for farm workers. The fruit, with a high vitamin C content, is a useful addition to the diet.

There are limits to the amount that women can earn from prickly pear brewing and selling, but these activities sustain them directly, and differ from other forms of informal hawking because women are involved in gathering and adding value. In addition to the money generated from sales and brewing, *itolofiya* provides a small supplementary income for those who regulate entry to picking sites, for bakkie owners, for farm workers who sell mula, for firewood suppliers and for spaza shop-owners. It keeps money circulating amongst poor people within the township, rather than going straight out to retailers or tavern owners who sell factory-manufactured, branded liquor. There is also a limited by-product in fodder for domestic animals.

While many other former uses have declined, *iqhilika* and fresh fruit remain popular – even if they are no longer as widespread as they were. Alcohol production may not seem to be an appropriate route for poor people to generate income. Alcoholism, especially amongst men, is a major problem in such communities, even within the families of brewers, including Nowinile's. But alcohol consumption will continue whether or not *iqhilika* is produced. There is a strong argument to support local brewers, rather than encourage even deeper penetration by large-scale liquor manufacturers and distributors. Prickly pear harvesting and brewing not only provides income, but it has long been deeply embedded in the lives of some of the Eastern Cape poor, and the fruit remains a valuable social focus in districts where it still thrives.

———————————

THE SPREAD
OF PRICKLY PEAR,
1750-1900

COLONISATION AND EXOTICS: THE GLOBAL SPREAD OF PRICKLY PEAR AND ITS ORIGINS IN SOUTH AFRICA

Prickly pear has become deeply embedded in Eastern Cape society. But how and when did these exotics from Mexico spread so widely in South Africa? There is not a great deal of specific information before the 1830s. We have to imagine the context and the different possibilities – the clues in names and odd references in texts. In general, however, prickly pear gained a foothold in part because of its remarkable properties of reproduction and survival, in part because of human intervention and in part because of the specific ecology of the Eastern Cape. The roots of its success lay in the interplay of human and environmental factors and it is important to note that not only people, but a number of indigenous species, found this spiny exotic to their liking and and – in their opportunistic search for nectar and fruit – helped it on its way. Invasives can displace some indigenous species, but they can benefit others.

Colonisation in general, and farming in particular, precipitated the introduction of many alien plant species with unpredictable results. Some were brought intentionally as food crops and some came by chance, either mixed with grain seeds or by other means along the trade routes of empire.[1] Dutch officials perceived a wood shortage from the very earliest years of their settlement in the seventeenth century. Exotic trees were planted for timber, shade and firewood.[2] Although the Cape proved rich in indigenous flowering plants, many new species were introduced for aesthetic reasons in gardens. Thunberg, the Swedish scientific traveller, commented sharply on the transformation of the Cape by the 1770s that '[in] a country where,

150 years ago … herds only grazed, one now sees several Indian and most of our European seeds cultivated, vineyards and orchards laid out, and culinary vegetables planted'.[3]

Prickly pear was the subject of curiosity from the beginning of transatlantic exchanges. The earliest Spanish conquistadors 'could not fail to notice the presence all around of *nopalli*'.[4] The term 'tuna', a Caribbean word meaning fruit or seed, was recorded when the Spanish ate the fruit in Haiti around 1515. Cortes was greeted in 1519 onto the Mexican plateau with opuntia fruits called *nochtli*. The Spanish were also very soon aware of the 'immense amounts of cochineal for sale' in Aztec markets and the role of opuntia in producing this startling, red dye.[5] Initially the promise of cochineal was overlooked in the quest for gold, silver and territory for sheep, but Native Americans continued to produce it and it became a valuable part of the Empire's tribute and trade.

Cochineal dye was rapidly adopted by European textile manufacturers and pieces of the 'perfect red' cloth soon bedecked royalty and their horses; painters in turn worked cochineal into their repertoire and palette of colours.[6] In her book called *The Perfect Red*, Amy Greenfield highlights Titian's famous portrait of Charles V on horseback in 1548, where his shining armour and black steed are counterbalanced by a sumptuous red saddle cloth, sash and plume. Courtiers, nobility and those with wealth followed suit, relieving the fashionable black with red flourishes. Elizabethan women offset their white face make-up with crimson lips.

From the start, opuntia fruit and seeds were compared to a fig – Europeans frequently gave familiar names to exotic plants and animals. An early illustration survives from 1535 and by the mid-century plants were well established in Spain – originally as ornamentals and for hedging. Prickly pear was adopted on the Canary Islands, the Azores, Madeira and along the Mediterranean coast. Hedges can still be seen in southern Spain and Morocco; on La Palma Island in the Canaries and in Madeira it has become an invader.[7] Prickly pear plants crop up in the backdrop of many postcards and pictures of the Mediterranean coast. Muslim communities apparently took to the fruit and it was passed through North Africa and into the horn of Africa. It travelled along the shipping routes of the Portuguese and Spanish empires. The cladode, which could remain relatively moist for months if stored carefully, was carried and eaten on board ships as 'a fresh vegetable to combat scurvy'.[8] The fruit rotted quickly but opuntia's capacity to store moisture in its cladodes for long periods, an adaption to its semi-arid habitat, was one factor in its rapid spread around the world.

Various species of prickly pear may have been introduced to the Cape from any of these sources. Ships sailing to Asia from Europe until the opening of the Suez Canal in 1868 stopped at the Cape. Many travelled with plants, seeds and animals of all kinds. By the mid-seventeenth century, colonisers, and particularly the Dutch, were highly attuned to the potential of introducing new plants. An estimated 50 crop plants, some of which became invaders, were introduced at the Cape within the first few years of settlement.[9] Exotic tree plantations sprung up around the company gardens and further afield within a few decades. As in the case of other imperial botanical gardens, Cape Town's was used as an experimental site for transferred plants.[10] Ships bound for the Cape often stopped at the Canaries and this is the most likely source for the first opuntia. Cape species, in turn, became established in the Atlantic islands. South African strelitzia, or bird of paradise plant, became the official flower of Madeira.

A.C. MacDonald, the first Cape agricultural officer in the 1890s, found that one of his earliest duties was to investigate opuntia. He suggested that prickly pear had been imported to South Africa from India – to which it was certainly taken by the seventeenth century. A few sources, probably following MacDonald, affirm that opuntia was introduced to the Cape in the seventeenth century. Although this is likely, we have not yet found definite evidence. An unexpected element of Jan van Riebeeck's diaries from the 1650s is that they include detailed information on plants, including those in the company gardens, but we could find no specific reference to cactus. Peter Kolbe, who worked at the Cape from 1705 to 1713, made extensive records of the food plants introduced by the colonists.[12] His list of species in the gardens also

Prickly pear, oleander and Greek ruins, Agrigento, Sicily, 2004

FURTHER SPECULATION ON THE ORIGINS OF PRICKLY PEAR IN SOUTH AFRICA

Gerhard de Kock, who worked at Grootfontein agricultural college for many years, and is one of South Africa's leading experts on opuntia, has an intriguing theory about its early arrival in South Africa.[11] He suggests that it may have preceded van Riebeeck's first Dutch settlement in 1652. It was possibly thrown overboard when vessels anchored along the coast to collect water or provisions on their route east; it was possibly planted by sailors in the hope that it would provide cladodes for future trips. The cladodes were certainly used in the sixteenth and seventeenth century as ballast and anti-scorbutics (to prevent scurvy) on sailing ships. Old cladodes could have been jettisoned and then floated to land and taken root. At present we do not have documentary evidence for this, nor is it clear how the theory could be tested by exploring species diversity or the genetic characteristics of remaining plants. Even one cladode could, however, have affected a significant plant transfer because the cladodes strike root so readily. Although they are largely composed of water, cladodes can float, especially in sea water, which is heavier than fresh. We have seen intact cladodes washed up on beaches in the Eastern Cape. They were probably washed down rivers into the sea, then deposited on the beach by waves.

omits cactus or opuntia. He refers to an Indian fig tree in his discussion of exotics but it is clear from the description that this is a fig not a prickly pear.[13] Kolbe makes one tantalising reference to a *Ficus americana*, and also calls it a cereus, with spines and needles. It was translated in the English edition as a 'torch thistle'. Cereus is a genus of cactus, later common in the Cape – and torch thistle was a name used for similar plants because Native Americans used the dried stems as fire torches. But Kolbe says that he did not actually see this plant himself, and his description of its reportedly milky sap suggests there may have been confusion with euphorbia.

Older Dutch dictionaries identify prickly pear as *Indisches Vijg* (Indian fig), but the term did not necessarily then imply the East. As is well-known, early Spanish explorers initially believed that they had found Asia by sailing west and the term Indian was carelessly applied to, and stuck to, American people and plants. Maize was called Indian corn. Indian was also used as a descriptive term for exotic objects and species (in the sense of mysterious and glamorous as well as foreign). The Latin binomial for the most common prickly pear species – *O. ficus-indica* – likely resulted from these associations.

The Afrikaans name, *turksvy*, or turkish fig, suggests a middle-eastern source. But confusingly, a few plants and animals of American origin acquired the name 'turkey', either because of confusion with eastern species, or because they were perceived to come by this route or simply to indicate an exotic origin. The Spanish names of 'nopal' for the plant (from a Native American word), 'nopales' for the cladodes and 'tuna' for the fruit do not seem to have travelled to South Africa although they are occasionally used in early sources. Prickly pear, the English term, was used in the Caribbean in the eighteenth century, where some species of opuntia were indigenous. Robert Percival, who visited in 1796 and 1801 on his way to and from India, made reference to 'the Nopal or prickly pear' around Cape Town but those few travellers who noticed the plant at the Cape around this time tended to talk of opuntia or cactus.[14] The term prickly pear was gradually generalised by British settlers in the first half of the nineteenth century and commonly used in written texts.

MacDonald noted that prickly pear was established in gardens in the Western Cape in the eighteenth century. Thunberg does not seem to mention it in his major *Travels at the Cape of Good Hope*, where he visited in the 1770s, which suggests that it was not common because he observed many plants. He recorded it in another publication as an introduced plant.[15] Percival saw it 'in abundance' around 1800 and noted that it was the plant 'on which feeds the cochineal insect'.[16] It had clearly been there for some time, but opuntia did not become a significant self-spreader in the Western Cape. Lucie Duff Gordon saw prickly pear only 'here and there' in hedges around Rondebosch and Wynberg nearly a century later in the early 1860s.[17]

THE ADVANCE OF OPUNTIA IN THE CAPE

Prickly pear can spread in two different ways. It reproduces most easily from its cladodes, which put out roots when they come into contact with soil, especially bare soil. As noted, the cladodes can remain moist and potentially fertile for long enough to survive sea journeys. Opuntia species can also reproduce from seed in the fruit – although this often requires assistance. The flowers have to be pollinated, usually by insects. Cape bees in particular took to the bright, yellow-orange, open blooms. Some bird species seemed to favour the nectar and bats could also have acted as pollinating agents. Once the fruit has matured, many animals, as will be illustrated, ate it and could have been vectors.

Non-human agency was undoubtedly involved in the transmission of prickly pear around the Eastern Cape, but documentary evidence suggests that people first took it there. The spread of prickly pear in South Africa coincided initially with the extension of more intensive pastoralism in areas that were often prone to drought. This to some degree replicated the American experience. In Mexico and Texas, where the plant originated, there was no significant indigenous pastoralism before colonisation. But this territory proved fertile ground for cattle and sheep – there were four million Spanish merinos in Mexico by the end of the sixteenth century, before South Africa was colonised. The demands of domesticated animals in these semi-arid lands resulted in widespread new use of indigenous prickly pear for fodder.[18] When the Catholic Franciscan brothers moved north from Mexico into California, they brought with them the most versatile species *O. ficus-indica*. This prickly pear was already semi-cultivated and there were probably a number of varieties. In turn it hybridised with local opuntia in California to produce a new variety, which was called mission fig.[19] Prickly pear was used by settlers as cattle fodder in Texas from the mid-nineteenth century. Fodder plantations of *O. ficus-indica* and other species were also established in north-eastern Brazil where a short, rainy season is followed by eight rainless months.[20]

If the plant did not establish itself as a castaway from ships along the coastal Eastern Cape, it was certainly taken by settler pastoralists on their migration eastwards. MacDonald heard a story that a farmer named Vanderberg had brought two cladodes from Cape Town to his farm in Buffels Hoek around 1750. This site is almost certainly a valley and farm close to the village of Petersburg in what was to become Graaff-Reinet district. It is a sheltered and well-watered spot, about 40 km east of the present town. The date of 1750 sounds early, and is likely to be an approximation. Although occasional settler hunting parties had reached this area, farms were only settled in the 1760s.[21] It is possible that Khoisan people spread prickly pear or that hunting parties planted it in anticipation of settlement – or even that animals spread it. But we found no evidence for this and the date of transfer was probably later than 1750.

Whatever the case, it is striking that prickly pear was sufficiently important to accompany Afrikaners to the furthest reaches of settlement almost immediately. Petersburg was amongst the first areas to become densely covered in later years. MacDonald also recorded that these plants had been the source for further cultivation by a farmer named de Bruyn in the Bruintjieshoogte, between Pearston and Somerset East. Sparrman, as noted in Chapter 1, was told in the 1770s that alcohol was made in the Camdeboo and elsewhere from a *'cactus* of considerable size'.[22] The Camdeboo, derived from a Khoikhoi word meaning green hollow, and also the name of a stream near present day Aberdeen, referred to the broad flat plains south of Graaff-Reinet town. This region, including parts of Somerset East, Pearston and Graaff-Reinet districts, became a hotspot for invasion in the nineteenth century.

Thus, prickly pear was certainly taken intentionally to some spots in the Eastern Cape in the eighteenth century, and there is evidence of planting, especially for fodder and hedging, throughout the nineteenth century. But once established, it began to spread itself. Observations from travellers and farmers suggested that by the 1850s, within about 80 years, it was quite widely dispersed.

Early routes followed by prickly pear included the livestock trekking and transport corridors. When the Quaker James Backhouse passed Mossel Bay on his route eastwards in 1838, he noted that the orange-flowered cactus 'seems to be naturalized here'.[23] He clearly had an eye for the plant. At Cradock he noted '[opuntia], bearing an edible fruit, is quite at home among the rocks; possibly it may be a naturalised plant, but it abounds in this latitude for many miles westward'. He also found it 'common in the Karroo, when it sometimes stands solitary 10 feet high'

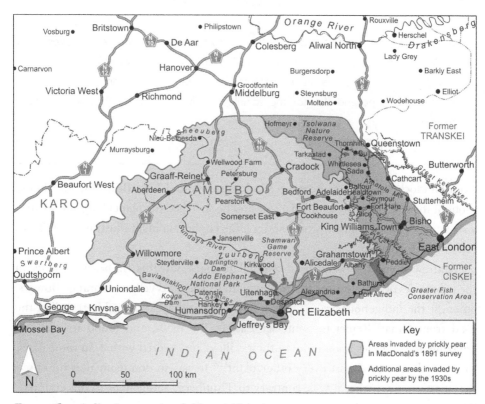

Eastern Cape indicating areas invaded by prickly pear

SCIENTIFIC NAMES FOR PRICKLY PEAR SPECIES

More than one species of opuntia was brought to South Africa, and at least 10 were established by the twentieth century. One of the difficulties in identifying the different species is not only that they are referred to by general and popular names in various languages, but that up to the 1950s there was a good deal of confusion about the botanical names. South Africa was not exceptional in this regard. The taxonomy of cacti has a long and complicated history, and the names for various genera and species were unstable until very recently.[24] Opuntia, in particular, was difficult to classify because there were so many (about 160), they hybridised and a few species were partly domesticated with a number of varieties. The botanical name *Opuntia ficus-indica* was used in some nineteenth-century sources and this was the main species brought to the Eastern Cape. However, MacDonald, referring to a book on the flora of Madeira, called the most common species *O. Juna L.* in his report of 1891.[25] It is likely that this is a misprint and he meant *Opuntia tuna*, a name which referred to the Spanish word for the fruit and which was in widespread use at the time. For part of the twentieth century, some scientists referred to this same species as *Opuntia megacantha* (big thorn).[26] They restricted the term *O. ficus-indica* to spineless, cultivated varieties, many of which also had sweet fruits. By the 1950s and 1960s, *O. megacantha* fell out of use. *O. ficus-indica* became fixed as the botanical name for the most common, wild prickly pear of the Cape and also for the spineless cultivated varieties that were derived from it.

The prickly pear established in the Western Cape was sometimes called *O.*

from Cradock to half way between Grahamstown and Fort Beaufort. Backhouse thought that the flower resembled a rose and he sketched the plant alongside an aloe, a strelitzia, a cycad, a small protea and a large euphorbia in an illustration of 'Trees etc. of South Africa'.[27]

Andrew Wylie, the first official colonial geologist, saw this 'fig-bearing cactus' in the tributaries of the Sundays River, 'gay with its splendid yellow or orange flowers' amongst the indigenous acacias, aloes, numnum and spekboom. He travelled the road from Graaff-Reinet to Somerset East in the 1850s, and found it 'perfectly amazing' to see 'miles upon miles of these valleys are covered with it, in some cases, to the exclusion of almost every other plant'.[28] It was so dominant that he raised the question of whether it was, contrary to Thunberg, 'indigenous to this country'. Thomas Baines found, as far north as Colesberg, that:

coccinellifera. It denoted a species on which cochineal insects thrived and had a smaller, sour fruit. The term *Opuntia vulgaris* was also used, probably for the same species. These were probably what is now called *O. monocantha* – although *O. vulgaris* is still sometimes used interchangeably. Both the cladode and the bush of this prickly pear are smaller, and it is more at home in humid, coastal patches. It grew at a variety of locations from Cape Town to Port Elizabeth and also on the KwaZulu/Natal coast. This was probably the species seen by Percival and by the English traveller Latrobe, which he called Indian fig, near Port Elizabeth in the 1810s. Lucie Duff Gordon saw it in hedges around Cape Town.

There were a number of attempts to establish cochineal dye production beyond Mexico. British imports of red dye from Spain, favoured for military uniforms, ran to about £200,000 a year in the late eighteenth century. Joseph Banks, the Director of Kew and President of the Royal Society in Britain, was involved in experiments to develop a source within the Empire.[29] Prickly pear was taken to Australia for this purpose in one of the earliest convict ships. Attempts were also made in India. We can find no record of similar experiments at the Cape at this time, but a dye industry flourished in the Canary Islands from the 1830s and this prompted Baron von Ludwig, the Cape Town plant collector, to import opuntia and cochineal at that time. Further unsuccessful attempts to nurture dye-producing cochineal on prickly pear were made in the 1860s in the southern Cape (see Chapter 7).[30] We do not know which species were imported for this experiment, but they were probably *O. monocantha*. This species is now rare in South Africa because it was so susceptible to cochineal.

the people had gathered a quantity of the fruit of the cactus or prickly pear. These are excellent eating but are so covered with little clumps of minute and almost invisible spines that a person is almost sure to get his fingers full. The best way is to cut off both ends and make a longitudinal slit in the rind, which may be turned back on each side, and the seeds and pulp laid bare.[31]

Rivers were another important route of transmission; South African ecologists still see them as one of the most susceptible habitats for plant invasions.[32] Prickly pear grew comfortably in rocky soils but thrived even better in deeper alluvial soil. Cape rivers and streams were often seasonal, and came down in flood after heavy rainfall in their large, dry catchments. Floods tore the cladodes from their bushes and carried them downstream. Thomas Baines and others saw it along the Fish River Valley in 1848. An area near Fort Brown was called Vyge Kraal because clumps of prickly pear grew there so luxuriantly. Wild bush pigs were reputed to feed off them. A few years later Thomas Stubbs described chasing after rebel Khoikhoi into the bottom of the Zwaartwaters Poort (near Grahamstown) which he found was 'very thickly studded with prickly pear and bush'.[33] The floods of 1874 reputedly spread opuntia further and more thoroughly down the Fish River from Cradock.

Prickly pear spread downstream from the original areas in which it was planted along seasonal rivers running southwards through the Camdeboo. R.P. Botha, a member of the Legislative Council, recalled in 1890 that he had lived on a 'prickly pear farm' in the Vogel (now Voel) River Valley in 1847; at this time relatively few farms were 'infested'.[34] The farm he mentioned was just north of present-day Pearston, near the source of the river coming out of Coetzeesberg. This watercourse proved to be one

important conduit. There are farms near Pearston called Turks Vyg Rivier and Turksvy Laagte as well as a Turksvykloof in the south of the district.[35] By 1861 Botha claimed that he had lost control of the prickly pear on his farm and was forced to sell it. Similarly, B.J. Keyter, MLA for Oudtshoorn, farmed for some years on the Melk River between Graaff-Reinet and Pearston in the 1860s.[36] The Buffels Hoek Valley, around Petersburg, was the source of the Melk, immediately to the west of the Voel River. So dense did the pear become on his farm, a century after the prickly pear was introduced

James Backhouse's Trees &c of S. Africa *with prickly pear as the only exotic between indigenous strelitzia, cycad and aloe with euphorbia in the background and small protea in the foreground*

upstream, that his sheep died and his herders could not get the cattle out of the thickets and into the kraals. As a result he sold up and moved to Oudtshoorn.

Transport corridors for ox-wagons and droving routes were conduits for prickly pear partly because they carried a large volume of people and livestock that were attracted to the fruits. Braving the glochids, animals ate them whether growing on the cladodes or rotting on the ground and deposited the seeds in their dung. As their casings were hard, the seeds did not grow easily if planted directly into the soil, but they would 'germinate more readily after passing through the stomach of any animal'.[37] This was known by the late nineteenth century, and probably before. Multitudes of prickly pear seedlings propagated like a miniature forest on cow dung, a natural fertiliser pack; the plants grew from the 'droppings of cattle as thick as grass'.[38] Human excreta were another potential vector and when Gerhard de Kock went in search of interesting varieties in the 1960s he made a point of visiting old farm homesteads.

CROWS AND BABOONS

Our evidence for mechanisms of transmission comes from observations recorded some decades after the initial period of invasion in the first half of the nineteenth century – notably a series of four enquiries undertaken by the Cape government between 1890 and 1906. Recent interviews and scientific studies enrich this material. We cannot be certain that ecological relationships observed in the 1890s or 1990s are applicable to the earlier years. Such interactions do change, and there were probably many different specific histories of adaption by domesticated and wild animals to a rich new source of sustenance such as opuntia. But some of these relationships are likely to have relevance for this earlier period. We need to think about the history of plant transfers and invasion in the context of unpredictable ecological interactions.

Prickly pear flourished under trees where birds perched or nested and spread their droppings or regurgitated seed.[39] Amongst many birds, crows were reputed to like the fruit and they were also attracted to the carrion along transport routes.[40] C.J. Skead, the ornithologist and naturalist who worked for many years at the Kaffrarian Museum in King William's Town, recorded this predilection in 1952, noting that the Cape crow (*Corvus capensis*) 'excavated the ... heavily-pipped interiors' of the fruit and discarded the harder, external covers.[41] In a fascinating piece of research done from 1987 to 1999, Sue Milton and Richard Dean tested this idea of crow dispersal.[42] They counted prickly pear plants and their relationship to telegraph poles and fences along thousands of miles of road in the western and southern Karoo. They found that there was a far higher concentration of opuntia along roads and next to these popular man-made bird perches. They also observed the location of Cape and pied crow (*C. albus*) nests – which occur frequently on telegraph poles. Patient and devoted researchers, they then analysed 300 crow pellets from five sites on the Prince Albert to Beaufort West route and found 86 opuntia seeds. This is not an area of particularly frequent prickly pear growth. They concluded that opuntia was far more likely to take root near telegraph poles and fences than elsewhere and that crows were major agents of dispersal. In the first half of the early nineteenth century, when prickly pear was first striding across country, there would not have been many man-made structures along the roads for crows to roost on, but their taste for prickly pear may well have been acquired early.

Cattle, sheep and crows could of course carry seeds away from river valleys and transport routes. Wild animals seem to have played a particularly significant role in this regard. Only the formidable digestive tracts of ostriches were thought to neutralise the seed. The fruit was eaten – and seed spread – by jackals, monkeys, porcupines, bush pigs and especially baboons. This is still the case. Gladman Tilasi, a guide in the Great Fish River Conservation Area, recounted to us his observations that baboons, warthogs and bush pigs eat the fruit, while black rhinos eat the whole plant, spines and all.[43]

Addo elephants also ate prickly pear fruit. One reason why so many (about 114 out of 130) were shot in 1919 to 1920 was because they roamed onto farm land before the National Park was declared to find water, enjoy prickly pear and oranges, as well as indigenous vegetation such as spekboom.[44] In the process they damaged crops and disturbed landowners. In retrospect, it was a devastating loss to the Cape's wildlife – although they were later protected. The Port Elizabeth Divisional Council may have had this relationship in mind when they put an Addo elephant, standing between two prickly pear plants, on their coat of arms. In the 1950s hundreds of tons of oranges were sent to the National Park for the elephants. These were piled near the ranger's house and a spotlight trained on them at night so that visitors could see elephants eating.

Baboons were widely linked with prickly pear fruit. Solly Zuckerman, one of the first zoologists to study omnivorous Chacma baboons systematically in the wild, recorded in 1930 that they ate largely roots, fruit of prickly pear, mealie cobs and plundered cultivated fruit – as well as a wide range of insects and small mammals. They were also said to spread prickly pear through their droppings.[45] P.W. Roux, former Director of Grootfontein and a close observer of Karoo ecology over many decades, recalled that baboon numbers had increased exponentially during the early decades of the twentieth century at the same time as the prickly pear.[46] He was sure that this was no coincidence, and that baboons had a symbiotic relationship with opuntia. On the one hand, they thrived on the growing supplies of fruit, and occasionally even cladodes. On the other, along with crows, they were probably the major agents of dispersal. In the same way that sheep provided additional food for jackals and contributed to an increase in their numbers, so prickly pear in some areas provided a new food for the wild species which thrived on it. When the biological campaign destroyed much of the prickly pear during the 1940s, farmers believed that omnivorous baboons switched their food sources and roamed the countryside killing sheep and young goats instead. There was a troublesome Grootfontein troop and more generally a scare about baboons in the Karoo in the 1930s and 1940s.[47] They reputedly tore open lambs' stomachs and ewes' udders to get at the milk, but some disputed this.

The story of a South African child, supposedly brought up by wild animals in the manner of Romulus and Remus in Rome, but in this case by baboons rather than wolves, sheds intriguing light on prickly pear. Captured by police in the eastern Cape around 1903, the youth was turned over to a hospital in Grahamstown. After observation, he was placed with a farmer near Port Alfred who named him Lucas or Lukas. The idea that baboons had raised him was later investigated and questioned, but the case received sufficient attention for a picture of Lucas to be deposited in the British Royal Geographical Society collection. It was recorded that as a wild boy he had eaten crickets, ostrich eggs, prickly pears, green mealies and wild honey. 'Although offered the best fare, he retained his old taste in food and preferred a meal of raw corn and cactus, once consuming as many as 89 prickly pears'.[48] For us, the interest is not so much the dubious truth of the story, nor how to interpret the racially informed, scientific interest at the time, but that prickly pear was represented at the heart of baboon diets.

Port Elizabeth Divisional Council Coat of Arms. An Addo elephant standing between two prickly pear cactuses

Our interviews suggest that this close relationship continues. A farmer in Hankey vividly described watching baboons and monkeys – equally fond of the fruit – climb up the spiny cladodes to get at it.[49] Baboons, in particular, cut and dissected the peel with their nails and dropped it on the ground below. According to people that we interviewed in Hewu, dassies also eat the fruit and there was a saying: 'the dassie lives in rocky, rugged areas with prickly pear' (*imbila zihlala emaxandikeni netolofiya*). Baboons, birds and other wild animals spread prickly pear to the most remote places, such as high and inaccessible krantzes.

The combination of growing numbers of livestock, together with so wide a variety of fruit-eating wild animals, provided particularly favourable ecological conditions for opuntia in the Cape. By the 1870s, about a century after its introduction, opuntia was seen in dense thickets in many parts of the area between the Sundays and Great Fish Rivers. *O. ficus-indica* clearly preferred semi-arid zones with a rainfall between about 300 and 600 mm a year and did not establish itself easily in the wetter, east-coast region of the Cape, east of the Kei, nor in the drier, western Karoo districts, with a rainfall under 300 mm a year. It adapted best to land below about 1,400 metres in altitiude although it could survive, especially if planted, at higher altitudes in more sheltered or north-facing spots in particular. Although frost damaged younger plants, opuntia certainly found niches on the highveld. Large clusters of prickly pear were effective in resisting fire.

PRICKLY PEAR IN THE INTERIOR

Mary Barber, the Cape's most noted woman botanist and illustrator in the nineteenth century, travelled south from Kimberley to the Orange River (Gariep) in 1879.[50] She saw American aloes (*Agave americana*), blue gum trees and figs – all exotics – planted on most of the farms, 'no matter how desolate – bravely holding their own in spite of the vicissitudes of wind and weather'. She also found 'a friendly Prickly Pear bush' on the roadside, 'offering us a capital shelter for our fire, which we gladly accepted: it was thick set, and well grown out, and a quiet nook within its sheltering recesses, was all but a chimney corner to us'. This led her to the consideration that:

> there are certain plants which follow civilization all over the world. It is true that many of them are 'ill weeds which grow apace', that we could gladly dispense with; whilst on the other hand, there are many useful plants. Amongst them we may mention the Prickly Pear (cactus opuntia) a native of America ... [which] may now be found through the colony.

Prickly pear was taken to Natal and the Transvaal, probably with the Voortrekkers in the 1830s. The Pedi adapted it further for military defence.

According to a story, probably from the 1850s, 'chief Sekwati, the father of old Sekukuni, built his main kraal on the top of Thaba Mosego (The Hill of Laughter). The Bapedi planted prickly pears and made a high fence of thorn trees around Thaba Mosego and also built stone walls with peep holes for shooting'.[51] Thabo Mosego was abandoned after Sekwati's death in 1861 and the reference to prickly pear seems to refer clearly to that period. We do not know how the plant reached African societies in the interior but it is striking that they adopted it so quickly. They may have taken cladodes from Afrikaner trekkers or it is possible that Pedi migrant workers carried it back with them. Peter Delius reports them going 'in some numbers' to the Eastern Cape by the early 1850s, mainly to acquire guns.[52] There were also trade routes to Delagoa Bay.

The strategy was carried elsewhere in Sekhukhuneland (now part of Limpopo and Mpumalanga provinces). 'At the time of the Swazi invasion in 1874', another tradition related, 'their [villages] were so well protected by barricades of prickly pear, that the Swazi warriors had to use their shields as platforms to cross over into them'.[53] In the late 1880s, 'most of the native kraals were defended by hedges of prickly pears' in this area.[54] The Ndzundza Ndebele stronghold of Erholweni (Mapoch se Grotte), conquered in 1882, despite its stone-wall fortifications, was covered with prickly pear in the early twenty-first century, and was probably then too. The fruits and cladodes would have made a valuable siege food. We have found no evidence of similar military uses in the Eastern Cape, where settlement was more dispersed. Near Pietersburg (Polokwane), prickly pear hedges were grown around African grain fields in the late nineteenth century.[55] Farmers in the Marico district also used it for hedging. Defensive hedges were a feature of some Mediterranean communities, and they are portrayed in nineteenth-century paintings in Seville's art gallery.

Prickly pear played a small part in the survival strategy of Boer families on the farms during the South African War (1899-1902). Kotie Steenkamp, a woman in her thirties, was left to manage the family farm and six children in the Free State when her husband was sent as a prisoner of war to St Helena. 'At the time of the scorched earth policy', her reminiscences record, 'fruit trees were destroyed but in most cases the prickly pear plants were left standing. The fruits of the prickly pears were ... used to supplement our diet, but the children were never allowed to eat more than three ... at a time'.[56] Perhaps the British troops were unfamiliar with the plant's potential. A Boer commando was reputed to have evaded the British by hiding in Camdeboo thickets, south of Graaff-Reinet.

PRICKLY PEAR AND CAPE CULTURE

Opuntia also began to enter the Cape's literature. Alfred de Jager Jackson, who grew up on a Beaufort West farm in the 1860s and 1870s, wrote a lyrical book towards the end of his life called *Manna in the Desert: A Revelation of the Great Karroo* (1920). His aim was 'to draw men towards a right and reverent regard of Nature'. His book is intensely conservation-minded. He was deeply aware of his natural surroundings and an advocate of indigenous vegetation as a way of fighting soil erosion.[57] Yet, he wrote of prickly pear as 'useful to feed the animals in a drought' as long as the thorns were 'scorched off over a blazing fire' and praised the 'delicious, oval-shaped fruit, the size of a hen's egg ... it is juicy, sweet, refreshing, wholesome, and strengthening'.[58] He told a story that both celebrated the value of the prickly pear and also vernacular knowledge at the Cape. A party of four men walking through the countryside were found dead from thirst under a large prickly pear that contained enough thirst-quenching liquid to have kept them alive for many days. They were strangers to the rural areas and did not know of the life-giving properties of the plant: 'those poor fellows', he wrote, 'did not know enough. Accompanied by a native lad, they would have been spared a needless, tragic fate'. He also rejoiced in another cactus producing a long, elegant snow-white flower: 'the sight of a sugar-bird in his coat of resplendent green, hovering before this beautiful flower, and sucking up its sweetness, is worth going far to see!'[59]

In *The Farm in the Karoo* (1883), a kind of docu-drama of 'adventure in South Africa', the narrator describes driving through 'miles of prickly pear shrubs; the soil was dry and sandy, every vestige of moisture being taken up by this troublesome cactus'.[60] But the author also affirmed its value: 'the fruit is very good, and is much liked by the natives. The Dutch make brandy and syrup from it, and the baboons and monkeys are ravenous after it.' In his novel *Gallows Gecko*, C. Louis Leipoldt, always interested in food, reminisced about the delicious cool fruit of the spiny cactus eaten as far west as Lamberts Bay, the seaside camp of Clanwilliam farmers, where he was brought up in the 1880s.[61] He made only brief mention of it, however, in his *Cape Cookery* – perhaps because this book concentrates very largely on early, Western Cape recipes and produce.[62]

Surprisingly, *itolofiya* does not seem to feature much in Xhosa-language literature, or African literature in English, but we have done no systematic trawl. *Imvo Zabantsundu*, the Xhosa-language newspaper, carried a report in the 1880s of '*itolofiya ityiwa isimanga*' – prickly pear as an unusual thing to eat.[63] And there is the suggestion, in a Xhosa author's pseudonym, Tolofiya Melitafa (prickly pear standing on the plain), that the plant was used as a literary symbol for endurance in 'a world scorched and made rainless by the black shadows of the sun' (*litshiswa lilang' ukubalela Zub' elimdaka, mat[u]nz' entaba*).[64] The poetess, Nontsizi Mgqwetho, used it in a different sense in a protest poem in the 1920s, where she seems to be complaining about a fellow-prisoner who would not share their prickly pear.[65]

By the late nineteenth century, prickly pear was thoroughly inserted into the culture, food supplies and farming practices of both Africans and whites as an all-purpose plant that required little care. Fruits were widely sold as well as eaten and brewed.[66] In Oudtshoorn, 'the blacks wander[ed] about from farm to farm selling the fruits to farmers at sixpence a hundred'; poor whites consumed it and brought it into town for sale.[67] There was a seasonal migration by farm workers to Graaff-Reinet in the fruiting season: 'fruit was hawked for sale in the town or converted into a concentrated syrup by boiling it in three-legged pots'.[68] Africans with ox-wagons or donkey carts took the fruit from Uitenhage into Port Elizabeth. Railway workers also ate it at work and used their favoured access to transport to carry it long distances, in bags, for sale.[69] Railways as well as rivers and roads became routes for the spread of prickly pear.

Nineteenth century Karoo farm with prickly pear

CACTUS INADVERTENTLY CAPTURED BY CAMERA

Cactus springs up in photographs, not often as the subject, but incidentally in the background.

A hunter with two dogs, probably George Chase, stands in front of a large cactus bush, probably a type of cereus or epiphyllum, near Port Elizabeth around 1870.[70] A photograph of Robert Godlonton's front hedge in Grahamstown had a specimen of prickly pear, close to a gum tree.[71] Burton's view of a valley in Graaff-Reinet district in 1903 includes an opuntia plant in the centre, and a postcard of a 'Walk in Botanical Gardens, Queenstown' sent in 1907 shows a large prickly pear bush on the left.

Similar evidence of prickly pear unnoticed in the background of pictures crops up further afield. Reenen van Reenen, the Free State engineer, illustrated a children's poem, Op Trek (1917), which celebrated the Afrikaner conquest of the interior.[72] He drew children playing at starting a farm with a large prickly pear bush in the background. Anthropologist Isaac Schapera's photographs of African society inadvertently show opuntia in Botswana in the 1930s.[73] The plant, called motoroko in Setswana, probably reached this area via transport routes in the mid-nineteenth century.

EARLY DEBATES ABOUT THE CONTROL OF PRICKLY PEAR

M ost early references to prickly pear are neutral in their tone, or like Mary Barber's, rejoiced in its familiarity and utility. Yet as early as the 1860s, when much of the rural Cape was being transformed into sheep territory, a few white farmers claimed that they were driven from their land by prickly pear. Soon afterwards key officials and experts became increasingly concerned about opuntia. One of these was Henry Bolus, a committed amateur botanist after whom the Bolus herbarium at the University of Cape Town is named. He lived for some years in Graaff-Reinet where he studied Karoo plants and landscape. In 1874 he wrote:

> Introduced at some unknown period from South America, [prickly pear] is now regarded as the greatest pest of the farmer in the first Karroo plateau between the Zuurbergen and Sneeuwbergen .... At this day very many thousands of acres are almost entirely covered with it, and some farms are said to be rendered almost worthless by its encroachments. Cattle, sheep, and goats, indeed, eat it; but the effect of the formidable spines, with which the whole plant is covered ... is very destructive, large numbers dying of inflammation of the mouth, caused by the wounds. In the kloof and by river sides it disputes the ground with the acacia and other trees, often killing them, and forming an impenetrable thicket from ten to fifteen feet in height. Many farmers have spent hundreds of pounds in endeavouring to eradicate it. But this is rendered extremely difficult by reason of its wonderfully rapid

propagation from any small portion of the flattened succulent stem, which quickly sends our roots and establishes itself, even in the dryest season, and on the most arid soil.'[1]

Bolus was struck by the 'sociable' nature of prickly pear which was rare amongst indigenous Cape plants. By sociable, he meant that large numbers of the plant grew together in dense thickets, whereas many indigenous Cape plants tended to be more solitary. This intensified its impact on indigenous vegetation. Peter MacOwan, who botanised with Bolus in the eastern Cape, and later became long-serving Government Botanist in Cape Town, kept a worried eye, during the 1870s and 1880s, on major thickets near the Bruintjieshoogte pass, and also at Cookhouse.[2] Walter Rubidge, son of one of the colony's leading sheep breeders, bought a farm in Aberdeen district and spent several hundred pounds eradicating prickly pear in the early 1870s. Their concerns were published by John Noble in his *Handbook of the Cape Colony* (1875), who reported that the 'cactus or prickly pear is becoming a source of trouble'. [3]

At this stage, the glochids on the fruit were the main issue. They caused swelling and sores around animals' mouths making it difficult for them to eat and sometimes resulting in death, especially for sheep and angora goats. The damage caused could extend down the gullet to the internal linings of the stomach and digestive organs. Duncan Hutcheon, the veterinary surgeon, reported later that animals 'will just stand and eat away till they die'.[4] He thought that it took six months for animals to recover from the severe inflammation caused by glochids on the fruit. Livestock particularly favoured cladodes and fruit in dry years, when the plant was one of the few sources of moisture. Prickly pear was thought to spread especially fast after a drought when the seeds in droppings were widely deposited. The Cape weathered a serious drought in the early 1860s and again in 1877.

Complaints about prickly pear had a social as well as an agricultural dimension. Poor whites around Graaff-Reinet, the bywoners or tenants on white-owned farms, were described as 'living on prickly pears' and thus escaping work.[5] In 1870, prickly pear on the Graaff-Reinet commonage was closely associated with 'squatting' by unemployed Africans.[6] Squatting, in the language of South Africa's white elite, was applied to Africans who subsisted independently on state or white-owned land. When the municipal authorities attempted to assert tighter control over the black location in 1879, they chopped down the prickly pear around it because this was thought to harbour 'a heterogeneous lot of rowdies'.[7] The area was again

THE IMPACT OF UNTREATED PRICKLY PEAR ON OSTRICHES

Between the 1860s and 1910s the number of farmed ostriches rose from very few to 800,000, and feathers became the third most important source of export revenue for the Cape, after diamonds and wool. Europe's fashion demands sent ripples through far-flung Cape districts and this wild animal, newly domesticated, became a creature of value. Ostriches could be blinded during the fruiting season, when the glochids blew or were shaken off, and some farmers had to fence prickly pear thickets so that their birds could be excluded at this time.[8] Annie Martin, who lived on an ostrich farm in the 1880s, gave a wry description of the problem of prickly pear, thus:

> Sometimes ostriches, with that equal disregard of their own health and of their possessor's pocket for which they are famous, help themselves to prickly pears, acquire a morbid taste for them, and go on indulging in them, reckless of the long, stiff spikes on the leaves, with which their poor heads and necks soon become so covered as to look like pin-cushions stuck full of pins; and of the still more cruel, almost invisible fruit-thorns which at last line the interior of their throats, besides so injuring their eyes that they become perfectly blind, and are unable to feed themselves. Many a time has a poor unhappy ostrich, the victim of prickly pear, been brought to me in a helpless, half-dead state, to be nursed and fed at the house ….There it would squat for a few days, the picture of misery; its long neck lying along the ground in a limp, despondent manner ….Two or three times a day I would feed it, forcing its unwilling bill open with one hand, while with the other I posted large handfuls of porridge, mealies, or chopped prickly pear leaves in the depths of its capacious letter-box of a throat. All to no purpose; it had made up its mind to die, as every ostrich does immediately when illness or accident befalls it.[9]

Prickly pear and ostriches in the late nineteenth century (photograph from William Roe Collection, National Library of South Africa (with permission), also used as frontispiece to Martin, Home Life*).*

cleared of prickly pear in 1883 because farmers living near town argued that stolen livestock were being secreted there. The first select committee on eradication in 1890 considered 'that unbroken thickets of this plant furnish shelter for thieving operations to a very serious extent'.[10] One of these around the Voel River, in the north of Pearston district, which harboured opuntia so dense that it was impossible to see more than twenty paces, was reputedly a veritable 'nest of thieves'.[11] Thickets also provided cover for jackals, the scourge of the Cape's valuable merino sheep, which found 'perfect safety from pursuit'.[12]

Prickly pear's contribution to African subsistence and the shortage of farm labour was mentioned by a number of farmers giving evidence to the Cape Labour Commission in 1894. A Scottish agriculturalist touring the Cape in the 1890s recorded that Africans avoided work during the three months when the fruit was at its best.[13] The 1898 committee heard an exaggerated argument that 'for six months of the year the fruit provides them with a means of subsistence, and they have consequently contracted idle and thievish habits'. These points were being made by eradicationists and were clouded by colonial prejudice, but they reflected the real value of this natural resource for poor communities in the eastern Cape.

We have discussed the brewing of *iqhilika* by African communities, probably ubiquitous in prickly pear districts by the late nineteenth century, and its perceived impact on the labour supply. One of the great rural skills, amongst whites as well as blacks in the Cape, was to turn any suitable natural substance into alcohol. Graaff-Reinet was a centre for wine and brandy making by white small holders until the 1880s when the vineyards were wiped out by phylloxera. Peach and other fruit brandy, later called mampoer, was legion in Afrikaner stories and folklore. (Mampoer is derived from a Sotho/Pedi word, or from the name of the Pedi chief Mampuru, and it was probably not used in the nineteenth century Cape.) Prickly pear fruit was equally suitable, and probably distilled from the eighteenth century. It was reputed to make a particularly 'intoxicating and maddening liquor'; this could be mixed with Cape brandy to produce 'a most villanous compound'.[14] Seen as a 'strong, coarse spirit' by British settlers, it was 'nectar to the Boers and Hottentots, who dr[a]nk large quantities of it'. Even the Cape elite, who thought it was 'abominable', recognised that 'great care' was taken in its preparation.[15]

During the late nineteenth century, white ruling groups in the eastern Cape, worried about the labour supply to farms, as well as many African clergy, anxious about the demoralisation of the black population, railed against alcohol and alcoholism.[16] Some thought that traditional brews such as *utywala* were becoming stronger, by admixture of brandy and honey. Their overriding concern, however, was cheap brandy itself and the proliferation of canteens and hotels selling it.

Gerhard de Kock, Grootfontein's retired opuntia expert, was convinced that the notorious 'Cape smoke' spirit – sold throughout South Africa in the nineteenth and early twentieth centuries – was in part distilled from prickly pear fruit.[17] The terms 'witblits' and 'Cape smoke' both referred in the nineteenth century to grape-based distilled liquors. The latter was given bite by additives such as tobacco and blue stone or sulphate of copper. According to the Civil Commissioner of Port Elizabeth, African drinkers preferred it adulterated so that it 'would cut like a saw all the way down the throat'.[18] Prickly pear may well have partly replaced grape-based spirits in the eastern Cape and even more widely for a period after phylloxera destroyed many of the vineyards in the mid-1880s. The rapidly growing Transvaal market, however, was largely closed to Cape producers after 1886 because of tariffs to protect the infant republican liquor industry.[19] Contrary to some opinion at that time, de Kock thought that the cactus 'produced beautiful pure alcohol' and 'beautiful brandy'.

In 1891, MacDonald, the Cape's first agricultural officer, was asked to survey the scale of wild prickly pear as one of his earliest tasks. He calculated that 478,000 morgen (over a million acres or about 400,000 hectares) were 'overrun', and much more 'infected' by prickly pear, largely in the semi-arid Cape midland districts: Jansenville, Graaff-Reinet, Aberdeen, Somerset East, Willowmore, Cradock and the drier parts of Albany, especially along the Fish River.[20] He cited the Buffels Hoek Valley – perhaps the first area in which it was planted – as a major problem, with 20,000 morgen densely infested. (See map on page 43.)[21]

Sections of white society in the midland districts and eastern Cape were clearly developing a strong hostility to prickly pear.[22] To its opponents the spread of prickly pear resembled that of a virus, as was reflected in their language about infection and infestation. It threatened health and social order, so that poor, white families on prickly pear farms 'degenerated'.[23] White poverty was increasingly being defined as a major social problem at the Cape in the late nineteenth century, and seemed to threaten the racial order as well.[24] Landowners associated the plant with poverty, jackals, African occupation and labour problems. In some respects, this was becoming a class issue. As J.J. Vosloo, a Somerset East farmer bluntly put it: 'the Kafirs and the poor whites are the people who are the friends of the prickly pear'.[25] But it was not simply so. Nor was it simply an English/Afrikaner divide, although the leading eradicationists tended to be English speakers. Any concerted action was difficult for a number of reasons. The fledgling Cape state, while eventually effective in conquest and maintaining order, had no highly developed bureaucracy to organise any widespread campaign against prickly pear. Opinion, even in white society, was divided. Many people from all social groups had an interest in using prickly pear rather than eradicating it. Moreover, the botanical and reproductive characteristics of the plant were not fully understood, making intervention difficult.

THE DOORNBLAD AND THE KAALBLAD

Prickly pear was divided by whites into two types: the doornblad, or thorny leaved, and the kaalblad, or bare-leaved variety. This difference lay at the heart of the dilemma about the plant in the late nineteenth century. Debates about the provenance and character of these two varieties proved important because they were central to discussions about the wisdom, or otherwise, of eradication. This issue became one key focus of the four parliamentary committees.

The kaalblad was valued far more highly as a stock feed because spines, harmful to stock, were largely absent from its cladodes; animals could eat it literally as it stood. A fodder or drought food that needed no water, little effort to plant and no labour to prepare was a godsend. As a Cradock farmer noted, however:

> the *Doornblad* greatly preponderated, not that it grew more readily, or was hardier, but because, on account of its thorny protection, stock could not eat it or destroy it, while the *Kaalblad* was eaten down to the bare stumps in many instances, and almost all animals greedily devoured the fruit. Further, the *Doornblad* nearly always threw true, while the *Kaalblad* always threw a heavy percentage of the *Doornblad*.[26]

Most agreed that the doornblad was spreading and that this was the Cape's tragedy. Some thought that kaalblad might be a different species from the doornblad. Those opposed to eradication had an interest in supporting this view in the hope that the doornblad could be eradicated and the kaalblad retained. Some farmers suggested that they might be male and female varieties, and talked of prickly 'mannetjies' and 'wyfies'; such differences were not unknown in plant species. It was also suggested that the kaalblad produced thorns when it was grazed very heavily as a means of protection.[27] Luther Burbank, the renowned American plant breeder (see Chapter 4), thought in broad evolutionary terms along the same lines. In general, he felt that opuntia plants developed spines over the long term as a protective response in the

Central American drylands, and he also thought that some species lost their spines if they grew in zones without browsing animals, such as the mountainsides of Hawaii or the South Sea Islands. Bolus suggested that the method of reproduction affected the variety: 'the plant grown from the fallen leaf, like its parent stock, produces but few prickles; while the seedling is bristling with them, and its fruit is very inferior. There is a decided tendency in South African plants to produce thorns'.[28]

All of these explanations indicate a curiosity about the plant but none were strictly accurate. By the end of the nineteenth century, the more general view, especially amongst those with botanical knowledge, was that these were both varieties of the same species, *O. ficus-indica*. MacDonald and the botanist Rupert Marloth were sure that the kaalblad originated as a cultivated variety of the *O. ficus-indica*. Such cultivars were in fact widespread in Mexico, and botanists now believe that *O. ficus-indica* is, in effect, a very diverse species which is essentially the result of centuries-old hybridisation and cultivation, and which no longer has a single identifiable wild forebear. Domesticated plants sometimes result from genetic mutations which by chance produce a variety more favourable for human use and which are then reproduced, where possible, by cloning or grafting. MacDonald thought that the kaalblad – in the manner of a semi-domesticated plant – grew better in deeper valley and alluvial soils.

The relatively spineless kaalblad may have been the only variety of this species originally introduced into the eastern Cape. Farmers in Aberdeen and Graaff-Reinet believed that at one time, in the earliest days of settlement, only kaalblad was found in their districts. Some reported a story that an isolated hedge of kaalblad in Aberdeen had produced doornblad plants by seeding. Charles Rubidge, a leading sheep farmer in nineteenth-century Graaff-Reinet, experimented by planting seeds from kaalblad and found that some produced doornblad. It was possible, but rare, for seeds from the doornblad to produce kaalblad. Thus, once reproduction from seed began, the doornblad spread far more quickly. It also survived better because it was not grazed so heavily. Botanists compared prickly pear to other cultivars that tended to revert to the wild, or in this case the spiny variety, if they were grown from seed.[29] Some thought that the doornblad variety hybridised with the kaalblad as both produced flowers and fruit and that this hastened the reversion.[30]

For MacOwan, a keen advocate of intensive agriculture, the growing predominance of doornblad was another sign of Cape carelessness. 'That the kaal-blad has not been spread purposely over the length and breadth of the land in otherwise useless wastes,' he wrote, 'is just one of those many things that make one wonder and pity poor Africa'; 'if by touch of a magician's wand the vast thickets of Prickly Pear along the Klyn Visch, Melk and Blyde Rivers could be turned into kaal-blad, there would be small chance of hearing of stock slowly perishing of combined hunger and thirst'.[31]

It seemed clear to the experts and committees that the kaalblad could only be reproduced with certainty by planting its cladodes. Some farmers used this technique purposely. In fact farmers who wished to propagate prickly pear to lay a fence, for example, invariably used the cladodes – whether thorny or bare – because this was the quickest and easiest way to establish the plant. In sum, kaalblad required direct human management if it was to remain widespread. The kaalblad was clearly superior as fodder but the only way to ensure its survival and predominance was to protect it, plant it and prevent fruiting and seeding. In order to understand why this was not done, we need to explore human priorities, neglect and ecological relationships. Clearly many rural people did not know that only cloning could ensure kaalblad, and many had interests in prickly pear which were not restricted to its fodder potential. Managing the wild plant was in any case enormously difficult.

OSTRICHES, OPUNTIA AND COUGH MIXTURE

The fodder content of the doornblad and kaalblad was much the same, although it was sometimes suggested that kaalblad leaves tended to be larger and juicier than doornblad. Ideally doornblad required preparation in which the spines were burnt or scraped off before cladodes were fed to livestock. Despite the labour involved, some farmers did organise such preparation which was widely done in other parts of the world, both by peasants and commercial farmers, from Madagascar and India to Texas.

By the late nineteenth century, those proposing more intensive and efficient methods of farming in South Africa saw fodder as a vital resource for drought years and dry seasons. They also envisaged that fodder, together with better water supplies, would help to end transhumance or trekking.[32] Many livestock owners still moved their livestock on a seasonal basis in order to find the best pastures, to follow the rain or avoid nutrition-related diseases. But Cape officials as well as wealthier and conservation-minded farmers frowned on the practice. They felt that it actually spread infectious disease and that the mass movement of animals exacerbated soil erosion. Lucerne, a protein-rich legume, was cultivated where irrigation was possible. In districts where water supplies were limited, edible exotics that could withstand the rigours of the Cape environment provided an alternative. The three most important for Cape livestock farmers were opuntia, *Agave americana* and Australian salt bush or atriplex species. They also found favour among some African livestock owners. The great advantage of these plants was that they needed little cultivation and no irrigation.

For a few officials and politicians, the idea of killing two birds with one stone was attractive: the costs of controlling opuntia would be much reduced and its effectiveness increased if the cladodes could be used on a large scale for animal feed. MacOwan eloquently advanced such a solution in his 1897 'Plea for the Pricklies'. He described Australian methods of preparing the cladodes by large-scale boiling or steaming in vats.[33] Euphorbia species had also been boiled to render them palatable for stock in droughts. In an experiment at Cookhouse thicket, cladodes were placed with water in a revolving barrel to rub off the spines. Some burnt them off.[34] One of the farmers at Cookhouse adopted an American strategy by using a machine to pulp the plant.[35] MacOwan hoped 'that some one down in the Opuntiaries of the Midlands' would evolve an economical machine to do this on a large scale, as in Arizona, Texas and New Mexico. In this way, it would be possible to 'clear a depreciated, pear-curst piece of land, and raise a mob of cattle at the same time'. He turned more against the plant in later years.

Although ripe prickly pear fruit damaged ostriches, the mushroom growth of commercial ostrich farming also resulted in intensive use of prickly pear cladodes. Lucerne was an ideal fodder for ostriches when mixed with a diet of natural veld. But farmers in the midlands and eastern districts, equally keen to profit from ostriches, found it difficult to replicate the intensive irrigation of Oudtshoorn and environs. Prickly pear was considered especially valuable in the 1880s and 1890s for ostriches in semi-arid districts. Occasionally it was used as an edible fence.[36] Ostriches devoured the fresh, green tops of young prickly pear and some reports suggested they could cope with the cladodes of larger wild bushes. More generally the cladodes were brazed and chopped. Arthur Douglass, a leading ostrich breeder who played a role in perfecting methods of artificial incubation, initially emphasised the dangers of prickly pear, but then allowed it to spread on his Albany farm and chopped cladodes for fodder on a large scale. Ostriches undermined any emerging unity by wealthier landowners against prickly pear.

Dr W.G. Atherstone, Grahamstown's multi-talented physician, a renaissance man with a wide range of scientific interests, keenly followed developments in the domestication and rearing of ostriches. He had worked with Douglass to find a suitable incubator. Down on the coast, he noted, in the 1880s: 'as a chick and young bird the ostrich drinks no water at all. Then seeing the parent bird drinking it does so too. The ostrich picks herbage and then picks gravel for his mill. Ostriches eat chopped prickly pear freely'.[37] Local companies developed chaffing machines in the 1880s which largely destroyed the spines of the doornblad. In Grahamstown C.J. Stirk and Son marketed an improved cutting machine for prickly pear and agave leaves in the early twentieth century.

Even in Oudtshoorn not all farmers had access to lucerne. A farmer there described how ostriches in his neighbourhood survived a serious drought in 1899 by consuming prickly pear.

> Mr P. Lategan, ... of Wynands River, had no mealie, oat or barley crops owing to the drought. He had about 120 valuable birds, and commenced feeding them exclusively with the leaves of Prickly Pear in November. For six months they had no other food, and not only were they kept alive, but were in ... good condition as if they were running in a lucerne camp, and several commenced laying and hatching. The leaves were freely given, so that after every feed some remained over. Many sent their mule and ox wagons long distances to get leaves ....[38]

Committed progressive farmers such as G.H. Maasdorp, MLA for Graaff-Reinet, affirmed in 1906 that 'there are many people who look upon it as a good fodder plant, and who during the last droughts have been keeping stock, especially ostriches, alive on it'.[39] To those who argued that prickly pear was not a particularly good stock food and produced a purgative effect, proponents responded that of course it should only be fed as part of a mixed diet.[40] Experiments were conducted in the 1890s to establish the most effective combinations. Lucerne, maize and veld were all suitable supplements.[41] Some farmers who kept ostriches in the drier districts where they were more reliant on Karoo bushes, actually valued the diarrhetic qualities of prickly pear.[42] Pigs also thrived on cladodes: 'we carry the leaves to them in the sty', a farmer told the 1891 committee, 'and we can fatten them on the fruit'.[43]

As noted both whites and Africans used the quick-growing thorny variety for hedges around gardens to keep stock out, or for hedges around kraals to keep stock in. It was favoured at one time in the Sneeuberg, north of Graaff-Reinet, because it was one of the few large plants that could withstand the extremes of climate.[44] On the Rubidge farm, Wellwood, they planted a hedge of spiny prickly pear around their garden in the 1860s. The family picked the fruit from the inside, and the farm workers on the outside. The Rubidges later destroyed the hedge. Some of the best capitalised farmers felt that they could benefit from the kaalblad and control the doornblad. They planted kaalblad at the same time as organising teams of workers to eradicate the doornblad every year.[45]

Aside from hedging, con-sumption, brewing and distilling, the 1891 committee heard about 'samples of vinegar, sugar, syrup, and dried prickly pear all made from the fruit' by an Afrikaner who thought 'there is nothing better in this country'.[46] In the midlands, some farmers collected the fruit 'in wagon loads' for the manufacture of preserves.[47] Hannah Brown of Glen Avon, a farm close to Somerset East town, wrote enthusiastically on 'The Prickly Pear: A Source of Wealth for the Union' in 1919.[48] She noted that the South African variety was so sweet that it could be used to make jam without sugar, and acted as a sweetener for preserving other fruits. Africans and poor whites made a coarse black sugar by boiling down the syrup. During the influenza epidemic of 1918, she had made a 'cough and bronchial medicine', mixing prickly pear syrup, watercress, wild mint and linseed oil. Versions of this recipe had long been known and were reputedly used by the Voortrekkers.

The yeast, or *karee moer*, was one of the best not only for beer but for bread and biscuits. Dried fruits served as a coffee extender and an amber-coloured oil could be extracted from crushed seeds. Brown, with her servants, had recently made 200 pounds of prickly pear soap: 'my factory consisted of a big three-legged iron pot and a wood fire under a willow tree'. Prickly pear soap was a particularly popular product made by thousands of rural families from all back-grounds. Another correspondent re-called how widely the fruit was used by English-speaking families around Cradock and Somerset East in the 1880s to make sweeteners, treacle, beer and 'a fine yeast powder – making most delicious light bread and pastry'[49] (see Chapter 5). There was even an attempt to make fuel for vehicle motors in Bloemfontein in the 1920s – an early excursion into biofuels.

Prickly pear cutting machine advertised in the Cape Agricultural Journal, 1909

In 1923 *Die Burger* headlined an article, 'Die Ironie van Turksvye', generally in praise of the plant and noting that *'wanneer hy nodig is, is hy daar'* (it is there when needed).[50] Because of all these different uses, many had an interest in allowing the prickly pear to fruit. The conditions were therefore established for the spread of the doornblad.

ERADICATION

Protagonists of eradication nevertheless made some headway in the Cape legislature, emphasising that prickly pear caused 'industrious and enterprising farmers' heavy expense. At the heart of their concern was not only the threat to faming, but that infested land and adjacent farms would decline in value. The problem with compulsory legislation, however, aside from lack of support, was the question of who would bear the expense of clearance. MacDonald estimated in 1891 that it would cost £320,000 to eradicate prickly pear in heavily infested districts. The government could not afford this and it far exceeded the Cape's small agricultural budget. Many private landowners and tenants were too poor to eradicate. Politicians did not wish to criminalise those who could not afford to clear.

Farmowners found that a single extirpation was seldom sufficient. A farm cleared in Jansenville in the 1870s had to be redone every three or four years as prickly pear spread from neighbours. Clearance required a month's labour by six farm workers. As in the case of sheep shearing, teams of African migrant workers were sometimes employed for these tasks. One man claimed to have spent between £7,000 and £8,000 over 25 years by 1906.[51] Where farmers lacked resources, they found it difficult to respond. In the words of one observer: 'some farmers would not eradicate it, because they only had a little, others because they had too much, others again actually tried to grow it'.[52] Where the cost of clearing exceeded the value of the land, it could become cheaper to sell.[53] The wages of 'prickly-pear-men' could amount to a major cost for landowners.

Eradicationists argued that there was not only a threat to individual incomes, but to the colonial economy as a whole in reduced production, declining land values and lower rental from public land. Most of all, they argued that a failure to act while the problem was containable would result in far greater costs at a later stage. Douglass, the ostrich pioneer from Grahamstown, asserted in 1893 that prickly pear was spreading so quickly that half the farming population in the Cape would be reduced to poverty if nothing was done.[54] An estimate was made of annual losses of £200,000 a year, which made MacDonald's figure for eradication costs, at £320,000, seem reasonable. Divisional councils were too poor, inefficient and politically divided to take control.[55] Eradicationists looked to the central government.

The figures produced were, however, one-sided. They represented the perceived losses to landowners and commercial farmers. They failed to cost the potential losses that might be caused by complete eradication to those who used the plants. It is very difficult to calculate these now, because so much of the value of prickly pear was in homestead-based, domestic production. The rural districts were economically and demographically much more significant at this time. Those with substantial amounts of prickly pear, mostly in the midland Cape, housed over 200,000 people in 1891. It would not be surprising if the value of prickly pear was more than £1 per person per year – and that the total value of benefits came close to the estimated costs. A similar problem bedevils calculations concerning the costs of some partly invasive plant species today, in the early twenty-first century. Environmental costs, such as the loss of water, or of biodiversity, or of other 'ecosystem services' are frequently calculated – they are now seen as more central than purely economic costs. Such calculations tend to omit the value of plants to poor people.

The Cape colonial state had begun to extend its interventionist reach in the late nineteenth and early twentieth centuries. Not only was railway and other transport expenditure growing quickly but the government also put funding into health and education. Self-consciously progressive landowners who were an influential voice in parliament successfully secured a Department of Agriculture in 1889. Officials tried to take action in such spheres as solving the phylloxera crisis in viticulture and developing larger-scale irrigation. Livestock diseases from scab to heartwater preoccupied the growing veterinary service. A system of bounties was designed to encourage extermination of animals considered as vermin (*ongedeerte* or non-animals), especially jackals. Baboons were included on the list. Not only were they a general nuisance for crop and fruit farmers, but some noted that they spread prickly pear.

It is no coincidence that government action on prickly pear first seemed possible in 1890 when Rhodes came to power as Prime Minister of an ambitious, modernising administration generally supported by commercial farmers, both English and Afrikaans-speaking. In the 1890s, however, key politicians such as Sprigg and Merriman, who were in favour of concerted action against scab, were reluctant to pursue prickly pear eradication. They felt that 'the business of the government was not to go and do what a man was capable of doing himself'.[56] As prickly pear became invasive in a restricted geographical area, they thought that state intervention would support a sectional interest. Merriman, a Western Cape politician, was rather disdainful about these rural concerns. 'I have just been on tour through the midlands', he wrote in 1892, shortly after he assumed ministerial responsibility for Agriculture: 'prickly pear and locusts *ad nauseum*, with an occasional excursion into other matters which agitate the bucolic mind'.[57] In his travels, he certainly did not look forward to the 'heat, the dust, the locust war and the prickly pear'.

Merriman was correct that rural communities and land owners in different regions had markedly different experiences with prickly pear. It was clear by the early twentieth century that some areas were more susceptible to invasion than others. Although prickly pear thrived in sweetveld zones and on rich soil in the valley bottoms, soil did not seem to be the major factor. It could spread quickly in stony terrain in certain districts. Climatic factors and rainfall appeared more significant.[58] In districts like Richmond, Middelburg and Colesberg, not far to the north of heavily infested areas such as Graaff-Reinet, prickly pear would grow wild but generally did not spread quickly. 'I have to plant and irrigate it', a farmer in Richmond noted.[59] This was the case throughout the dryer, western and northern Karoo districts, the southern Free State and the western littoral of the colony. Marloth, the botanist at Stellenbosch, thought that frosts in the interior, at higher altitudes, were too hard and regular for opuntia to thrive. Young plants seemed especially susceptible so that invasion was unlikely.

The grasslands to the east of a line from East London to Queenstown were generally too wet and humid for prickly pear to spread easily. Again, the plant would grow there, and it is still found as far east as Lusikisiki, but it had to be planted and nurtured. Khotso Sehuntsa, 'the millionaire medicine man', established a hedge next to his blue-tiled villa on the edge of the town, and it is still (2009) there.[60] Prickly pear also found it far more difficult to compete where there was a denser cover of grass. Even in Graaff-Reinet, wild plants were less likely to take root in the grassier, sourveld, elevated areas of the Sneeuberg. Humidity was another influence. The Kei River Valley in the east of Stutterheim district had a similar rainfall to infested areas elsewhere, yet doornblad did not spread vigorously there. Marloth thought that its higher humidity and sea winds made it less likely to provide favourable conditions for invasion. Eric Nobbs, a recent recruit to the Department of Agriculture, affirmed in 1906 this preference for dry air and a hot summer.[61] Parts of Albany and Uitenhage districts, with a relatively high rainfall, were nevertheless susceptible to invasion. In addition to their location down-river from key areas of infestation, lower humidity might have provided conducive conditions.

In view of these differences, it was difficult to find unanimity in favour of spending government money on eradication. However, those most committed to state involvement argued that it would be pointless to eradicate prickly pear in particular pockets: the central problem was that doornblad in inaccessible areas could re-infest land that had been cleared.[62] A colony-wide campaign was needed. There were many reports in the Cape's *Agricultural Journal* on the 'extirpation of prickly pear' in the couple of decades after the first parliamentary committee in 1891. Some made reference to Australian conditions; in New South Wales, eradication was compulsory.

The Cape Department of Agriculture compromised by distributing plant poison at half of cost price from 1893. To the large quantities of strychnine laid down for vermin control in the Cape, and the increasing amount of chemical dip used for livestock, arsenic compounds for eradication of prickly pear were added.[63] Various solutions were tried, including Cooper's Dip, an Australian Scrub Exterminator, arsenite of soda and sodium arsenate.[64] Arsenite of soda seemed the most promising. It was adopted by the government and proved to be the cheapest successful compound, convenient to distribute in powder form.[65] MacDonald demonstrated its use in Graaff-Reinet, Pearston, Bedford and Fort Beaufort. This also put the responsibility on landowners to eradicate on a voluntary basis. Those who wished to plant or use prickly pear were free to do so.

Eradication proved to be both time-consuming and technically difficult. By the 1890s, the consensus was that doornblad succumbed best when chopped down to its roots, piled in stacks, dried, turned so that any sprouts on the outside of the pile would be destroyed, and then burnt as soon as this was feasible, after about one year. This was a labour intensive and expensive process that required commitment, organisation and careful supervision. Eradicators had to be vigilant throughout so that cladodes were not dropped on the ground. Stacks could become a source of rotting fruit attractive to birds and animals and hence a new node for spreading the seeds. Seeds could survive inadequate burning.[66] In some cases, the area on which cladodes were piled had to be cut and treated again.

An alternative method was to poison the plant where it stood, which saved costs and labour. The problem was that sprayed arsenic solutions tended to kill only parts of the plant. The result was that live cladodes dropped to the ground and sprouted again, compounding the problem rather than solving it. Poisoning worked better if the plants were first punctured and injected, especially in the stems and stem joints, before spraying. Access to plants in denser thickets could prove difficult and even when the tops of the plants were killed, the roots could sprout. Poison worked most effectively on plants cut down and stacked: it hastened the process of decomposition and reduced the risk of reproduction from stacks.[67] MacDonald's experiments suggested that poison could reduce the time before burning to six weeks after the materials were piled.[68] Burying cladodes with poison, as done in India, could also be effective. The dry winter months, when prickly pear grew very slowly, were best for eradication. Some farmers employed large teams – thirty men for two months – for this difficult work.

Opuntia, like scab, jackals and locusts was a perennial subject of intense discussion in the rural midland and eastern Cape. The 1898 committee found that in some districts, farmers were highly motivated to eradicate: 'the traveller by rail through the midlands can see for himself in every direction piles of the extirpated pear heaped up to rot and dry off'.[69] Government expenditure was minimal, averaging less than £1,000 a year between 1893 and 1899. But over 200,000 pounds of chemical exterminator was distributed in these years. In one of the worst-affected areas along the Great Fish River near Cookhouse, the 'champion nest of Prickly Pear', landowners 'got rid of the pest wholesale; and large agricultural areas are now under the plough and carrying crops which had for fifty years been impenetrable thickets of the Prickly Pear'.[70] Here, the fact that the thickest growth was concentrated on the most valuable riverine land provided an added incentive. There were similar initiatives between Port Elizabeth and Uitenhage: 'the interest in the matter was very general and … lively'.

Yet the success was patchy. Impoverished people on pear-infested farms ironically became more dependent on it. 'Owners and occupiers have become so poor that they are dragging out a miserable existence living principally upon the fruit'. Farms subjected to internal subdivision after partible inheritance were thought to be particularly vulnerable. From 1898 to 1905, following the committee's report, poison – or 'Government exterminator' – was distributed free. Expenditure doubled. Thus enabled, Uitenhage municipality destroyed 25,000 bushes on its commonage.

In 1905, acute recesssion resulted in a return to charging half of cost price and there was a fall in demand for poison.[71] The 1906 select committee was less optimistic about the success of control; the area heavily infested was still estimated at about half a million morgen.[72] While this could be calculated as the equivalent of about 300 average-sized midland farms, or about one district, the problem was that prickly pear was scattered so widely, in such variable concentrations, that the dangers of further spread remained. As Nobbs put it, no other weed 'has become such a characteristic of the landscape'.[73] The South African War, during which farms were neglected, and the subsequent drought of 1903 to 1904, militated against effective control.

By this time, jointed cactus (*Opuntia aurantiaca*, then sometimes called *O. pusilla*) was becoming identified as an equally important scourge. This was a hybrid that originated in eastern South America and came to South Africa as an ornamental via Britain. Moran and Annecke are convinced that Baron von Ludwig first imported it for his famous garden in Cape Town; it was transferred to the botanical gardens from where it was distributed in the 1850s.[74] This cactus was indestructible, which made it attractive to those starting gardens in the eastern Cape: the missions at Hertzog, Hankey and Salem are all mentioned as early sites. It probably spread invasively from a farm in Bedford. The story recorded is that a farmer named Botha, when taking possession of the property called Goliath's Wagen Drift, disliked the plant, ordered it to be dug up and thrown away into the nearby Gobas River. During the 1874 floods it was swept downstream to a number of riverine properties in Bedford and from there fanned out through adjoining districts. Later versions attribute the start of the invasion to the mission station in Hertzog, in the Kat River Valley, where Olive and William Schreiner's parents were located in the 1870s, and to the town clerk in Fort Beaufort. There, as elsewhere, jointed cactus was grown in cemeteries. When it invaded the graves, he ordered it to be thrown over the fence and it started its deadly journey.[75]

Jointed cactus is still widespread in this area. Its cladodes or leaf joints were smaller and spinier than prickly pear, and small joints broke off far more easily. It was first called *injubalani* in Xhosa, to signify its capacity to stick fast to passing livestock. This name came from the root *ukujuba* which can mean to hold fast or rebound and scratch in the manner of a thorn tree.[76] More recently *ukatyi* has been used in Xhosa and *katjie* or *litjieskaktus* in Afrikaans. These popular names probably refer to cat's claws. Joints carried by flood water or livestock reproduced as quickly as prickly pear. Not only was it very difficult to eradicate, but this opuntia had no value for fodder or fruit either. An Act of 1889 enabled divisional councils to declare weeds 'noxious' and order their eradication. Some did list jointed cactus but the expense of eradication made it impossible to enforce.[77]

Nobbs, who later became Director of Agriculture in colonial Rhodesia (Zimbabwe), brought for the first time a systematic eye to the various poisons available for extirpation in 1907. He tested 50 plots, using a number of different solutions and four different methods: digging up plants and spraying heaps; injecting standing trees; injecting stumps after felling and spraying. He found, with some relief, that 'in every instance the Arsenite of Soda imported by the Government prove[d] to be the best material' and the cheapest. It also had the advantage of being distributed in lighter, powder form. Nobbs recommended different methods for particular purposes – thorough digging up for arable land, but the less-effective spraying for dispersed plants 'on steep hillsides and on krantzes'. Somewhat surprisingly, he found that kaalblad was hardier than doornblad. Whether eradication by any of these methods was financially worthwhile, except where land was used for crops, was questionable.

Nobbs was sufficiently sensitive to record the human costs of poison. All of the chemicals caused 'a painful and unpleasant rash, developing into yellow watery pustules'. One of them penetrated more deeply under the fingernails, burnt the skin painfully, and, 'in spite of masks, caused choking and coughing'. Agricultural work in the age of manufactured poison was not always safe. The costs to some bird species was also beginning to be counted. Simultaneously, he and R.W. Thornton turned their attention to jointed cactus. They found it equally susceptible to heavy doses of arsenite of soda and more easily burnt in situ (after only 12 days) than prickly pear.[78]

While it seemed that effective strategies of control had been devised, this was far from the case. After Union in 1910, noxious weeds, as in the case of vermin control, became a provincial responsibility. Alarms about opuntia were soon sounded in the Cape administrator's office. Eradication costs were now estimated at £20 per morgen in densely infested areas, or £10 million for the 500,000 morgen identified as the major problem areas. This was 30 times the estimated amount in 1891, barely 20 years before.

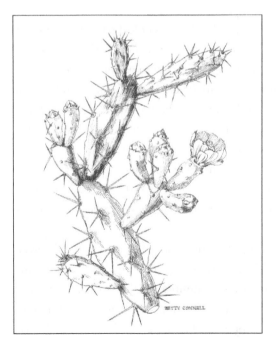

Commonages and crown lands were especially susceptible to invasion and here control was a government responsibility. In any case, local and private action seemed increasingly inadequate. The question was whether, like the jackal, opuntia should be viewed 'as a national danger.'[79] Free

The jointed cactus

distribution of poison was resumed. At the Congress of Cape Divisional Councils in 1914, a delegate argued that if the provincial council did not 'eradicate the pest ... then jointed cactus would eradicate the farmer'.[80] Representatives of infested areas pointed to the special assistance given to Western Cape farmers over phylloxera.

The South African Agricultural Union argued at its congress in 1916 for more concerted action. The president of the Cape Province Agricultural Association, P.M. Michau, was 'horrified to see the cavalier way in which that terrible scourge "jointed cactus"... [was] allowed to grow'.[81] Districts such as Albany and Uitenhage, previously on the peripheries of the problem, were increasingly affected. The best option still seemed to be a chemical solution. When Rademeyer's new 'exterminator' solution came onto the market, experiments were held in Bedford in 1917 and its inventor was funded by the provincial council to manufacture the product on a large scale to a uniform standard. The province retained an option to purchase the secret of his mixture for £10,000.[82] Basson's 'Destroyer', analysed as arsenious sulphide in alkaline solution, proved less effective.[83] Rival Australian solutions were not pursued.[84] The province distributed Rademeyer's mixture for some years, but the contract was terminated in the 1920s because it was found to be more expensive, yet no more effective, than generic arsenic pentoxide. As the chairman of the Uitenhage farmers association wrote in 1925, 'proprietary dips and compounds in the market today for inoculating and spraying of plants are not a success'.[85]

In the 1920s, however, expenditure on eradication began to escalate. Following a change in local authority financing systems, Divisional Councils were permitted to raise loans and opuntia proved to be one of the first priorities in a few councils. Specific legislation on the jointed cactus was passed in 1928. Local and provincial government employed eradication teams. But just as finance for larger scale mechanical and chemical eradication seemed to be available, new options were opening up in the shape of insects from the Americas (Chapter 5).

Prickly pear poisoned with arsenic pentoxide

EXPERIMENTS WITH CACTUS IN THE CAPE

A MIRACLE FODDER, 1900-1930

THE SPINELESS CACTUS

At the time of Union (1910), opinions were sharply divided in South Africa on the value of spiny *O. ficus-indica*. But in the next couple of decades, a new option opened up for advocates and users of cactus. Spineless cactus varieties (now called cactus pear) were bred that seemed to be far more productive than the South African kaalblad. At the same time, the Union Department of Agriculture, which commanded increasingly sophisticated capacity for research, initiated a series of investigations and experiments on wild prickly pear. Officials were determined, once and for all, to clarify whether opuntia could make a major contribution to livestock production and whether it could be useful for other industrial purposes. This chapter explores the application of science to opuntia, as well as the plant's systematic adoption by some leading livestock farmers in the Karoo.

Plants can be malleable both in nature and in human hands. This biological capacity to modify changed the social balance of interest around cactus. At the very moment that many wealthier landowners seemed to be uniting against opuntia, their interests and attitudes diverged again in the early decades of the twentieth century. The story is, however, more complex. Just as these experiments on usage were developing under the aegis of one branch of the Department of Agriculture, so another, the entomological section, was finding common cause with the advocates of eradication. Entomologists were beginning to advertise their capacity to deal with unwanted, wild prickly pear through completely different methods. Their campaign is the subject of the next chapter.

In the reconstruction period after the South African War (1899-1902), the agricultural bureaucracies of the Transvaal and Free State, as well as the better-established departments in the Cape and Natal, expanded quickly. A number of specialists were employed. Joseph Burtt-Davy was an energetic British botanist who trained and worked in California in the 1890s before coming to the Transvaal in 1903. He was typical of a new generation of South African scientists, most from outside the country, who had wide international networks. Burtt-Davy was an avid collector of indigenous plants. He made a number of important field trips and wrote extensively on trees. However, he was equally interested in the potential of introduced species. Maize, already the dominant crop on the highveld, could hardly fail to absorb his attention and he published a book on it in 1914, shortly after leaving government employment to take up farming. Burtt-Davy was responsible for a number of key introductions into South Africa, including Kikuyu grass from East Africa which soon became widespread in pastures, gardens and golf courses. After returning to England, he was appointed one of the first lecturers at the Imperial Forestry Institute in Oxford.

Spineless cactus was one of Burtt-Davy's many interests. He collected specimens of a type of kaalblad that was brought to the Transvaal by the 'early settlers'.[1] By 1907 this was being grown at Skinners Court, the Department of Agriculture's experimental site in Pretoria. This may have been the origins of the cultivar later called Skinners Court. Burtt-Davy was aware that Louis Trabut, a French botanist who worked in Algeria for many years, was breeding improved varieties of spineless cactus and he imported one type from this source in 1907. It was later widely distributed in the Transvaal.[2]

As we noted, wild prickly pear had penetrated the northern and eastern Transvaal by the 1880s. Tudor Trevor, who travelled all over the Transvaal in the late nineteenth century, wrote to Burtt-Davy detailing its incidence in Sekhukhuneland, the Soutpansberg and on his own farm at Barberton. Prickly pear had been planted by African people for defence, hedging and food. 'Cattle will eat them', he confirmed, 'and thrive when there is no other food in the country, and in famine times they are the saving of thousands of native lives'. Burtt-Davy claimed that the new department was keeping an eye on them and that they were not spreading: 'because a plant becomes a weed in one country it does not at all follow that it will be troublesome in places where the climate is different'. In later years, Burtt-Davy discussed the many different methods of treating prickly pear, especially in the United States. He was a plant entrepreneur and bricoleur like a number of his predecessors in South Africa, with profligate interests in the potential of everything he could lay his hands on.

The most successful varieties of spineless cactus were developed in the United States by the innovative plant breeder Luther Burbank of Santa Rosa, California. He was responsible for many new varieties of deciduous fruits as well as a classic and widely grown potato. In the 1890s, he wrote that:

> while testing the availability of a great number of proposed forage plants from the various arid regions of the world, with a view to the improvement of the most promising, I was greatly impressed with the apparent possibilities in this line, amongst the Opuntias, which from their well-known vigor and rapidity of growth, easy multiplication and universal adaptability to conditions of drought, flood, heat, cold, rich or arid soil, place them as a class far ahead of all other members of the great cactus family, both as forage plants and for their most attractive, wholesome and delicious fruits, which are produced abundantly and without fail each season.[3]

Burbank produced a richly illustrated, multi-volume book in 1914 detailing his many experiments, including a fascinating account of his work on opuntia. He cross-bred opuntia species and varieties, scouring the world for varieties that were, like the kaalblad, largely spineless. In addition to Mexico, some of his most valuable breeding material came from France and Sicily and some was Californian. Samples were sent from North Africa and from South Africa. Some of these varieties had already been subject to breeding or hybridised. Natural hybrids were particularly vigorous and it seems that these provided critical building blocks in his experiments. Burbank was benefitting and working from, long-established processes of local plant selection especially in the Americas and Europe. In fact, he was accused at the time of simply adopting and replicating known spineless species. It seems clear that his breeding programme went beyond the available stock.

Sometimes Burbank found it difficult to tell which species and varieties he was dealing with and he did not keep good records – there was not, at this time, an internationally accepted nomenclature. He retained some of the common names of varieties that he received. One from the United States was called Anacantha (from the Greek meaning 'without spines'), and he thought it was identical to plants received from Mexico and Italy called Gymnocarpa (meaning a naked, bare or

LUTHER BURBANK'S THEORIES ON SPINELESS CACTUS

Burbank was convinced that none of the apparently spineless varieties sent to him were truly so. Many either developed a few spines, or patches of glochids, on at least some of their cladodes. He believed that varieties found in Hawaii and the South Sea Islands, which were not browsed, had lost their spines. Some Cape farmers, it will be remembered, had an inverse idea, that plants became spinier when they were heavily grazed. Burbank argued that historically cactus developed spines to protect themselves from predation in dry zones where their moisture was so valuable to all living creatures. He believed that environmental conditions could affect spininess over the longer term and noted that in his first generation of spineless cultivars, there was a tendency to produce some spines if they grew in unfavourable conditions or were short of water. We have not seen recent scientific papers that might verify these observations.

huskless fruit). This latter name was retained for one of the most successful, South African spineless varieties. He also found that the variety called Morada, from southern Europe, was the same as that called Amarillo from Mexico.

Burbank and his team handled millions of seedlings, plants and fruits at all stages of growth. This, he recalled, was 'the most arduous and soul-testing experience I have ever undergone'.[4] The spicules (as he called the glochids) frequently stuck in his fingers or in his skin and clothing and he had to remove them painstakingly with magnifying glass and tweezers. Many plants turned spiny but a small number of his crosses produced increasingly spineless plants, with larger cladodes and bigger fruit. He was lucky in that it was possible to detect spiny characteristics very early in the plants' growth so that the failures could be quickly discarded. He was convinced that he had discovered 'one of the most important food-producers of this age'. After selecting from millions of cross-bred seedlings, he produced a number of 'hybrid Opuntias that grow to enormous size, producing an unbelievable quantity of succulent forage; the slabs of which are as free from spines or spicules as a watermelon; and that produce enormous quantities of delicious fruits'.[5]

His plants reproduced effectively from cladodes, but he recognised that they may not be stable if they were reproduced from seed. Burbank knew he had not bred out

Cladodes of Burbank's spineless cactus in California, ready for shipment.[6]

Image from Burbank, Luther, 1849-1926/*Luther Burbank: his methods and discoveries and their practical application* (1914). University of Wisconsin Digital Collections Center.

the spines, so deeply set in the 'germ plasm' of opuntia, entirely. However, he had no major fears about this. He contended that 'the new hybrid Opuntias had been found to be seedless; or where the seeds are not entirely eliminated, they are reduced in size and have lost their vitality'. When fruits dropped to the ground they produced few seedlings in contrast to the wild species. After a few generations, he thought, the seeds of some of the spineless varieties that did germinate were actually producing largely spineless offspring, so that over the long term, it seemed feasible to breed out the spines completely. He hoped also to improve the fodder value of spineless cactus. The variability in protein and fat content between different species and varieties indicated to him possibilities for improvement. A South African scientist later attempted to breed a higher protein content into spineless cactus (Chapter 7).

Burbank does not seem to have made, or even tried to make, a huge amount of money from his experiments. He sold the rights to distribute spineless cactus in the southern hemisphere for $1,000 dollars. In fact it was difficult to keep the reproduction of such plants under control because they were so easy to clone from cladodes, but he was by no means shy about advertising his achievements and would 'rub his face against the pads to determine whether the spines [were] really there'.[7] He was not at all constrained in promoting his wares.

The value of a plant that need not be cultivated and needs no preparation yet which will perpetually hold in reserve a colossal quantity of food per acre, constantly adding to it (the annual increasse being measured in scores or even in hundreds of tons), offers a refuge to populations that are threatened with years of drought and failure of cereal crops that is not duplicated by any other food produced hitherto under cultivation.[8]

Compared with the kaalblad, new spineless cactus seemed to offer three advantages. Firstly, some of the varieties were more truly spineless (though occasional spines were reported later). Secondly, they were more productive and he bred varieties that had special potential either for fodder or fruit. Thirdly, his plants were more stable and less likely to produce large quantities of spiny offspring should they reproduce from seed.

News about the spineless cactus soon reached South Africa. Burtt-Davy was one conduit of information. In 1906 Burbank was visited in California by William MacDonald, former farm manager at Lovedale Mission School in the Eastern Cape, who had moved to Milner's reconstruction Transvaal as an agricultural officer. He also edited the *Transvaal Agricultural Journal* and published a long account of his American adventures.[9] MacDonald wrote about Burbank's breeding successes but included a rather sceptical report from an American academic who wondered whether spineless cactus could really remain spineless and could really be planted economically on a large scale in desert areas. Burbank was accused of breeding for the sake of breeding: 'because he can make them take on new forms'. This was unfair in relation to the spineless cactus cultivars. MacDonald himself was more absorbed in American experiments with dry farming and the breeding of drought-resistant cereals to make the deserts bloom. Dry farming turned out to be a problematic enterprise in South Africa, although this method brought significant agricultural gains in particular areas.[10] But the Transvaal botanists were enthused, and in 1908 the Department received cladodes of two Burbank varieties, Anacantha (probably the type later called Gymnocarpa in South Africa) and Morada.[11] Thus, the Transvaal Department of Agriculture started its spineless cactus distribution in 1907 to 1908 with varieties from three different sources: local Skinners Court, Algerian and Californian.

In the Cape, any doubts about spineless cactus soon dissolved. A nursery at Grahamstown imported cladodes of Burbank's Santa Rosa cultivar in 1909. The

Department of Agriculture tested them in 1912 and quoted approvingly from a report of their American counterparts: they were 'the camels of the vegetable world. They must have water but they can get along for long periods without it'.[12] After two years, cladodes from Santa Rosa plants were 'almost absolutely smooth' and more than twice the size of comparable kaalblad. Individual farmers such as Sydney Rubidge in Graaff-Reinet imported their own plants direct from California.[13]

A snapshot of how clusters of farmers innovated in this sphere was given to the entomologist F.W. Pettey in 1938.[14] An angora goat farmer named Colborne in Willowmore imported cladodes in 1909 and sold to others around him. One of these was W.H. Morris who was also a shop owner and purchased a large farm near Miller village in Willowmore in 1921. Morris, in turn, sold cladodes, including some to the 'very wealthy' Brunsdon family who had 'eleven valuable farms' in this and neighbouring districts. They developed a large spineless cactus area of 800 morgen (about 1,700 acres or 700 hectares). When Pettey investigated in 1938, there were about 2,000 morgen planted to spineless cactus around Miller village alone by at least five farmers. Others had smaller plots – and Pettey, as will become clear, tended to underestimate these plantations.

After Union in 1910, the Department of Agriculture established an experimental farm and agricultural college at Grootfontein, close to Middelburg town, in the heart of the sheep-farming districts of the Karoo. It was one of five colleges in the country and it specialised in pastoral farming. Grootfontein had been used as a military remount and grazing farm during the South African War and its vegetation was in poor condition. It was a good place to experiment with conservation techniques and fodder plants. R.W. Thornton, who had worked in the Cape department for a few years, became its first director. He was deeply committed to improving pastoral production and one of his priorities in the 1910s was growing, testing and distributing Burbank varieties. Experimental plots of spineless cactus were instituted at Grootfontein in 1913 soon after its foundation. Despite occasional complaints from commercial nurseries, officials were so enthusiastic that the government engaged directly in the production and marketing of spineless cactus.[15] Demand could hardly be met. In 1916, Grootfontein distributed 8,000 cladodes and by 1918, 20,000. Between 1918 and 1930 an average of roughly 25,000 cladodes a year were sold. In 1924, when farmers were alarmed by a severe drought, sales topped 100,000. Farmers could reproduce the plants themselves easily by cloning and after three or four years would have plenty of cladodes to use.

The Department advertised methods of planting and cultivation and emphasised the plants' potential in combating soil erosion.[16] In the 1920s it released circulars in praise of the spineless cactus as 'capable of doing as much for the stock industry of our country as turnips and mangels have done for that of Western Europe'.[17] No crop was 'so easy to grow'. By the 1930s, Grootfontein had experimented with 37 varieties. Chemical analysis showed that they did not differ greatly from the spiny varieties. They would grow in the same areas, and were even more palatable to livestock. The leaves grown in nursery conditions were bigger and heavier than the ordinary kaalblad. Each cultivar had its own characteristics and name. One of the most productive was a lighter green type with large long cladodes and an upright habit, called Fusicaulis. All varieties except one grown at Grootfontein produced some fruit, but Fusicaulis was amongst the sparsest fruiters. It was recommended to farmers not only on account of its succulence but because the Department was concerned that fruit production might lead to fertile seeds and reversion to spiny varieties.

Officials who worked with the plants over the first couple of decades found that they seemed to produce little fertile seed. By the early 1940s there was more clarity as to which cultivars produced more spines and glochids. Only two, Protectorate and Arbiter, were found to be totally smooth, but they were low yielders. Skinners Court, obtained from the Transvaal, was favoured at that time for its all-round properties. When we interviewed at Grootfontein in 2003, August Wenaar and Isak Abels, two long-serving technical assistants, told us that livestock always went for Fusicaulis first.

Just how much of this new fodder crop was planted became a matter of dispute. Somewhat surprisingly, spineless cactus was not recorded in the agricultural census.

EXPERIMENTS WITH PRICKLY PEAR

While spiny prickly pear had been widely used, little systematic research had been done on the plant in South Africa prior to Union in 1910. Preliminary experiments conducted by R.W. Thornton confirmed that prickly pear was a valuable fodder when properly prepared and mixed with lucerne, a legume with a high protein content, and maize.[18]

This expansion of spineless cactus did not resolve the problems posed by spiny cactus, so the Department also re-examined potential uses for the plant, as well as ways of processing it. Heavier use – as MacOwan advocated in the 1890s – might have resulted in effective clearing from areas where it was not wanted. The

Department's anxiety about the problem of prickly pear prompted four published reports in the early 1920s.[19]

Charles Juritz, long-serving agricultural chemist, focussed especially on the comparative literature concerning industrial uses for prickly pear. In general, he was negative about the prospects. Interestingly enough, he saw Australia as most advanced in discussion of utilisation, and South Africa more focussed on eradication. In fact, Australian officials were already committed to eradication and – partly because of the predominance of *Opuntia stricta* there – it had not played so significant a role in pastoral farming. In respect of South Africa, his views were shaped by the official elite rather than poorer, rural communities who made such extensive use of the plants. He underestimated its value to them. Juritz was well aware of fruit consumption by Native Americans, southern Europeans and North Africans. In the Mediterranean, he noted, it was cared for as an orchard plant and there was a significant export of fruits to the Italian communities in the United States and to London. There it was a curiosity rather than a popular addition to the imperial capital's food supplies, and was said to mingle the flavour of cucumber

REPORTED USES FOR PRICKLY PEAR

Although Juritz was not an enthusiast for prickly pear, he came up with a surprising number of reported uses. MacOwan had suggested, years before, that machine pulping of cladodes could make an excellent green manure and Juritz confirmed that their high potash and lime content enriched soils. In India prickly pear compost was made in trenches rather than pulped by machine. In Spain cladodes were used to fertilise vineyards and in Morocco to prepare soil for planting fruit trees. It was occasionally used as a feed for citrus in South Africa. However, Juritz felt that the costs of bulk pulping or processing for fertiliser would be prohibitive. Similarly, while it could be used to make an industrial alcohol it could not compete with the product made from a range of other crops. He heard of opuntia used as an ingredient for textiles, paint, glue, whitewash additive, oxalic acid (for dye and bleach), paper fibre and soap. But the chemical composition of prickly pear meant that it was by no means the best source for any of these products on a commercial scale. Juritz concluded that its advantages in mass industrial use, particularly if the aim was also to eradicate wild prickly pear in rural districts, were 'nebulous'. Prickly pear was valuable, after the application of household labour, where other alternatives were not available.

and melon. From his Cape Town base, Juritz mistakenly believed that it was also of marginal interest in South Africa: 'Like the mighty snoek of Table Bay, it has made itself too common with us, and familiarity has bred contempt'.[20] He did not suggest there was an export opportunity for South Africa. While he knew of the African fruit beer he did not report on distillation of spirits for human consumption in South Africa.

Ambitious ideas about industrial use were not followed up, but Grootfontein's staff was still interested in fodder potential. A process was developed in Graaff-Reinet for converting prickly pear into dry, fodder balls.[21] The severe drought in South Africa from 1919 to 1920 destroyed an estimated 5.4 million small stock and 200,000 cattle. Their worth was calculated at £16 million, much the same as the average annual value of wool exports through the 1920s. It should be remembered that diamond exports averaged about £10 million in these years, less than wool, and gold about £40 million. Wool was the second most valuable export overall. These were large sums in the Union's economy and the losses focussed the government's mind on drought, soil erosion and environmental degradation. One result was the appointment of the Drought Commission, which delivered its widely circulated report in 1922.[22]

In response to the crisis, Thornton instituted a new experiment at Grootfontein designed to clarify whether sheep ate chopped prickly pear readily, whether they also needed water and how long they could survive on prickly pear alone.[23] Ten, large 95 pound (43 kg) hamels (castrated rams) were kept in a small enclosure and fed with cladodes cut from wild plants that were not thornless, but not very spiny and were not treated by singeing or braising. The fodder was machine chopped, weighed and then placed in troughs so that the remains at the end of the day could be weighed again and a reasonably accurate figure of total consumption calculated. For 25 days, the sheep ate an average of 10.75 pounds (4.9 kg) of prickly pear and 0.6 pounds (270g) of lucerne per day and maintained their weight. From then on, they received prickly pear only for long periods, averaging over 12 pounds a day. (This seemed to be the upper limit of their capacity.) It was supplemented occasionally for a few days with lucerne when their condition deteriorated too quickly.

The experiment showed that sheep would eat prickly pear continuously – at least if they had no other options. Although an opuntia-only diet did not maintain their condition, small additions of lucerne could make a major difference. The sheep could survive for over 70 days at a time with no supplements and most animals rapidly regained condition when lucerne, maize or natural, veld vegetation was also available. Little internal damage was done despite frequent purging. (The purging was later ascribed to the relatively high level of oxalic acid in prickly pear.)

What most excited the investigators was that four of the animals survived for 525 days without any additional water, and with only occasional lucerne and maize supplements. This was an experiment that demanded a good deal of patience, but it cut across the eradicationist argument. Although prickly pear's fodder value was again proved as inadequate in itself, 10 pounds (4.5 kg) of cladodes a day, suitably treated and supplemented with small amounts of lucerne and maize, provided enough water and nutrients for sheep to thrive. In ordinary conditions sheep would also have access to natural veld, which would add variety to their diet even during droughts. Agricultural experts now knew, for the first time, the precise nutritional content of prickly pear and could specify the weight of supplements required for its use as fodder. Although their experiments were conducted with wild prickly pear, they knew that spineless cactus had a very similar composition.

This was an important finding from the Department's perspective. It was particularly keen to end transhumance in South Africa and was also trying to discourage farmers from long, daily treks to water sources. More systematic use of prickly pear or spineless cactus promised to contribute to both of these goals. 'No water supply is so proof against the effects of drought as the prickly pear plantation', a report concluded, 'and no fodder crop makes such perfect use of a scanty and irregular rainfall'.[24] New ideas about the significance of vitamins in nutrition also informed research and officials speculated that these plants might provide a good supply.[25] In fact, prickly pear is quite rich in vitamin C – the sailors of earlier centuries did not know about vitamins but they had realised this property of opuntia cladodes. Experiments suggested that while the nutritional value of opuntia was low compared with similar weight of other fodders, the actual quantity of digestible nutrients obtainable from an acre of mature plantation was higher than any other fodder, including maize, mangels and lucerne.[26]

A further experiment in 1930, conducted on Graaff-Reinet commonage in conditions similar to those on farms, supported many of the conclusions reached in the early 1920s.[27] Sheep were kept alive for 250 days on prickly pear, bonemeal and salt lick. They became emaciated but recovered condition when returned to a normal diet.[28] Both maize and lucerne were tested in mixes with freshly pulped cladodes. Unlimited supplies of pulped cladodes mixed with as little as 10 ounces (283 gms) of lucerne per day was found to be both the best and cheapest feed. The condition of sheep and quality of wool was not affected and researchers concluded that purging actually helped to clear internal parasites. However, lambs did not do well on prickly pear, and losses were quite high without other fodder. Lucerne, rather than maize or groundnuts, was confirmed as the optimum supplement in further experiments at Grootfontein in the 1930s. Sheep receiving lucerne also ate more opuntia and showed higher overall weights.[29]

South African experiments were confirmed by experience in the United States. In 1928 David Griffiths of the United States Department of Agriculture, who had researched extensively on these issues, summed up the benefits that native prickly pear offered livestock farmers in Texas:

> Live-stock values are large, and droughty seasons are certain to occur in our southwestern 'cow country'. ... In such emergencies a store of reserve feed is needed which will carry stock through the period of shortage until rains come again and the normal supply of forage is restored. In southern Texas, and similar regions, where prickly pear is native and rampant, fortunately the reserve is always ready. All that is necessary is to 'limber up' the prickly-pear torch, destroy the spiny armature of the plant which has protected it from destruction by live-stock ... and the herd is saved from the effects of a moderate drought.[30]

This wild crop enabled ranchers to keep herds intact through droughts ranging from three months to three years. 'Prickly pear is a decided asset to southern Texas', Griffiths concluded. 'Probably 50 per cent more cattle are marketed over a term of years than could be produced were it not for this reserve supply of feed'. Experiments were also conducted there on the best fodder mix. Calculations based on the *Opuntia lindheimeri* recommended rather higher supplements, of about 15 per cent each of wheat bran and lucerne, in a prickly-pear-based feeding mix. However this was a calculation for an optimum balanced fodder for cattle rather than an experiment designed to test how long animals could survive on prickly pear. Australian atriplex (saltbush) was also found to be a good complement to cactus and suitable in non-irrigated, semi-arid lands.

Although the experiments done in the 1920s confirmed a good deal of general knowledge about the value of prickly pear, three problems were never fully overcome with respect to the spiny variety. Given the scattered distribution of wild prickly pear, it was very difficult to keep livestock away from damaging engagements with thorny cladodes and glochid-covered fruit. Dried fruits fallen to the ground were just as attractive and dangerous to the animals as the fresh fruits. In order to overcome this difficulty, farmers would have to separate their livestock from plants during and after the fruiting season. Secondly, wild prickly pear became particularly dense in richer alluvial land which was suitable for cultivation and sometimes for irrigation. Land for cultivation was desperately short in the Cape midlands and money was being invested in irrigation on both the Sundays and Fish River systems.

Thirdly, although mechanical choppers, pulpers and burners were all available on the market, and quite widely used, relatively few commercial farmers seemed to find it profitable to process thorny cladodes on a mass scale and on a daily basis. New and more powerful paraffin torches were developed in the United States that singed spines on the plant, without cutting. One version, the B&H Pear Burner sold by Mangold Bros of Port Elizabeth, was touted in the 1920s as 'Worth It's Weight in Gold'. It competed with the New Mercantile Pear Burner.[31] These burners did not seem to make a major difference. Similarly, African livestock owners in the Ciskeian districts such as Peddie and Middledrift used prickly pear in drought years, but – in contrast to Madagascar – they did not make processing a central element in the peasant economy.[32] At this stage, in the 1920s at least, both white farmers in southern Texas and indigenous livestock owners in southern Madagascar were more prepared to process on a systematic basis.

It is difficult to be definite about South African constraints. In part, white commercial farmers had other options in the shape of Karoo bushes, lucerne, saltbush, agave, spekboom in the wetter, coastal districts and, increasingly, spineless cactus. While labour was relatively cheap, some farmers were heavily indebted and lacked the capital to organise mass processing of opuntia. Ciskeian homesteads were often impoverished, their men absent as migrant workers and family labour was stretched. After the 1920s, for reasons that will become clear, the Department showed less interest in researching the fodder value of spiny prickly pear.

OPUNTIA AND PRODUCTIVITY ON WELLWOOD FARM

Government experiments showed the value of prickly pear as drought fodder and continuous feed, but they did not attempt to measure whether opuntia increased productivity on Grootfontein or private farms. One example of the impact of spineless cactus is offered by Wellwood farm in Graaff-Reinet district. The area has a highly variable average annual rainfall of about 13 inches (330 mm). Natural grazing resources largely consisted of Karoo bush on the lower lying flats, and sourveld grass on higher lands that were used for seasonal pastures during the spring and summer rainy season (October to February).

Wellwood was purchased by the Rubidge family in 1838 and they still owned it in the early twentieth century.[33] From the start it was developed as a sheep farm, one of the most successful Merino studs in the country over the long term. In 1913 Sidney Rubidge inherited the farm and he kept a detailed daily diary and also other files. Most farm diaries are laconic and record only brief comments about the weather, stock numbers or major incidents. Some on stud farms are specifically focussed on breeding. Sidney Rubidge was unusual in that he also commented on a range of farming activities, and sometimes mentioned his general ideas about pastoral strategies. Although he was seldom in financial difficulties, he did not expand the area of the farm by purchasing land. His holdings were stable up to the late 1940s at about 5,600 hectares. This was well above average for the district but by no means the largest farm. Rather than expanding his landholdings, he concentrated his energies on improving the productivity of the farm and the livestock.

Rubidge's predecessors had constructed dams in order to provide water for livestock and to irrigate gardens and crops. Fodder was all the more important to farmers who invested heavily in breeding programmes because of the value of individual animals. When he started farming, Rubidge generally planted about 50 hectares of irrigated land mostly under lucerne, oats for hay and other grains, but water supplies proved too unreliable to secure irrigated fodder crops on any scale. He saw very limited yields in many years, and in 1924 crops failed completely. Instead, Rubidge devoted an increasing amount of time and energy to dryland perennial fodder plants.

Agave americana was used over many decades as stock feed at Wellwood. It was planted along contour lines to control soil erosion, sometimes interspersed with indigenous *Acacia karoo*. With perhaps 40 to 50 kilometres of agave on the farm by the 1920s, Rubidge's problem was not supply of the plant, but the labour involved in preparing it for fodder. Workers had to cut away the sharp tips and serrated edges of the leaves, leaving only the moist bulbous base. This had to be chopped across the grain into small blocks so that animals did not choke on long strands of fibre.

Like opuntia, agave had to be combined with other fodders or natural veld. It could also act as a purgative or cause deficiency diseases if fed alone. Although Rubidge noted in 1921 that agave was 'king of fodder plants' in the Karoo, he used it largely as a drought supplement. The high water content of the bulbous leaf-base made it particularly suitable for this purpose. Rubidge confided to his diary that he would not attempt to keep so many expensive breeding animals on the farm without agave because of the dangers of drought losses.

Rubidge imported seven varieties of atriplex (saltbush) seed from Australia in 1913.[34] These were already being pushed by the Department of Agriculture. He chose 'old man saltbush' (*Atriplex nummularia*) – a grey-green, leafy shrub with more leaf cover than most Karoo bushes, which seemed to flourish under the toughest conditions. A saltbush camp (paddock) was selected and fenced, and the plant spread slowly by planting and self-seeding. It seemed to do better than indigenous shrubs in drought, but did not become an invader at that stage. (It still does not spread quickly on the farm but in recent years, environmental scientists have seen saltbush as invasive.) When Rubidge made a calculation of the carrying capacity of the farm in 1933, he estimated the saltbush camp to have the highest capacity per area.[35] The plant could be eaten direct by livestock and it had a high mineral and protein content.

Graaff-Reinet, as we have noted, was among the districts most infested by spiny prickly pear.[36] Even on a well-run farm, birds, baboons and monkeys could spread spiny varieties. Throughout the 1910s and 1920s, Rubidge had teams of farm workers eradicating prickly pear in the veld. However, the Burbank varieties of spineless cactus were of great interest to him. As part of his systematic attempt to increase fodder resources, he imported cladodes direct in 1915 and 1920, experimenting to find those most suitable. He became convinced that spineless cactus was a better all-round fodder than agave. He found that sheep could survive longer on a diet very largely derived from spineless cactus and unlike wild prickly pear and agave, they could eat it direct from the plant.

In 1925, Rubidge began large-scale plantings. In 1927, he lost a few hundred sheep from drought despite having established 20,000 spineless cactus plants on which they could graze. He calculated, on the basis of the average consumption of one sheep per day, that he needed 146,000 plants for 2,000 sheep.[37] By 1945 an estimated 258,000 cladodes had been planted on over 200, enclosed hectares.[38] On average, there were about 1,300 plants per hectare and he thought this enough for 15 sheep. Livestock also had access to other fodder resources and natural veld. The benefits, he reckoned, were reaped in more ewes and an average 250 extra and better fed lambs annually between 1930 and 1944. The plantations cost about £1,000 to establish, but he reckoned they were worth £900 a year: 'the most profitable investment in the recorded history of the farm'. Cattle stocks were also increased, including 16 Jersey dairy cows. In his perception, spineless cactus made a major difference to the fodder resources of the farm, more so than agave and saltbush.

A variety of evidence can be used to test Rubidges's perceptions that opuntia was the most beneficial and successful fodder. Most important are livestock numbers on the farm. Although there are annual records from the early 1920s, enumeration sometimes took place at different times and figures can be difficult to interpret. Lambing inflated numbers and livestock were often sold and sometimes purchased, causing irregular rises and falls. Nevertheless, the unusual stability of Wellwood's size, together with the fact that Rubidge did not generally move his livestock to other farms or hire or rent out land, provides us with more stable parameters for making such a calculation than would generally be possible.

Average Livestock Numbers on Wellwood Farm (n = number of enumerations)				
Average:	**Merinos**	**All small stock**	**Cattle**	**Ostriches**
1910s (n=2)	1,909	2,204	73	130
1920s (n=7)	2,206 (n=6)	2,384	31	29
1930s (n=15)	2,508 (n=14)	2,740	71	16
1941-2 (n=2)	3,065	3,512		
1946 (n=1)	1,758	2,008	70	11

The figures show a clear and sustained increase, both in the numbers of merino sheep and in the total of all small stock. Cattle numbers, after falling in the 1920s, increased again. Ostrich numbers did decline over the long term, and this was one reason he reduced irrigated lucerne and fodder production. However, ostrich numbers had become negligible before large-scale plantations of spineless cactus were established.

Aside from agave and saltbush, what other factors could have affected the striking increase in livestock numbers, especially in the 1930s and early 1940s? Perhaps most important were water supplies. In 1911, 24 dams, two wells and two boreholes were recorded on the farm.[39] By 1946, 43 dams were fed from rainwater and 14 water storage facilities from boreholes.[40] In 1935 alone, four successful new boreholes were sunk.[41] Rainfall may have been an additional factor. Rubidge had a gauge on the farm and recorded averages of 11.6 inches (295 mm) in the 1910s, 11.2 (284 mm) in the 1920s and 14.6 (371 mm) in the 1930s. This is a sharp relative increase in the 1930s after the devastating national drought of 1932 to 1933. Better water supplies facilitated higher stocking rates and reduced dry season, winter losses, but extra fodder was also essential.

More complex is the question of his grazing strategies, which were partly related to water supplies. Firstly, Rubidge completed the construction of jackal proof, 'netted' perimeter fencing and successfully eradicated jackals from the farm in 1920. He also increased the number of internally fenced camps. This allowed him to leave animals out overnight and to run freely in the day. Previously, the sheep had been kraaled (penned) nightly at dispersed sites around the farm. It was argued powerfully at the time that leaving animals to run freely in camps for longer periods could lead to more efficient and systematic grazing, as well as obviating long, daily treks and thus increase carrying capacity and productivity. As Rubidge noted in 1938, 'Year after Year, since netting 18 years ago, I took courage to fully-stock the veldt'.[42]

Secondly, Rubidge became convinced that understocking presented dangers for the wool farmer, especially in wetter years. He was an increasingly committed conservationist who invested a good deal of his workers' time and his own money in controlling soil erosion and was cognisant of government warnings about overstocking. But during the 1930s, he became more convinced that wet years produced too much grass. This inhibited the growth of Karoo bush, the best natural pasture for sheep. It may seem anomalous that a Karoo farmer would complain of a surfeit of grass, but the pioneer species that grew most quickly, especially when rain came after droughts, were often unpalatable. *Steekgras* (an andropogon species) was inedible except when very young and its sharp seeds stuck in the wool and skin of merinos, diminishing the value of the product and causing septic sores. In 1934 after the great drought of 1932 to 1933, *steekgras* threatened to ruin the wool completely. For Rubidge, the answer seemed to be heavier rates of stocking to ensure that the *steekgras* was eaten down before it seeded. By 1938, he thought that the most heavily grazed camp produced the best lambing rates and best wool.[43] In sum, his grazing strategies contributed to the growing number of animals, but they would not have been possible without the accompaniment of new fodder and water resources.

The evidence suggests that spineless cactus was not the main food of sheep on the farm, which still depended largely upon natural pastures. Yet it was a central element in enhancing productivity by up to 60 per cent between the 1910s and the early 1940s. Wool yields continued to increase and the farm maintained valuable stud rams that fetched high prices at the national sales.

Extrapolating to the provincial scale, there is little doubt that the availability of opuntia fodder was a factor, though probably not a major factor, in the rise of the number of sheep and livestock in general in the Cape during the period 1900 to 1930. Merino sheep numbers climbed from 11 million in 1898 to 23 million in 1930 and the total number of small stock numbers from 18.2 to 33 million. Wool exports increased from 35 million pounds to 133 million, showing a doubling of wool yield from about 3 to 6 pounds per sheep. (Rubidge was getting close to 12 pounds per sheep.) Cattle numbers also more than doubled to 3.5 million.[44]

Stock numbers and quality are affected by a range of factors, including veterinary intervention, changing pastures, rainfall cycles, water provision, rising and falling global markets in livestock products and fiscal policy. It is difficult to isolate the effect of one factor, such as a fodder plant, from the many other variables. The major reasons for the gains in numbers and productivity in the Cape were probably improved disease control by dipping, water supplies, rotational grazing and fodder. Poverty, falling wool prices and debt probably also played a role in the case of poorer livestock owners, in that farmers stocked more heavily in order to survive. Spineless cactus was significant on a limited number of well-capitalised farms. On less-developed farms and in African reserve areas, where livestock numbers also peaked in the early 1930s, wild prickly pear was probably a contributing factor. The distribution of prickly pear was at its height in the 1930s and 1940s.

The Wellwood spineless cactus reserve was clearly useful but never fully tested in a serious drought. It was useful to Rubidge in the drought of the early 1930s, but he had not yet completed plantings. By the time of the next major drought in 1946, his plantation was destroyed. The events in that year give us a further means of testing the significance of spineless cactus on Wellwood. The biological campaign against prickly pear, begun in the early 1930s, took some time to reach this farm but in 1946 the insects devoured his spineless cactus plantations. 'Today I am viewing hungry ewes and dying stud rams', he wrote in September 1946.[45] He had to dispose of his dairy herd. The number of merinos on the farm declined to 1,500 by 1948 and the total of small stock to the lowest since 1919, or even earlier.[46] 450 lambs survived, rather than the usual number of between 700 and 800. Drought exacerbated the problem, as rainfall in 1947 dipped below 10 inches for the first time since 1927. But it seems clear that the major problem was the destruction of the spineless cactus plantations. Agave and saltbush were not an adequate backstop.

We turn our attention to this destruction in the next chapter.

———————————

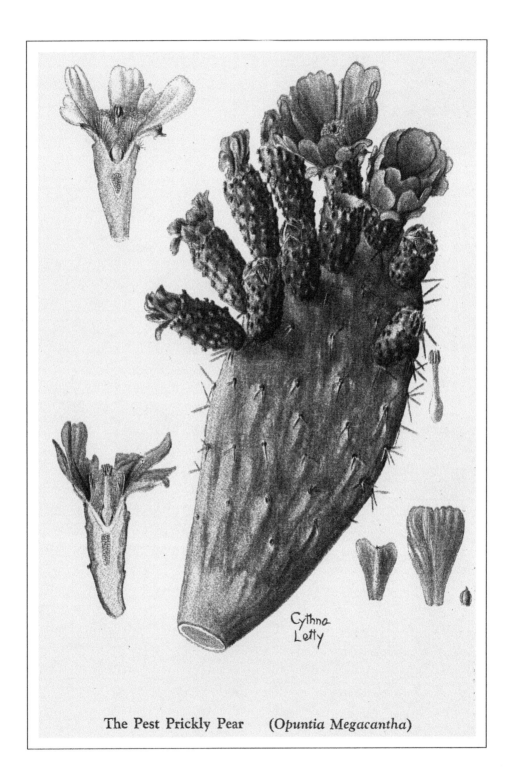

Cythna
Letty

The Pest Prickly Pear   (*Opuntia Megacantha*)

ERADICATING AN INVADER

ENTOMOLOGISTS, CACTOBLASTIS AND COCHINEAL,

1930-1960

ENTER THE ENTOMOLOGISTS

In order to understand the next phase of the history of prickly pear, we should turn to the state and entomologists. In the 1930s, the white-controlled South African state found new confidence and new money.[1] The depression years (1929 to 1933) hit the country hard. Yet recovery was relatively rapid as the gold price soared in the 1930s. State revenues and employment expanded quickly. Hertzog's electoral victories in 1924 and 1929 enabled Afrikaners to flex their nationalist political muscle. Although bruised by the depression, Hertzog hung on to some power in a new fusion government with Smuts (1934). They launched ambitious projects in a number of spheres – not least intensifying racial segregation. They shared in a widespread, global, post-depression conviction that the state should and could take a greater part in shaping and improving society. They resolved to address the poor white problem and they funnelled finance into agriculture.

The Department of Agriculture was built around scientific expertise. During this period it had one of the largest concentrations of applied scientists in the country. Embedded directly in the bureaucracy, they turned their skills to pressing national problems. While South Africa's fractious and divided white society was not a global leader in many spheres, the natural sciences were becoming comparatively strong. Scientists in many spheres – from engineers to parasitologists – had long believed that they could contribute to resolve social problems. South Africa had, for example, embarked on major government dam-building projects for irrigation and had instituted a massive, national, livestock dipping programme. The expansion of the state gave scientists greater scope.

At the very moment that cactus seemed to offer a panacea for droughts, so too was a new urgency articulated about the need to control spiny, wild prickly pear. The tilting of the balance in favour of attempted eradication is a complex story. It was not simply a victory for wealthy, white landowners. As we will see, they remained split on the issue because the new techniques of eradication threatened their plantations of spineless cactus. But it was, overall, a policy that reflected and encouraged a scientific approach to agriculture and natural resources. In the minds of officials, they were promoting both the improvement of farming and conservation of natural resources. They believed that various species of opuntia were rapidly colonising new zones, and they were gradually gaining increasing insight into complex ecological relationships. A sub-text in our narrative concerns a shift from provincial and local control to national responsibility for environmental policy and governance. As in the case of locusts and livestock diseases, the central state took increasing financial and technical control.

In the late nineteenth and early twentieth centuries, the United States was at the forefront of applied entomology.[2] The discipline was developed not least to support intensive agriculture as settlers moved westwards across America onto the Great Plains and encountered new scourges such as locusts. Entomologists in a number of countries urgently addressed insect pests in fruit and crops, and they assisted in the veterinary battle with animal diseases carried by ticks, flies, midges and other insect vectors. While the vets were always numerically predominant in the South African Department of Agriculture, the entomology section grew quickly after Union and by the 1930s supported about 30 professional officers. Four of South Africa's key entomologists in these years were American and the country's first South African-born chief entomologist was trained there.

Charles Lounsbury, born in New York and trained in Massachusetts, was employed by the Cape government in 1895, aged 23. His highly innovative research into ticks revealed patterns of transmission for some of the most damaging livestock diseases such as redwater, heartwater and East Coast fever. Such work was the basis for the national programme of dipping that helped to transform livestock management. He remained chief entomologist until his retirement early in 1927. After a brief interregnum under another American, Claude Fuller, Theunis Naude was appointed to the post, aged 31, in 1928.[3] Hertzog's government, which came to power in 1924, was keen to promote South Africans, and especially Afrikaners, in the Department. Born in the Free State, Naude did his doctoral research on leaf hoppers – insect pests of both maize and cotton – at Ohio State University from

1921 to 1923. He later worked on locusts and harvester termites. Naude oversaw the initial stages of the prickly pear eradication campaign. The main responsibility fell to Frank William Pettey, an American who trained at the Universities of Maine, where he excelled in the student dramatic society, and Cornell, where he received a Master's degree. He was appointed in 1914 as a lecturer in Entomology at Elsenburg government agricultural college in Stellenbosch. Pettey, who always used his initials F.W., researched on apple codling moth and other insect pests in deciduous fruit.

The eradication campaign in South Africa is copiously documented in the archives because so many professional officers were involved. Lounsbury was initially the key figure in favour of biological strategies.[4] He believed not only in the eradication of troublesome insects but also that beneficial insects, in the hands of skilled entomologists, could provide incalculable benefits for human society. He was involved as early as 1901 in a trial introduction of ladybirds to combat fruit pests. Later he hoped to find a Brazilian wasp to attack fruit fly. Although chemical spraying became established as the preferred mode of control, Lounsbury remained alert in the 1910s to the potential of ladybirds especially to control scale insects in citrus. Such techniques of introducing biological agents, usually insects, to control pests or weeds were gaining currency globally. Many scientists were, however, cautious. They were aware that, on occasion, unintentional transfers had unexpected outcomes or had damaged plants. This was the danger of biological campaigns: would new insects restrict themselves to their intended prey?

The link between cochineal and prickly pear had, of course, long been known and as early as the 1880s the insects were mentioned as a possible strategy for eradication in the Cape.[5] The potential for cochineal not only to co-exist with, but to destroy, opuntia was also known by entomologists in South Africa. In Mexico, a particular species of cochineal, *Dactylopius coccus*, had been bred over centuries for dye. It was larger than many wild species and produced far more red pigment per dried weight. It seldom flourished without careful management. In late eighteenth-century India, a wild species had been inadvertently introduced for dye production and had caused some damage in peasant prickly pear resources.[6] When the Canary Islands became an important centre for dye production in the nineteenth century, some people objected to the introduction of cochineal for this purpose because they felt it might destroy their fruit supply.

By the early twentieth century, Australia suffered more than any other country from rampant invasion by prickly pear – with perhaps 25 million acres (10 million hectares) swallowed up by the plant. An Australian Commission reported in 1914 after visiting India, South Africa, the United States and South America in search of possible biological controls.[7] (They also looked into uses.) By chance their visit to India coincided with a devastating attack by cochineal on the *O. monacantha* in southern India.[8] The Australian Commission, which clearly travelled with insect samples, gave Lounsbury some of this cochineal species in Pretoria in 1913. It was transferred for experiments to Natal.[9] With little public debate or even departmental discussion, the insect was then released near Pietermaritzburg where there were some prickly pear thickets. The results were initially limited. Cochineal required a critical mass to have any major impact, otherwise it would find a balance with the host plant. But Fuller, Lounsbury's deputy, found in 1921 that it was 'rapidly exterminating' a thin-leaved variety of pest pear prevalent in Zululand and Natal.[10] This was probably the *O. monacantha* which preferred coastal sites. Pettey later noted that the *O. monacantha* (or *O. vulgaris*), which had been scattered for over a century along the Cape coast, was also largely destroyed by this cochineal.[11]

Immediately after the Natal experiment was publicised in 1914, there were calls of alarm about the danger of an uncontrollable insect pest.[12] Some feared that a biological campaign could produce self-spreading insects that might devour other crops, including spineless cactus, and turn invasive themselves. But the entomologists were fairly sure that the two species of cochineal already established in South Africa – one long present in the Western Cape and the other recently released in Natal – had very specific habits. The 1914 Queensland Commission believed that most cochineal species subsisted on opuntia alone, and some on specific species of opuntia. Cochineal insects from the Western Cape were introduced into Graaff-Reinet around 1915 and had been spread further by farmers. They established very slowly on the wild doornblad and to the extent that they survived, seemed to subsist with, rather than destroy, the plant.[13]

Lounsbury had great faith in the capacity of science to regulate environments. South Africa's great dipping campaign was, by the 1910s and 1920s, proving a success in controlling tick-borne diseases in cattle and scab in sheep. He felt that the potential of cochineal for eradication of pest prickly pear outweighed its possible impact on spineless cactus. He was convinced that his division of entomology could manage a biological campaign. The involvement of entomologists would ensure that his department took over responsibility from the provincial councils that directed mechanical and chemical eradication. He sent samples of both kaalblad and doornblad to the Australian Prickly Pear Board, which was further ahead in investigating suitable insect species.

In 1924 a moth called *Cactoblastis cactorum* introduced earlier in Australia without success was identified as particularly promising. Unlike surface grazing cochineal, the moth's larvae burrowed into and devoured opuntia cladodes from the inside. Lounsbury tried to persuade the Department to experiment with cactoblastis at Grootfontein. Thornton, the principal, was particularly keen to find an enemy for the jointed cactus, that 'most deadly weed',[14] but he was unprepared to take the risk. Even if cactoblastis restricted itself to opuntia, it might devour his heavily promoted spineless cactus.

Lounsbury secured some cactoblastis when the ship carrying them from Argentina to Australia stopped at Cape Town. They were bred at the entomological laboratory in Rosebank.[15] The Cape samples were also intended as a safeguard for the Australians in case their supply died on the long, onward, sea journey. This initiative deeply split South African scientists. It is important to note that scientists did not always speak with one voice. The entomologist in charge of cactoblastis breeding in Cape Town felt that the first results on jointed cactus were successful and that biological methods might be 'a comparatively rapid and workable proposition'.[16] While cactoblastis attacked two other varieties of spiny cactus, he said that it had not attacked spineless varieties. Farmers could in any case destroy eggs on spineless plantations. But another of the American entomologists working in Cape Town, Mally, then researching on locusts, agreed with Thornton that the risks were too great. Behind Lounsbury's back, Mally warned the Western Province Agricultural Society. Reprimanded by the Secretary of Agriculture, he left government service for the University of Stellenbosch.[17] Fuller also called for caution. Lounsbury was confronted by his opponents at the second conference of South African entomologists in 1925. He was uncompromising: he had 'no intention of destroying the insects' and would take responsibility for them.[18] Prickly pear was dividing scientists, just as it had divided landowners.

The cactoblastis had the advantage of feeding on a number of different species, including jointed cactus, the worst Australian pest pear *O. stricta*, as well as *O. monocantha*. It is interesting that some of the most successful biological campaigns have used insects on plants other than their usual hosts. Cactoblastis came from Argentina and Uruguay, while its main victims in Australia, then called *O. inermis* and *O. stricta*, were from Mexico and Central America. (These are now seen as the same species.)[19] Its adaptability is still evident. In the early twenty-first century, cactoblastis moths were spreading through the Caribbean and into the southern United States, into places where they were not indigenous, and they threatened indigenous opuntia species there.

Australian scientists had shown in the 1920s that cactoblastis had no damaging effect on over 70 economically valuable plants. South African experiments later confirmed that although cactoblastis larvae survived up to 21 days on cultivated fruit, the insect seemed unable to reproduce or complete its life cycle except on opuntia species. Critically, biological control could be relatively inexpensive once the insect was established. Australia had already shouldered much of the financial burden of procurement and testing.

In 1926 Lounsbury reported that the Australian results were 'phenomenal'.[20] A new testing station was established at Port Elizabeth. Thornton now changed his position and lined up behind Lounsbury to recommend liberation of cactoblastis, subject to confirmation that it would not attack important indigenous fodder plants such as spekboom.[21] Although he had directed experiments that showed the value of prickly pear as drought fodder, the growing threat of jointed cactus helped to change his opinion.[22] If spineless cactus succumbed, other exotic drought fodder plants, such as agave and saltbush, would have to suffice. In 1926, Thornton moved to head office in Pretoria as chief of the Division of Plant and Animal Husbandry, but his former colleagues at Grootfontein supported his new position. Pettey later reported that 'the sheep men' agreed that prickly pear 'caused havoc with small stock'.

While it seemed that a biological campaign was imminent, the momentum ebbed in 1927 when Lounsbury retired. Claude Fuller replaced him as Chief Entomologist and entomology was absorbed by the Botany and Horticulture Division under I.B. Pole-Evans. The latter was a committed veld conservationist who had long been concerned about the possible impact of introduced plant and insect species on both indigenous plants and economic crops in South Africa. The Cape Town and Port Elizabeth breeding stations were closed. A misunderstanding at Grootfontein resulted in the destruction of the final South African colony of the American moth. For Fuller it was a 'profound relief' as the discussion had generated strong personal feelings in South Africa's small group of entomologists.[23] In July 1930, after careful observation of the Australian experience, the Department issued a circular and press release arguing that the costs of releasing cactoblastis, especially in the loss of livestock fodder and the dangers of renewed transhumance, still outweighed the benefits.[24]

JOINTED CACTUS

While the entomologists debated about cactoblastis, local authorities in the midlands and eastern Cape found themselves in an increasing quandary about jointed cactus (*O. aurantiaca* or *uḵatyi* and called tiger pear in Australia). Aside from its ornamental interest in rockeries, it was used occasionally in South Africa for hedging and some believed it offered protection against snakes. Jointed cactus did not cover anything like the same area as prickly pear, but it damaged livestock, sticking in their hides and wool, sometimes

Photo from Department of Agriculture leaflet showing jointed cactus stuck to a sheep's face

on their faces, and it was creeping down ever more river valleys. Rising anxieties about jointed cactus, and the incapacity of local authorities to deal with it, were significant in prompting national action against opuntia in general.

Prickly pear tended to be less dense in reserved districts settled by Africans, because they used the plant so heavily, and it was grazed so intensively, but *uḵatyi* proved to be a major problem in areas such as Middledrift. By the early 1920s the Keiskamma River was identified as a conduit, especially around the old Methodist mission station at Annshaw near Middledrift village; so too, by 1930, was the Kat River, including land around the famous school of Healdtown.[25] Jointed cactus was classified as a noxious weed and, under an ordinance of 1917, responsibility placed on headmen to take action. While officials could try to enforce the law, they had little effect.

> Time after time convictions for non-eradication have been obtained in the Middledrift Magistrate's Court, and sentences passed and fines paid, but with little practical result in thorough eradication. At present time there are three or four Headmen under six months suspended sentence.[26]

The imposition of fines for failure to deal with weeds clearly irked African communities, and this came as yet another regulatory and financial burden. It was difficult to eradicate jointed cactus; few government bodies or white farmers were successful in doing so. The Divisional Council at least recognised that 'being unable to do so, [they] *will not*, eradicate the weed'. The council was empowered to eradicate and claim a third of the expense from the landowners, but it could not devise a means of collecting the money in a communal area such as Middledrift. Strapped for cash, the council decided not to unleash its team with their drums of Rademeyer Exterminator.

Jointed cactus became a running sore; *ukatyi* scratched at local communities, metaphorically as well as literally. White farmers downstream of Middledrift complained that their land was being infected. The opposite pattern was also evident. Headman Mamotela in Peddie found it washed down the Fish River from white-owned farms upstream.[27] By 1927 the Native Affairs Department, which had unwillingly taken some responsibility in the past, resumed energetic action with a novel method.

> The thorns on the cactus are first burnt with any grass that may be growing in the cactus and then a patent paraffin burning machine is used to remove all the remaining thorns. After this the cactus is dug out with picks, collected with forks, rakes, and shovels, and moved in wheelbarrows to big heaps, which are burnt with manure from the kraals. Stock eat the cactus after it is burnt and in this way a good deal of it is destroyed before it is collected into [the] big heaps.[28]

The intricacies of 'methods of extermination', as they were called at one meeting, were now part of the regular correspondence of senior officials.

Annshaw was largely cleared but problems arose with this method, as well as poisoning jointed cactus on the spot. Livestock and people were vulnerable to poison and any rooted tubers (locally called bulbs) that remained in the ground could resprout. It was very difficult to control livestock movements in the open communal grazing of the African districts. The Ciskeian white authorities were clearly concerned about alienating their charges by enforcing eradication with inadequate methods and funds. Matters came to a head at Healdtown in 1930. The neighbouring Fort Beaufort commonage had been partly cleared by the Town Council with paid teams, but the magistrate recognised that 'the native point of view is that the white man, from whose landed property infection spread to Healdtown commonage, is receiving assistance'.[29] African communities therefore refused to offer labour for free on communal land. Officials feared 'passive resistance' if clearance was enforced. By 1932, the Fort Beaufort Town Council had spent £20,000 on eradication and claimed that jointed cactus was being spread again by goats from Healdtown.[30] In Fort Beaufort, poisoning teams found it essential to dig the plant up by the roots and carry the whole to a fenced trench before dousing with arsenate of soda and then burning.

In 1929 Rhodes University hosted a conference of local councils and government

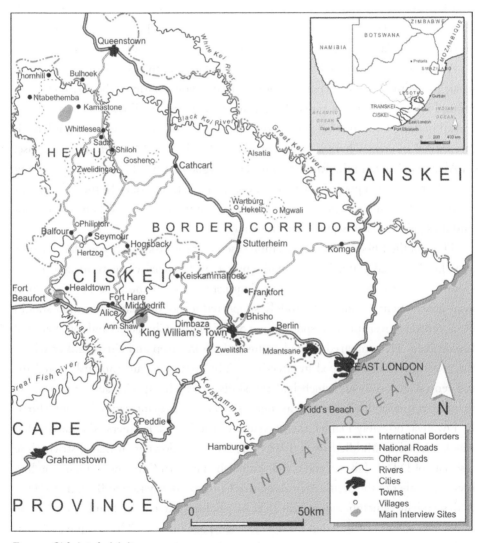

Former Ciskei and vicinity

officials to discuss 'government neglect and culpability' for the 'Jointed Cactus menace'.[31] Rhodes's leading botanist, Prof. Selmar Schonland, who was also a member of Albany Divisional Council, took a lead in the proceedings. In 1924 Schonland had published forcefully on jointed cactus in the Department's journal.[32] He distinguished between weeds that just occupied ground to the detriment of other plants, and weeds that did severe damage – none more so than jointed cactus. He also provided the first attempt to audit its spread, largely in lower lying districts within about 100 kilometres from the coast. Jansenville, Bedford, Adelaide, Fort Beaufort and King William's Town seemed to be the worst affected with 35,000 morgen of farmland and 14,000 of commonages invaded. The latter areas of public and communal land was generally in a 'shocking condition' and 'useless for grazing'.

All agreed on the 'incredible vitality' of the plant and the capacity of small joints to survive without water, separate from the main plant, waiting to be carried to new ground where they struck roots. As few animals ate the small fruit, seeds were not spread in dung but could fall close to the main plant. Many landowners found 'fresh infestation' in areas where it had been repeatedly cleared. Like a dormant disease, an Albany delegate to the Rhodes conference argued, 'it had been known to spring long after it was supposed to have been completely cleared out'. In the veld, it was 'scattered often in small pieces you can hardly see with the eye. Where one cannot find these pieces, Cactus cannot be eradicated'.

Those at the Rhodes conference emphasised that the task was beyond landowners and the divisional councils, even with their new financial capacity to take loans. Opuntia eradication was becoming a significant issue in the debates about rural local government. Schonland strongly supported a motion that eradication should be a central government responsibility of 'National Character and of National Importance'. He compared jointed cactus to scab in sheep and citrus canker where the government had stepped in effectively. The conference unanimously voted for the central government, which had the skills, research capacity and organisation, to take responsibility. There was one African participant out of about thirty, D. Dwanya, probably Daniel, the president of the Native Farmers Association that was launched in Middledrift in 1918.[33] He was a landowner in that district, close associate of D.D.T. Jabavu, and a well-established eastern Cape spokesman who had been a member of the South African Native Congress delegation to Britain in 1909.[34] A descendent remembered a great deal of prickly pear on the family farm. If he spoke, this was not recorded in the detailed, ten-page minutes. The fledgling African nationalist movement does not seem to have taken up the cause of prickly pear.

In 1929 Thornton moved from the Department of Agriculture to become the first national Director of Native Agriculture. His new post reinforced his support for the release of cactoblastis – a low-cost, nationally-funded solution to jointed cactus. In the meantime, he and other officials haggled over money for clearance and payment to African workers with all levels of government. His new boss, the Secretary of Native Affairs, took a hard line, arguing that as it was the legal duty of African communities to keep their lands clear. The Department would offer only food or 9d a day, less than half the usual wage, for clearance. It was very difficult to find workers, and by 1935 people in Healdtown were refusing to eradicate.

WAS PRICKLY PEAR STILL SPREADING?

A central part of the renewed eradicationist argument for quick release of masses of cactoblastis eggs was the perception that spiny, wild prickly pear, as well as jointed cactus, was still spreading rapidly. The evidence suggests a steady expansion, although officials were prone to exaggerate the scale of invasion. A figure of eight million morgen, or 27,000 square miles, 'entirely taken up by cactus' was published in an article in *Farming in South Africa*, the Department's journal, in 1930.[35] This number, amounting to over one-tenth of the surface area of the Cape, and clearly an exaggeration, was attributed to a participant in the 1929 debate on eradication at the South African Agricultural Union. It implied that more than 50 per cent of the midlands was covered by prickly pear. No systematic survey was conducted, but the Department, spurred by uneasy livestock farmers, made enquiries in 1931. There was some baseline for comparison over time in that MacDonald had estimated prickly pear infestation in 11 districts in 1891. Of four districts for which comparable estimates in 1931 are available, the returns from Somerset East and Jansenville actually showed a significant reduction in densely infested areas, while Uitenhage and Albany showed an increase.[36] These lower figures were not made public and hence were not of significance in the debate.

The Department changed its mind about cactoblastis a few months later, before any systematic survey was done. Perceptions and interest groups, rather than closely researched numbers, shaped this outcome. In 1932, Chief Entomologist Naude sent Pettey from Pretoria on a two-week tour of infested districts of the Cape to confirm the government's decision.[37] His initial estimate of the infested area was six million morgen; he clearly included areas of scattered plants. A more comprehensive survey in 1933, which included 27 districts, produced a figure of about 412,000 morgen densely infested and 328,000 lightly infested – a far lower total of 740,000 morgen.[38]

Over 30,000 morgen were estimated to be infested with jointed cactus, somewhat less than Schonland's figure.[39] Calculations suggested £20 million would now be required to clear prickly pear and jointed cactus – as much as £25 per morgen. A national survey published in 1942 put the area at about 1,1 million morgen (about 1 million hectares) with over 80 per cent in the eastern Cape.

Even though eradicationists exaggerated their figures before the 1933 survey, there were a number of predisposing factors for the spread of doornblad during the first few decades of the twentieth century. The sudden fall in ostrich numbers during the First World War, when feathers went out of fashion in Europe, removed one major consumer. As Pettey commented of Albany district in 1932 'not only was much fed to the birds but they destroyed the young plants by feeding on them. Prickly pear is increasing 100 per cent more rapidly now that ostriches are absent'.[40]

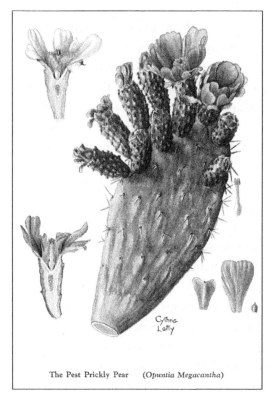

The Pest Prickly Pear   (Opuntia Megacantha)

Drawing from Pettey's 1947 report. The name Opuntia megacantha *was abandoned soon after this time for* Opuntia ficus-indica

Secondly, although wealthier livestock farmers were devoting resources to clearing prickly pear, poor whiteism and farm subdivision was intensifying simultaneously.[41] In some districts poverty and African tenancy had been closely associated with spreading prickly pear. Undercapitalised owners could do little to manage opuntia effectively and some positively encouraged it. The depression years, from 1929 to 1933, probably exacerbated such trends. As one farmer in Bedford noted in 1931: 'our country is becoming more and more infested with prickly pear and in these depressed times our farmers are not able to cope with the pest'.[42] The price of wool plummeted during the depression so sheep farmers were amongst

EVIDENCE FOR THE EXPANSION OF PRICKLY PEAR 1891-1933

It is difficult to make a direct comparison between MacDonald's 1891 estimate of 457,000 morgen and Pettey's of 740,000 morgen in 1933. By his own admission, MacDonald's numbers were approximate and he used the criteria 'overrun'. Later figures distinguished between heavy and light infestation. Pettey's 1933 figures do, however, suggest a small increase in eleven districts also surveyed by MacDonald.

Prickly Pear invasion in morgen

	MacDonald 1891	Pettey 1933		
	'Overrun'	Dense	Light	Total
Aberdeen	64,000	29,000	37,000	66,000
Albany	25,000	23,000	36,000	59,000
Bedford	18,000	23,000	10,000	33,000
Cradock	35,000	31,000	54,000	85,000
Fort Beaufort	6,000	3,000	3,000	6,000
Graaff-Reinet	92,000	94,000	62,000	156,000
Humansdorp	5,000	18,000	5,000	23,000
Jansenville	105,000	20,000	7,000	27,000
Somerset East	50,000	16,000	22,000	38,000
Uitenhage	15,000	21,000	18,000	39,000
Willowmore	42,000	26,000	7,000	33,000
Total:	**457,000**			**565,000**

The total figure produced by Pettey of 740,000 morgen included a further 16 districts. The major anomaly was Jansenville, where the estimated area infested had declined from 105,000 to 27,000 morgen. Perhaps this was an overestimate in 1891 and perhaps it was the result of mechanical and chemical eradication. There were some large and successful angora goat farmers in the district who had the capital to clear land systematically.

the major casualties. Tom Murray in Graaff-Reinet told Pettey that 'in hard times like the present no farmer can afford to spend a penny in preventing prickly pear from increasing in sheep lands'.[43] Pettey saw dense thickets on a number of municipal commonages where clearing had ceased by cash strapped councils.

This included commonages around towns such as Middelburg which observers remembered had little prickly pear 30 years before.

Thirdly, invasion could be an exponential phenomenon; once doornblad had taken hold in a district it was more likely to spread if it was not cleared. Infestation along inaccessible river valleys had become particularly serious. At Uitenhage, Pettey heard that 'prickly pear forms a jungle the whole length of the Sunday's River ... for a distance of 75 to 100 miles' and had invaded the valley lands on either side for up to 15 miles.[44] Jointed cactus overhung the Keiskamma River, near Middledrift, and 'broken off joints were resting on the rocks waiting for the next storm to bring them down the river to reinfest the lands of private farms lower down'. Pettey found that 'in places the jointed cactus was so thick that no paths existed to allow walking in it'. In Patensie, a beautiful valley on the Gamtoos River north of Hankey, prickly pear was so dense in some places that you could not walk through it.

And fourth, the rise in the number of sheep, though in some small part facilitated by opuntia fodder supplies, was also, ironically, linked to the spread of spiny prickly pear. As sheep numbers soared to about 23 million in the Cape alone in 1931, double that in the 1890s, there was a concomitant denudation of vegetation. Prickly pear cladodes were more likely to take root in bare soil than on land covered with grass and other vegetation. Periodic droughts in 1913, 1916, 1919 to 1920, 1926 to 1927 and 1932 to 1933 may have hastened the process, both because animals depended more on fruit and because vegetation cover was even sparser. Pettey found that the doornblad took hold not least in sweetveld areas, which were favoured by sheep for grazing and were more quickly denuded. More dung with opuntia seeds in it was also probably deposited on them.

AGRICULTURAL POLITICS OVER ERADICATION

The politics around prickly pear eradication were becoming increasingly intricate in the early 1930s. The files of the Department of Agriculture preserve not only detailed scientific and policy reports but a cacophony of letters arguing different points of view. By and large, the key debates were held amongst white officials and farmers; African opinion was not sought, although we will illustrate some involvement by the Native Affairs Department (NAD). As noted above, the reluctance of African communities in the former Ciskeian districts to clear jointed cactus, especially as this work was not properly paid, prompted Thornton to back a biological solution, but a couple of NAD officials, recognising the value of fruit, were less enthusiastic.

The division over biological methods was not simply between Afrikaners and English-speakers, or wealthy and poor. Despite Afrikaner nationalist dominance from 1924 to 1933, most key posts in the Department of Agriculture were still held by English-speakers. They were gradually replaced when trained officers from Afrikaner backgrounds became available. The battle between the various entomologists in the 1920s was very largely an English-speaking affair and even the Americans Lounsbury, Fuller, Mally and Pettey ended up on different sides.

Under the Cape government, Afrikaners had generally been opposed to compulsory eradication. General Kemp, Minister of Agriculture in Hertzog's government, had initially authorised Lounsbury's experiments with cactoblastis. He then changed his mind in the face of the spineless cactus lobby.[45] There was a clear geographical split on the issue. Spineless cactus growers in the Northern Cape and Free State, districts largely free of the invasive prickly pear, were adamantly opposed to biological campaigns. These areas were generally dominated by Afrikaner landowners who were nationalist in sympathy. An Afrikaner wrote about the dangers for South Africa *'met sy besondere gunstige klimaat vir insekteplae'* (with its particularly favourable climate for insect plagues)'. He argued, perhaps mistakenly, that introduced ladybirds and Australian bugs now ate melons and pumpkins.[46] When pressed to introduce cactoblastis at the 1930 South African Agricultural Union congress, 'General Kemp shook his head and was not at all interested'. Visiting the Cradock show in the same year, the Afrikaner Minister of Mines and Industries joked about the insects. 'You are very hospitable', he said. 'You are so hospitable that you have even invited the Cactoblastis germ to come. But let me just add that, when once it arrives in Cradock, it will never leave you.'[47]

The Willowmore Farmers Union wrote to Kemp in 1932 that Afrikaners were against the cactoblastis. This district also housed some very substantial, English-speaking angora farmers. Spineless cactus, they maintained, was the *'enigste oplossing teen die droogtes in die land ... Veral nou dat ons op genette plase boer'* (the only solution to drought, especially now that we farm on netted farms). In other words, fencing of paddocks or camps within the farm boundaries, rotation of livestock between them and discouragement of transhumance, placed a premium on fodder and water resources in the camps.[48] But the Willowmore MP supported eradication, pointing to the fact that the Baviaanskloof was seriously infested (*vreeslik besmet*), and suggested that this area provided an excellent opportunity for experiment because of its isolation from the spineless cactus plantations.[49] The archives give the impression of intense local debate.

Although Kemp saw Afrikaner nationalist opinion as primarily opposed to biological eradication, the issue cut across party loyalties. Some of the strongest advocates of cactoblastis in the early 1930s proved to be Nationalist MPs. English-speaking farmers were equally split. Districts towards the coast where prickly pear and jointed cactus were an increasing threat supported the South African Party, later the United Party, as well as cactoblastis. *Farmers Weekly*, the leading English-language agricultural journal ran a series of articles in 1930, some reporting on Australian successes which were generally in favour of cactoblastis. After a talk by Bernard Smit, an entomologist at Grootfontien (who had focussed on blowfly in sheep), Cradock farmers passed a motion at their show in 1930 asking for the moth. Leading farmers such as Tom Murray in Graaff-Reinet who had planted 200 acres of spineless cactus, were pro-eradication despite the potential cost to themselves. It was agitation from English-speaking farmers at this time, especially some sheep farmers around Graaff-Reinet, that helped to place biological control back on the political agenda. They wrote a rash of letters to the press, to *Farmer's Weekly*, to parliamentarians and officials.

Yet even they were split. Some members of the oldest, established, settler families opposed release. John G. Collett, secretary of the Midland Farmers Association, sponsored a resolution against a biological campaign. Sidney Rubidge lined up on this side (Chapter 4). Jack Bowker in Middelburg spoke of the extensive spineless cactus planting taking place: 'one can hardly place the potential value too high'.[50] Wealthier, self-consciously progressive farmers felt that they could, and did, keep their land clear by mechanical means. They believed that others should be compelled to do so. On Cranemere, a well-developed farm in Pearston district, the owner worked assiduously to ensure that the prickly pear, 'a monstrous weed', which formed a thick jungle to the north of the farm around the oldest areas of infestation, never crossed his boundary. He 'ranged up and down the farm', burning every invading cladode, but he also grew spineless cactus.[51]

When he became Director of Native Agriculture in 1929, Thornton's position in favour of biological control was cemented. He did not want to force Africans to dig up jointed cactus manually and preferred to pay them properly – a battle that he lost. So he then pushed hard to re-import cactoblastis himself on the grounds that he had supervised the first brief trials at Grootfontein in 1925.[52] The entomologists were able to convince the Department that they alone had the expertise to manage the insect.

Thornton was not unaware of the potential social costs of a biological campaign to poor, African communities. Paul Germond, manager of the farm at the South

African Native College, Fort Hare, warned him that prickly pear fruit 'constitutes the basis of an impoverished people's diet during certain months of the year'.[53] The magistrate in Peddie had similar reservations. Despite the fact that some of the centres of rural African nationalism were affected, we have not found evidence that prickly pear eradication became an issue for organised African politics. But for Thornton and other senior officials, the economic and political costs of manual and chemical extirpation were mounting. In 1933, the Chief Native Commissioner suspended work by clearance gangs in Ciskeian districts much to the annoyance of the provincial authorities, in anticipation of the release of cactoblastis. He wanted to keep departmental money for other purposes.

An underlying issue in the debate was not only the question of how much land was overrun but how much land had been planted with spineless cactus. Pettey, who strongly supported release, hugely – and perhaps deliberately – underestimated the area of plantations in the midland and eastern districts as 'apparently ... a few hundred morgen'.[54] Evidence from Grootfontein and from individual farmers shows that by the early 1930s far more had been planted. We know that the area around Miller village in Willowmore had more than 2,000 morgen in the 1930s. In 1947, a survey of losses calculated that Graaff-Reinet and Aberdeen districts alone had over 7,000 morgen.[55] As a number of farmers planted over 200 morgen, this would appear to be a reasonable assessment. In Hofmeyr district one farmer claimed to have planted 500 morgen. There are records of plantations in perhaps 20 Cape districts and there may have been over 50,000 morgen planted in all, at least by the early 1940s. Surprisingly, given the political significance of spineless cactus growers and the department's initial enthusiasm for the crop, they did not survey the plantations or record them in the agricultural census.

THE TURNING POINT

Emphasis on the scale of dense infestation and underestimates of spineless cactus plantations helped to frame the debate. The turning point came in mid-1931 as a result of a trip to Australia by the Secretary of Agriculture, Colonel Williams (the last person of British background to serve in this position) and Gerhard Bekker, Nationalist MP for Steynsburg. They travelled with a South Africa delegation for a wool conference and used the opportunity to examine biological control methods. They enjoyed great hospitality, including flights to successfully cleared areas. Both were bowled over by the Australian programme and Williams telegrammed home: 'Bekker and I convinced cactoblastis complete solution'.[56] They were intrigued to find that South African spekboom had been introduced into Queensland and grew 'abundantly' in areas cleared of prickly pear by cactoblastis.[57]

Williams's enthusiasm, together with the perceived intensification of the problem in South Africa and the support of more nationalist MPs, shifted Kemp's position yet again. Rumours circulated that farmers would take the matter into their own hands and introduce cactoblastis. This had always been the entomologists' fear. A chance introduction might have unpredictable results. If South African officials knew of events in southern Madagascar at this time, their fears would have been confirmed. Karen Middleton has shown that an unauthorised introduction of cochineal had a major effect on that region's prickly pear which had become central to the rural economy. Widespread hardship followed.[58]

The Department's hand was forced when Bekker raised money for cactoblastis importation from the Provincial Council and farmers. Williams insisted that the Department had to control all insect introductions centrally. So sensitive was the issue that the order for new cactoblastis eggs was sent to Australia in code; the authorities there had great difficulty in interpreting the message. The Department was reasonably open about the possibility that spineless cactus would be lost and South Africa might have to live with an imported insect in the long term.[59] In 1932, legislation was passed indemnifying the government against financial claims arising from damage to spineless cactus plantations.

Pettey took his two-week car trip through the eastern Cape as this time. He wrote a detailed and fascinating travelogue and we can see the landscape freshly through his eyes. He traversed many districts – in which he was to spend much of the rest of his career – for the first time. Given the time constraints, he travelled mainly to small towns and farms along the main transport routes. Extension officers and the cactus inspector of the Cape Provincial Council who had 'long tactical experience' with the plant accompanied him for periods of the trip. Pettey also met magistrates, members of divisional councils, farmers associations and farmers. He favoured Uitenhage as the key breeding station because its milder climate might produce bumper yields of cactoblastis and it had rich stocks of the invasive cacti as well as good transport links.

Any reader of his notes in the Department would have taken them as support for their new decision. Major areas of infestation were identified in Uitenhage, Bedford and southern Graaff-Reinet. At Cookhouse, where clearing had seemed temporarily successful in the late nineteenth century, he estimated 50,000 morgen of farmland, some along the Fish River, was 'a dense jungle of prickly pear as far as one could see, right up and over the top of hills and koppies'. Some plants were 15 to 20 feet high and could not be penetrated. He recorded dense infestations around Cradock town, along rivers and railways. Fort Cox agricultural school for black students, near Middledrift, had succeeded in removing cactus through long and persistent poisoning but he saw opuntia everywhere near African settlements and schools. With his eyes attuned he also saw other plant invaders.

At the end of 1932 Pettey visited Australia to study cactoblastis breeding. He soon warned against unrealistic expectations. South Africa's prickly pear species differed from those in Australia. They were taller, tended to have harder stems and were usually less dense.[60] The most prolific Australian invader, estimated to cover 25 million acres (about 12 million morgen or over 10 million hectares), was the dwarf species *O. stricta* with softer cladodes and generally under 5 feet high. Cactoblastis had not controlled the giant species in Australia, such as a 20,000 acre patch of what was called *O. streptacantha* or *O. megacantha*, similar to the doornblad, in Queensland. At best it seemed to kill young plants of these species.

Cactoblastis eggs were brought back to Pretoria under quarantine late in 1932. Some tests had been carried out on the larvae's predilection for other plants during the 1920s and these were repeated with 29 commercial species and 16 indigenous species particularly succulents such as aloes, spekboom, euphorbia and mesembryanthemum. The larvae managed to bore into ripe tomatoes, a paw paw and six avocado pears. Minor injury was caused to other plants when the larvae had no alternative food but they always went for opuntia first. With Australian evidence to back him up, Pettey concluded that cactoblastis was safe for other plant species and this opened the way to release.

South Africa, however, proved to be less hospitable to the cactoblastis than Australia. Within a couple of months, a parasite attacked the larvae in their Pretoria cages causing high mortality.[61] On hot days the cactoblastis larvae crawled through the mosquito mesh of their cages. The decision to locate breeding in Pretoria had been taken partly because the entomologists were concentrated there, and partly because it was seen to be a safer location, away from the main spineless cactus plantations. It had been a mistake because it was not the best climate and elevation for reproduction. When a station was opened at Graaff-Reinet in November 1933, cactoblastis breeding rates improved although they were still half those achieved in Australia.[62] By 1935 they switched to breeding on spineless cactus, rather than wild prickly pear, as it was easier to handle and gave a higher egg yield.

In March 1934 the first eggs were put in the veld in Graaff-Reinet, Cradock and Uitenhage. Australian experience suggested that success depended upon a single rapid campaign with wide insect distribution before the enemies of the cactoblastis gathered their forces. A critical mass was also essential in order to minimise the possibility of balance being reached quickly between the insect and its host. Pettey and his team were not producing sufficient insects to achieve optimum results. It was a year before the first releases were supplemented with more systematic egg-laying at ten-mile intervals.[63] Political problems still hampered activities. In the headman Zalase's location, Middledrift, people opposed the egg-laying. They 'strongly support[ed] the eradication of jointed cactus but they resent the eradication of prickly pear'.[64]

A further decision facing the Department was whether to continue the mechanical eradication and poisoning programmes under the provincial and local authorities. With additional funding these were now making more impact. In 1934, some operations were curtailed. Pettey was concerned that there would not be enough prickly pear leaf to sustain the cactoblastis, and that the insects themselves might be poisoned.[65] He wanted a five-mile gap between biological control areas and poison areas. This issue bred heated disputes between officials on the ground about national and provincial authority, and about techniques of eradication, especially of jointed cactus.[66] Pettey wanted preference given to cactoblastis.[67]

From 1935, Uitenhage became the major national insect-breeding station and the headquarters for the eradication campaign. We interviewed a retired Uitenhage teacher called Jean van Onselen, then in her eighties, at the town's prickly pear festival in 2005. She remembered the Petteys well. They lived close to the centre of town in Caledon street, opposite the Crown Hotel, until the early 1950s. They were part of the substantial English-speaking elite, though he was one of the few with an American accent. As in his student days, Pettey was an enthusiastic member of the amateur dramatic society, which staged popular plays and musicals – sometimes to packed houses of hundreds in the town hall. He also spent a great deal of time travelling.

THE IMPACT OF THE INSECTS

By 1936, Naude recognised that the campaign had started 'in a ridiculously modest way' and, as Pettey predicted, cactoblastis had limited impact on large prickly pear.[68] It soon also transpired that cactoblastis only destroyed the aerial growth of jointed cactus and not the root systems or tubers which could sprout new growth. Further problems arose in relation to what were called the rondeblaar varieties of prickly pear, which was then classified as *O. spinulifera* and *O. tordospina* (later given as

O. lindheimeri) spreading around Stockenstrom and Fort Beaufort.[69] Larvae were hampered or killed by the sap they exuded when attacked. Most of these plants had longer spines on their cladodes that hampered the moths' capacity to lay eggs. The local lawyer and MP, Fenner-Solomon, was particularly dissatisfied with progress and conducted a sustained campaign for more effective action. He had become a large landowner in the area, purchasing properties from coloured freeholders, sometimes by unscrupulous means.[70] He certainly stood to benefit from state expenditure to clear land that he had obtained cheaply. Pettey thought that this area along the Kat River was one of the most heavily covered with huge prickly pear plants mixed with indigehous bush. He found five invasive opuntia species in the district, including the dangerous jointed cactus, which had been planted on mission stations there in the nineteenth century.

In 1934 following the Jointed Cactus Eradication Act, responsibility for this weed shifted from the provincial to the national level. The Department of Agriculture decided to pursue mechanical eradication itself. As in the case of locust control, the work was combined with a scheme to relieve unemployment in these post-depression years. Between 1934 and 1936, 750 European and coloured men worked on eradication gangs in the white-owned farming areas and about 1,000 Africans in the Ciskei. When private farms were cleared, a certificate was issued to the owner who had to take responsibility for keeping the land clean. In Act 42 of 1937, all species of opuntia except for the cultivated Burbank spineless varieties were proclaimed as weeds. The state was now empowered to require eradication by farmers, but the Department exempted landowners in the districts where the biological campaign was being pursued.

The entomologists fully recognised the difficulties that they were encountering in the field and were engaged in a continuous process of testing and experimentation. Meticulous records were kept. Accepting the limits of cactoblastis, they turned to cochineal. In 1932 a cochineal species called *Dactylopius confusus* was imported and bred in Port Elizabeth. It was released on Uitenhage commonage and in Zalase's location of Middledrift between 1935 and 1936.[71] By mid-1937 it seemed very promising in destroying the above-ground growth of jointed cactus.[72] Pettey focussed cochineal release in areas south of Graaff-Reinet town, well away from the main spineless cactus plantations, and initially declined to meet requests for eggs further north.[73] In 1937, 30 million eggs were bred at three stations; 200 colonies were distributed in 16 districts.[74] The *Graaff-Reinet Advertiser* published a portentous report on the 'Doom of Opuntia' following successes against dense thickets in the

Camdeboo and around Petersburg.[75] Denys Reitz, the new United Party Minister of Agriculture, threw his support behind the campaign and at least within government, Naude wrote, 'nobody' now denied that eradicating prickly pear, rather than salvaging spineless cactus, was 'the larger national issue'.[76]

Gaining some momentum, the Department imported new species of cochineal, *D. opuntiae* and *D. coccus*, tested by Australian researchers. Reared at Uitenhage, they were then added to the repertoire. Pettey argued that it was a waste of money to poison and uproot.[77] Around Hankey mechanical clearance had led to the destruction of valuable indigenous plant species because it was so difficult to separate out the jointed cactus. Insects could be more precise in their plant targets. Mechanical eradication by the government was stopped.

Yet the South African biological campaign never ran smoothly. Cactoblastis was infected by a parasite of the genus nosema, similar to that identified by Pasteur on silkworms in France.[78] A third breeding station had to be started at Fort Beaufort in 1936 with more rigid systems of sanitation. Techniques of breeding changed – a departure from the Australian example – and eggs were increasingly collected from established breeding colonies in the veld, where they were less susceptible to disease. In Australia it had been necessary to breed for only 18 months because the rate of reproduction both in the cages and on the wild prickly pear was so high. By contrast, Pettey and his team had to breed for seven years until he was satisfied that they were reaching a critical mass. He calculated that by 1941 they had 'mass produced' 120 million eggs in cages in Uitenhage and 280 million in all. A further 300 million were collected from the veld, especially in Graaff-Reinet.[79]

Distribution of cactoblastis eggs reached a peak in 1939 and 1940, when roughly 200 million were placed annually in over 2,000 colonies in 24 districts.[80] They aimed to start colonies roughly every five miles. Moths could fly perhaps 20 miles so that once they reproduced in the veld, they could cover the zones between. By this time Pettey supervised a team of three entomologists, 20 white staff, a larger group of black labourers and about 12 vehicles. Preparation, breeding, collection and transport was more time-consuming than placing the eggs. 'Working at high pressure' it was possible for one man in eight hours to distribute about 600 quills each containing about 100 eggs – so that about 400 days of work by a single egg-layer, concentrated in the summer months, was sufficient for each of the two peak years. The small, inconspicuous moths that eventually emerged between 100 and 250 days later, depending on the season and climate, became a feature of the Cape countryside. Like other moth species they were attracted to light. Pettey found female moths 'flying into [my] lighted residence in the centre of the town of Uitenhage at least a mile distance from the nearest prickly pear'.

Despite all these predators, cactoblastis made an impact, especially in the lower-lying, warmer Karoo areas in Graff-Reinet, Steyterville, Jansenville, Aberdeen and Pearston. It was less effective in frosty districts and on higher mountains. The larvae were most effective on opuntia in richer soils, because the external skins of the cladodes tended to be thinner and they contained less mucilage – the thick aqueous or gummy material within the cladodes. Of 275 colonies monitored closely over seven years to 1945, half reached population densities that achieved major defoliation in the first peak of numbers. In Australia the first peaks were often within two years, clearing 50 to 80 per cent, and the cactoblastis recovered sufficiently from destroying their food source for up to three waves or peaks, achieving total destruction in many areas. By contrast, Pettey despaired that in South Africa 'nowhere has even an acre of prickly pear ... ever been completely cleared ... by this insect'.[82] Cactoblastis in the Cape found it especially difficult to recover after the first rash of defoliation. However, it did stop further spread by destroying young plants, as well as some newer, more succulent, fruiting cladodes. Because moths could fly, they found isolated plants away from main concentrations and in this way could stop some re-growth in areas that were especially difficult to get at.

Cochineal breeding operated in a different way. *Dactylopius opuntiae* proved to be the most effective species released on Uitenhage commonage in 1938. Unusually, its eggs hatched within the female which gave birth to minute, live larvae. In this case it was difficult to separate eggs or larvae so that cladodes with the breeding insect itself were distributed. From the start supplies were taken from more disease-free colonies that reproduced in the veld. The cochineal lifecycle could be as short as two months in the summer and its increase could be exponential. By 1939 general distribution proved possible. For the next four years, 30 men, with nine lorries spread cladodes seething with cochineal in clumps of prickly pear all around the Cape. As the insect was less mobile than cactoblastis, colonies were placed much closer together, 30 yards apart along roadsides and then 200 yards beyond. However, it could spread unpredictably over long distances because the tiny larvae adhered to birds and passing animals, or were swept away by wind. As in the case of prickly pear, it sometimes followed routes of animal movement.

Cochineal was initially more destructive than cactoblastis, especially in hotter, drier districts and in dense thickets with alluvial soils. Cochineal managed to destroy some larger plants, which cactoblastis could not. The males did not eat but 'the

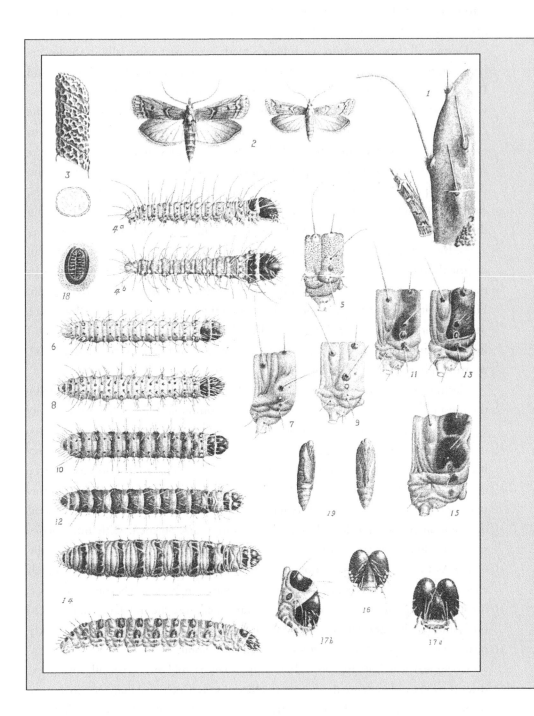

LIFE-CYCLE AND ENEMIES OF THE CACTOBLASTIS

In this illustration from Pettey's 1947 report, the moths and egg-sticks are at the top and the stages of the larvae and pupae lower down. He and his assistants developed an intimate knowledge of every phase of growth.

Even with the new volume of breeding, with cactoblastis naturally completing two generations in a year, and with each female laying perhaps 200 eggs, the moths were vulnerable. Their major enemies were ants and baboons. Widespread, aggressive, flesh-eating Anoplolepis ant species were the worst predators, attacking eggs, larvae and pupae and seriously affecting nearly half of the colonies in the Karoo. We need to explore briefly the life-cycle of cactoblastis in order to understand this vulnerability. Female moths, which survived for five to 13 days, depending on the climate and ecology, laid cylindrical egg 'sticks', two to three times, on cactus spines. These took between 35 and 55 days to incubate. The emerging larvae in turn went through a number of moults, taking between about 50 days (in summer) and 170 days (in winter) during which they ate, burrowing tunnels into the cladode and sealing the entrance hole with silk. This is when they did their damage, but when decimated, rotting cladodes fell to the ground taking the larvae with them, which died of starvation or were eaten by ants. When the larvae were mature, they crawled onto the ground to spin their cocoons, usually under the shelter of a fallen cladode or other plant growth. It was then also that they were most susceptible to ants.

Wasps, monkeys and baboons also fed on the larvae.[81] Baboons tore open the cladodes to eat them. In one area, 800 baboons were trapped and killed in order to protect the cactoblastis colonies. Inadvertently, the baboons were protecting their source of fruit, and for a few seasons, these omnivores benefitted from a surfeit of another food.

young female crawler', Pettey reported, 'soon inserts her fine needle-like proboscis deep in the plant tissue, begins feeding and remains stationary for the rest of her life'.[83] They favoured the sheltered side of cladodes away from wind and rain. The insects displayed their presence by covering themselves with a white, waxy secretion. In the dry years of 1944 to 1946 the cochineal thrived and this helps to account for its rapid spread through the Karoo and the demise of Rubidge's spineless plantations in 1946. Cochineal attacked the much favoured, thin-skinned Fusicaulis variety with relish. They were able to recover after a first peak of cladode consumption and breed sufficiently rapidly for a second wave.

Cochineal was by no means immune from local predators and this soon hampered its impact. Rodent droppings were found to be purple from the typical dye and when their stomachs were cut open for investigation, the contents were similarly stained. Field mice and the brown rat both thrived on this new stationary insect. Baboons and some birds adapted their diets to include it. Fort Beaufort commonage, cleared in the 1930s and treated three times with cochineal releases, proved very intractable. By 1941, many plants had re-sprouted and rodents were playing havoc with the cochineal. The only solution seemed to be for the municipality to control the rodents.[84] We know from interviewing in Fort Beaufort that some prickly pear around the old townships and commonage survived this phase of eradication.

Cochineal on jointed cactus in the 1940s (right) and on prickly pear in the 1990s

Overwhelmingly the most important predators of cochineal were the Australian ladybird, *Cryptolaemus montrouzieri,* in the Karoo districts and the beetle, *Exochomus flavipes*, indigenous to South Africa, in the coastal districts. Cryptolaemus, a small, black and brown ladybird, was transferred from Australia to California in 1891 to control citrus mealybug (*Planococcus citri*), an insect related to cochineal. It was this ladybird that Lounsbury introduced in 1900, with little public debate, to control grape and pineapple mealybug in South Africa in his first biological experiment. It was liberated at Bathurst, King William's Town and Grahamstown and proved more successful on citrus scale insects. The first record of ladybird predation on cochineal was in 1939 at Amanzi estate, formerly the citrus orchard of Sir Percy Fitzpatrick near Uitenhage. In fact, citrus growers started collecting cryptolaemus ladybirds from prickly pear, where it was feeding on the introduced cochineal,

CRYPTOLAEMUS MONTROUZIERI (LADYBIRD)

This beetle was imported into the United States in 1891 from Australia by one of the early biological control pioneers, Albert Koebele, to control citrus mealybug in California. Although *C. montrouzieri* initially devastated the citrus mealybug populations in citrus groves, it was unable to survive the winter except in coastal areas. Lounsbury then imported it from California into the Cape around 1900.
Courtesy University of California Statewide IPM Project.

Photo: Whitney Cranshaw, Colorado State University, Bugwood.org

and transferring it to their plantations.[85] Boosted by the cochineal, the overflow of ladybirds contributed to control citrus pests, though it undermined the biological campaign against prickly pear.

The indigenous exochomus was generally seen as beneficial to farmers in the control of fruit pests such as mealybugs and aphids, but it destroyed the biological control campaign in the Gamtoos Valley and possibly spread its range on the back of the introduced cochineal insects. This beetle was not, however, the only problem in coastal districts. It soon became clear that cochineal reproduced less effectively in damper climates and areas with cooler summers where it was also susceptible to a fungus called empusa. Cochineal was never as effective on opuntia in the coastal districts of Uitenhage, Albany and Peddie as it was in the Karoo.

Directly and indirectly, insects introduced for biological control campaigns were interacting with one another and with transferred plants. They had, in effect, become a complicated part of South Africa's ecological and agrarian systems. Questions were raised as to whether different insect species actually hampered one another's destructive capacities. Entomologists had to deal with a range of unpredictable outcomes.

INSECTS, ITALIANS AND HARD LABOUR

Following the uncertain beginnings of the campaign, the Department now had the resources for eradication. South African state revenues expanded quickly after the depression. When Hertzog eventually left the Gold Standard and the currency devalued, the income from a booming gold industry in the 1930s rose exponentially. A significant proportion was transferred to the Department of Agriculture. Over £1 million was spent on locust eradication between 1934 and 1935 and over £2.5 million on conservation and water supplies in eight years following the 1932 Soil Erosion Act. The sums devoted to eradicating opuntia were not insignificant. The Chief Entomologist later calculated that the Cape Provincial Council spent about £120,000 between 1928 and 1934, and the central government a further £180,000 between 1934 and 1944 on jointed cactus eradication alone.[86] Overall prickly pear expenditure was probably about £500,000 in this decade and individual farmers had cumulatively spent large sums themselves. Local ecological conditions proved far more unpredictable than in Australia and there was a new twist to the saga that required a further change in strategy and huge expenditure.

Between 1939 and 1941 the Weed Inspectors of the new Division of Soil and Veld Conservation, which now shared responsibility with entomologists for eradication, made the first systematic investigation of opuntia invasion. The Department formally distinguished a 'biological area' of 17 districts in the eastern and midland Cape, as well as portions of 13 more, where insect releases were concentrated. Here, they believed that about one million morgen were still sufficiently infested to curtail farming activities.[87] 200,000 morgen of dense pear survived in the eight worst districts.[88] Outside of the main biological areas where no insect releases were allowed because of the spineless cactus plantations, 21,000 morgen were recorded as densely infested and 350,000 lightly.[89] There were pockets of dense infestation in the Transvaal and Natal, and widespread light infestation in the Free State and Northern Cape. Officials thought that while dense stands of opuntia were being reduced, the area penetrated by different species of cactus was still expanding.

Re-involving farmers on a more compulsory basis was a necessary part of this strategy and the recently passed Weeds Acts (1937 and 1939) provided scope for doing so.[90] This was not imposed on farmers in the 'biological area' of dense infestation because the state was taking responsibility for eradication, but the Department felt that it could be extended to areas of light infestation, especially to the north of Graaff-Reinet and Cradock, where spineless cactus plantations were widespread. Arsenic pentoxide was again distributed for free in such areas. If wild opuntia was cleared in such areas there would be no bridging plants which could serve to spread the insects to spineless cactus plantations. Farmers could then keep their spineless plantations clean by organising manual clearance of any eggs or larvae.

The Department was still attempting to follow a strategy that might protect some spineless cactus growers by distinguishing between biological and non-biological areas. Ultimately, farmers themselves made this impossible. Individuals in a wide variety of districts in the Transvaal and Natal, as well as in the non-biological areas of the Cape, called for insects.[91] The Division of Soil and Veld Conservation emphasised new conservationist arguments in favour of total eradication: prickly pear was an enemy of the natural veld and some officials were hostile to all introduced plants. These arguments had not been as important before. After much internal debate, the Department sent cochineal and cactoblastis consignments to nearly 200 farms in 14 districts outside of the biological control area in 1941.[92] Unauthorised transfer continued.

By the early 1940s it became clear that biological control, which had initially been touted as a cheaper and universal solution, was working only in patches; in coastal districts Naude anxiously reported that there was 'retrogression'.[93] Entomologists recognised that they had a good deal to learn about the social as well as ecological complexities involved. Some farmers waited for the state campaign and were now less inclined to spend money themselves. It seemed clear that the halting of mechanical clearing was beginning to result in further spread in some districts.

The *D. opuntiae* cochineal flourished best close to the ground and, it was discovered, best of all when the large plants were cut down. Near the ground it was better protected from the rain and wind, could shelter under cladodes and was less susceptible to the predatory ladybirds. They also consumed any fresh re-growth at ground level. Naude accepted that systematic felling of the larger cactus bushes should accompany *D. opuntiae* releases; eradication would require simultaneous mechanical and biological control.

Bulldozers and tractors were used briefly to fell plants for cochineal consumption but the terrain was often difficult and indigenous vegetation was also destroyed. There was little alternative to hard, manual labour. In 1943 Smuts approved the use of Italian prisoners of war – well-known for their work on roads in South Africa – to cut the plants.[94] This was a high-level, cabinet decision in the war years when resources were short and Smuts would only approve an experiment in a few districts.[95] Intriguingly, Sicilians were preferred; they were supposed to be more suited to such rural work. The most successful European prickly pear fruit orchards were based in Sicily. The Department of Agriculture paid the Defence Force for their services. A complex scheme was devised whereby farmers paid the Department up to five shillings per morgen and the Department subsidised the remaining costs. Old established thickets near Cookhouse were chosen as the first target.

The project fell under a new Grahamstown-based official with the resounding title of Chief Weed Inspector. He was hardly equipped to face all the problems that arose, not least the attitude of the landowners. A few farmers had over 1,000 morgen covered with prickly pear and baulked at the considerable bills. Negotiations had to be entered into with scores of individual farmers some of whom still did not want to eradicate prickly pear completely. Farmers also complained that the military was getting supplies for the Italian POW camp from Jewish storekeepers in town, rather than themselves.[96]

Camps had to be built for the Italian prisoners and the army insisted on higher standards than the Department would normally have provided for labourers. The brackish borehole water was considered inadequate for prisoners so lorries had to be mobilised for a fresh water supply. Fifty defence force guards were needed. The Department was working on a cost of about ten shillings a morgen for felling – of which they hoped to collect half from the farmers. But the standards required in the Cookhouse camp, together with the density of prickly pear, resulted in costs of up to £4 a morgen.[97] Farmers tended to underestimate the extent of infestation and, as always, prickly pear was more difficult to get at in dense thickets or in rocky areas. In sharply undulating ground the actual surface area covered was far greater than it appeared on the map.[98]

Starting at around 6 am on the cooler mornings, the Italians were very reluctant to work for more than six hours a day and did very little after 11 am. They demanded hot food in camp at midday. Transporting them to and from the clearance sites took over an hour so that they sometimes did little more than three hours of work a day. When officials tried to increase hours they were faced with sit-down strikes. The POWs, despite their Sicilian origins, did not like the hard labour nor the sharp spines of these large plants. Towards the end of the fruiting season in particular, from February to April, they found themselves victims of the fine glochids of the ripe fruit. They started to report sick in numbers, but this was an important season for felling because the cochineal appeared to be most active in the dry months from March to June. This was also the period when ladybird attacks on cochineal were lowest. (Peak ladybird activity appeared to be August to January.) The ecological and social complexities of eradication in South Africa were considerable.

Piecework rates were offered to the POWs but did little to improve matters. The camp commander found it very difficult to impose harsher discipline. After six largely wasted months, the Department decided to abandon this experiment. They recognised that 'hard manual labour' was required and fell back on African workers.[99] African workers reduced the costs of felling to about 14 shillings per morgen in Cookhouse and 11 shillings per morgen in Graaff-Reinet. The programme now entered a more successful phase.[100] From 1945, felling teams worked widely through the southern, midland and eastern Cape, especially from March to June when the cochineal was at its most active and the prickly pear semi-dormant. In mid-1947 they had made sufficient progress to transfer the onus onto landowners to maintain clearance. As in the case of conservation works, landowners were now able to claim subsidies to clear prickly pear themselves. Old trouble spots proved intractable, with constant re-growth reported. The analogy of cancer was used. Yet the prickly pear was at last driven back across a wide front.

CONSEQUENCES OF ERADICATION

Growing success in building up the insect populations brought with it a crescendo of complaints by spineless cactus growers. Hofmeyr district, immediately to the north of Cradock, was the centre of political agitation. It was led by W.J.J. van Heerden, secretary of the local Farmers Association, who had planted 500 morgen of spineless cactus which was grazed by livestock in a systematic rotation.[101] Officials were not unmindful of their problems, although they sometimes felt that compensation rather than protection was the major aim of complainants.[102] A sceptical entomologist who visited Sidney Rubidge's plantation in 1940 found there was 'much talk of the great value of spineless cactus, but very few of the growers are prepared to go to a little expense and trouble in order to save it'.[103] This observation was frequently repeated.

Demonstrators were sent to Hofmeyr in 1943 to show how spineless plantations could be kept clear. Cactoblastis eggs could be removed manually. Cochineals were easy to spot because the sedentary females produced white, waxy filaments which sheltered them. Males wove a white cocoon towards the end of their life cycle.

Prickly pear on Fonteinplaas, Graaff-Reinet, before and after eradication[104]

The problem for the farmers was time and labour. The beauty of spineless cactus for them was that it needed little attention once planted. Manual control required constant vigilance. In 1945 an attempt was made to introduce ladybirds on a large scale into the Hofmeyr spineless cactus plantations to eat cochineal. This inverse biological experiment was not effective.[105] With felling, *D. opuntiae* had spread more rapidly than was anticipated and in unpredictable directions. Tests were carried out with pyrethrum and DDT for spraying insects in the spineless plantations – although even then there was some awareness that milk might be affected.[106] The Department could find no effective antidote and most spineless plantations in the Karoo succumbed.

By the late 1940s, the area of dense prickly pear infestation was probably reduced by three-quarters.[107] Pettey, who published regularly on the campaign in the departmental journal, *Farming in South Africa*, wrote up his experiences and findings in a major 160-page report published in 1947. It is a testament to the intense curiosity of a man who devoted nearly 20 years of his life to observing opuntia and its insect predators. He ended with a realistic assessment. While there had been significant success against most prickly pear species, and especially *O. ficus-indica*, he thought future prospects of biological control of jointed cactus 'not at all bright'.[108] Tubers persistently sprouted new growth and fresh segments seemed to break off even more easily. Some farmers complained that jointed cactus had been 'sewn' (*gesaai*) by the Department when it placed segments infested with cochineal on their land.

While officials felt that some of the worst concentrations had been thinned out, a 1953 estimate gave 750,000 morgen, or 20 times the 1920s figure, as the new area seriously affected with jointed cactus.[109] The entomology division was gradually sidelined and arsenic pentoxide, injected rather than sprayed, was reintroduced. During the 1950s, the Department tried a new hormone weed killer, 2,4,5T and this was increasingly favoured for all opuntia eradication. It was a powerful defoliant, later used as one of the ingredients of Agent Orange – notoriously sprayed in the Vietnam war. Between 1957 and 1960 1.5 million gallons was distributed. Annual expenditure rose to close on £200,000 a year by 1960. In a vigorous new campaign, school children were encouraged to become '*kaktusjagters*' (cactus hunters).

ERADICATION, ECOLOGY AND SOCIETY

Prickly pear eradication was supported in the early twentieth century largely by the same group of better-capitalised, livestock-improving farmers and state officials who pushed for such measures as compulsory veterinary controls and predator eradication. Some called for enforcement of universal legislation because eradication of the doornblad presented the same problems as scab or jackals. A voluntary system of eradication, even if subsidised, could not get around the problem of re-infestation from 'infected' flocks or land. Initially the government was hesitant. The state had limited resources, invasive opuntia affected only a limited number of districts and many found the plant useful.

The social base of support for eradication changed in the 1920s and 1930s because of two scientific and technical developments. The first was spineless cactus which was less susceptible to seeding and reversion to doornblad. Officials saw its potential and it effectively became a crop plant, popular with wealthier livestock farmers in the semi-arid and arid districts because of its value as a supplementary and drought fodder. Secondly, biological control strategies using insects promised a total solution to eradication, but they could not differentiate between spiny prickly pear and spineless cactus. As a result some of the well-capitalised farmers, especially in areas less infested with prickly pear, turned against a national eradication campaign. They preferred to use mechanical and chemical methods on their own farms, with subsidy if possible. Ironically, some rich whites, poor whites and most Africans landed up as joint opponents of the cactoblastis and cochineal, although they did not organise together.

By contrast, some less-capitalised landowners, whose forebears may have earlier valued these multi-purpose plants, saw in the biological campaign a means to clear their land at very little cost. By the inter-war years, farming families were less dependent upon home manufacture for their requirements. Livestock were the priority. The mobilisation of the majority of landowners in favour coincided with a more far-reaching attempt by the South African Department of Agriculture to reach out to Afrikaner farmers and incorporate them in more scientific, progressive and intensive forms of production. This policy outcome was not simply the result of a switch of government from the South African Party, supported by wealthier Anglophone farmers, to the Nationalist Party, supported by Afrikaners and poor whites. Kemp, the NP minister, changed his position on more than one occasion. Some English-speaking entomologists had always favoured the cactoblastis. It was an English-speaking official and Afrikaner MP who swung the balance of the debate in 1931. The campaign was begun under Hertzog but was pursued very largely when Smuts led the United Party government (1934 to 1948), and against the interests of some of his strongest rural supporters in the midland Cape.

The eventual losers were both wealthier landowners with large spineless cactus plantations, and poorer rural communities, especially Africans, who used prickly pear fruit. Not all Africans were opposed to the campaigns, especially in respect of the jointed cactus; both poor whites and Africans found local employment on the biological and felling campaigns. The Native Affairs Department strongly supported eradication. In the longer term, the survival of a higher proportion of prickly pear in the coastal districts meant that everyday use of the fruit for consumption, localised sale and brewing to some degree continued (Chapters 1 and 6).

Prickly pear control was a divisive and emotive issue over a long period of time in South Africa. Officials, especially entomologists within the Department of Agriculture, generated much of the momentum for the biological campaign, as well as the strategies adopted. Scientific knowledge and expertise were at the heart of the enterprise. Partly because of the scientific expertise required, the central state effectively absorbed functions that had been assigned earlier to provincial and local government. The prickly pear campaigns ensured that applied entomology remained a flourishing field in South Africa. In turn, scientific knowledge and experiment shaped the development of policy. Although Australian scientists did the basic research on suitable insect species in the Americas, South African entomologists, led by Pettey, faced a more challenging environment on the ground. Scientific strategies were continually modified in the light of experiment and experience. New insects were introduced and mechanical felling and biological methods were eventually combined, despite the expense. Science was playing an increasingly important role in environmental management and state policy.

The state was reasonably successful in suppressing spiny prickly pear over the long term. Much has been written on the transfer of new species through the colonised world during the centuries of European expansion; less so on the way in which species suppression by governments has helped to shape ecological outcomes. Cactoblastis and cochineal have survived in South Africa to the present, and continue to exercise some control over the recrudescence of opuntia. In this sense, species suppression has had significant ecological impact in the country. There is little doubt that indigenous vegetation and South Africa's biodiversity benefited from the twenty-year programme. Some species of wildlife actually thrived on prickly pear but conservationists certainly saw its eradication in national and provincial parks as benefitting a wider range of indigenous animals.

Conservation, or what would now be called the protection of biodiversity, was not initially a significant aim of eradication. The arguments for eradication were primarily economic rather than ecological. Although there was certainly a growing interest in the Cape's indigenous flora at the time, this was largely focussed on Western Cape fynbos rather than Eastern Cape bushveld or Karoo shrubs.[110] There is not much evidence of hostility to prickly pear on the grounds of its foreign origins. Some individuals, such as botanist Schonland, were devotees of indigenous vegetation and a number of landowners were keen to maintain some 'balance of nature'. He did much to build up Rhodes University's herbarium. F.W. Fitzsimons, Director of the Port Elizabeth Museum from 1906 to 1936, also campaigned on indigenous species – particularly birds, reptiles and mammals rather than plants. Eradication was increasingly influenced by conservationist ideas in the 1940s and 1950s when the Division of Soil and Veld Conservation took more responsibility, but they did not do detailed research into the impact of opuntia on indigenous species. The campaign was more strongly guided by the expectation of economic gains, increased agricultural production, social improvement and environmental control. For those that owned land in the valleys formerly covered with prickly pear, there was certainly a significant economic benefit over the longer term. For example, clearance facilitated the expansion of irrigated citrus and fodder production in the Gamtoos, Sundays, Kat and Fish River Valleys.

The controversy over eradication gave rise to frequent explanations, articles and debates on related botanical, entomological and ecological topics – at least in expert circles and among those farmers who read the agricultural journals. Environmental concerns were being promoted more generally in connection with soil conservation. At least for the literate elite, the prickly pear campaigns unintentionally contributed to expanded popular environmental knowledge. New insects and complex ecological interactions became part of everyday rural discourse because so many people were involved in the campaigns. Recent eradication campaigns aimed at exotic species have been more strongly influenced by aesthetic and ecological considerations. The Working for Water Programme, however, has also been guided by strong economic incentives. Economists and ecologists have tried to calculate the value of water saved by the eradication of plants such as black wattle. One reason that the ANC has supported this project is the opportunity to provide employment opportunities for poor rural communities.

In the longer term, knowledge about the properties and usage of prickly pear, along with some of the plants, also survived. This is the focus of the next chapter.

THE MULTI-PURPOSE PLANT, 1950-2006

MEMORIES OF JAM IN HEWU

In the mid-1990s, when we were both working for the Border Rural Committee research group on land reform and popular politics, we got to know Hewu and Nthabathemba districts, south-west of Queenstown, in the northern part of the former Ciskei.[1] It was a fascinating but troubled and impoverished area. In the nineteenth century this locality was the centre of thriving mission stations and Christian communities such as Kamastone and Shiloh. Radical and millennial Christianity took root in the difficult, early decades of segregation and in 1922 the Israelites were massacred at nearby Bulhoek where a monument has recently been erected. In the homeland era tens of thousands of people were removed to, or flocked into, these districts and one of the resettlement camps, Thornhill, became particularly notorious as an apartheid dumping ground. During the early 1990s activists had organised a mass occupation of state-owned land to form new communities, such as Tambo village. These districts were a central focus of Luvuyo Wotshela's doctoral thesis.[2] We had seen prickly pear in the vicinity and on a later visit asked speculatively about it. As responses proved to be rich, we returned on a few occasions.

One of our most intriguing interviews was with Fezeka Thelma Mpendukana (b. 1944), wife of the former headman of Kamastone.[3] The settlement around this former Methodist mission station, established in 1835, still retains some of its identity. The old stone church has been refurbished and the homes nearby are traditionally built bungalows with stoeps (verandahs). Some have unusual stone cattle kraals. Many of the older families had quitrent tenure. Mpendukana reminisced about her teenage years in the 1950s. She lived then, before marriage, in a nearby village where prickly pear was planted on many of the homestead sites: 'those who started without it, would transplant it from the veld'.

While our interviews in Fort Beaufort focused on the risky activity of brewing, Mpendukana's memory of prickly pear was very different. Her mother did not brew because they were a respectable Christian family. She associated prickly pear with African church circles and agricultural associations. Self-help and self-organisation through *Zenzele* (do it yourself) were a central feature of the Methodist womens' groups. 'A number of older women', she recalled, 'who were experienced in food production and processing, as well as cooking, would run workshops and imparted knowledge and experience to the younger ones'.[4] In the 1950s:

> Hewu women were part of the *Zenzele* Cooperatives. Women were trained in church circles and ... agricultural societies in social and household skills and particularly they used *itolofiya* and other summer fruits such as peaches (*iipesika*) and figs (*amafiya*) to process a number of products such as jam (*inyhobanyhoba*) .... My mother taught me how to cook prickly pear fruit with a little water then filter away the stones, add a bit of syrup to the cooked, thick liquid and then boil slowly again. When simmering, a bit of gelatine would be added to the mixture and it would be left for a day to cool down. When cool it attained a soft, thickish consistency.

The jam stored for several months. In both Hewu and Middledrift it was used with homemade, baked bread (*umbhako*) 'which tasted very good with prickly pear jam'.[5]

In this chapter we focus on changing prickly pear incidence and use since the 1950s. We explore whether plants were still accessible, whether they were still valuable and for whom.[6] Our findings confirm that people found an extraordinary range of uses for prickly pear, but that processing and detailed local knowledge has dwindled in recent years.

PERCEPTIONS OF THE INCIDENCE OF OPUNTIA

By the 1950s, a couple of decades after the start of the biological eradication campaign, perhaps three-quarters of the wild prickly pear in South Africa had been destroyed.[7] The campaigns in South Africa proved more difficult than in Australia and there was no similar sudden collapse of opuntia as experienced in Madagascar. But by the 1980s, a combination of the remaining insects, together with chemical poisoning, reduced the incidence of dense growth to an estimated ten per cent of its 1930s climax. By this time, Helmuth Zimmermann, a leading scientist working on eradication, estimated that 900,000 hectares of dense stands had been reduced to about 100,000 hectares – although scattered prickly pear remained over a far larger area.[8]

Wild prickly pear was one of the nine species named as an invader plant under the Conservation of Agricultural Resources Act of 1983.[9] Ten opuntia species were listed in the condensed official *Declared Weeds* publication of 1987.[10] Jointed cactus was still spreading and by 1982 affected over 800,000 hectares – though little of this was densely overgrown.[11] In sum, most opuntia species were greatly reduced in range but it was possible for them to coexist with the introduced insects.

Given the scale of the biological eradication campaign, as well as felling and poisoning, it is interesting how much prickly pear survived. Most of Graaff-Reinet, Aberdeen, Jansenville, Cradock and Bedford districts, and the eastern Karoo more generally, which had some of the heaviest stands of opuntia, was cleared. But eradication was less successful in the coastal districts, especially parts of Hankey, Uitenhage and Albany, as well as in Peddie, part of the former Ciskei. These areas had higher rainfall and it was more difficult to clear prickly pear among the denser vegetation.[12] As Pettey noted, predatory mammals, ladybirds, beetles and ants attacked the cactus-feeding insects and reduced their effectiveness. Cochineal was less prolific in the damper coastal districts which have cooler summers. Heavy downpours also hampered its work. The eradication campaign was resisted in a few places.[13]

Between 2001 and 2006 we interviewed about the historical incidence and use of prickly pear in four areas of the Eastern Cape: Hewu, Fort Beaufort, Middledrift and the Gamtoos Valley around Hankey and Patensie. Somewhat surprisingly, given the timing of the eradication campaign, people remembered that prickly pear was quite widespread at least up to the 1960s. Some did note that they had heard of even denser coverage before this in their parents' time but most agreed that a significant decline in the incidence had occurred in recent decades, since about the 1970s, and – as will be illustrated – they sometimes cited reasons other than the biological campaign.

Five types of opuntia were mentioned in the interviews. We should sound a warning about identifications because we are inexperienced in this field and informants used local or colloquial names in three languages. Opuntia species hybridise and vary in their shape and colour. Sometimes they may also be confused with other introduced cactus, such as cereus species, borzi cactus or with indigenous plants such as noors, a type of euphorbia. For example, we found that the word *isihlehle*, which originally

137

referred to a small type of indigenous euphorbia may also be applied to some kinds of exotic cactus, but usage is unclear. Kropf translates *isihlehle* as noorsdoorn, the various species of euphorbia found especially around Jansenville that provided valuable fodder for small stock.

We should also note that while some informants knew that prickly pear was an introduced plant, some believed it to be indigenous. This view was echoed in a recent survey in Mpofu (formerly Stockenstrom): 'participants revealed that they were unaware that prickly pear was an alien species; so much so that one woman insisted that it was "the plant of my ancestors"'.[14] She was not, of course, entirely incorrect in that her forebears in the area may have lived with prickly pear for over 150 years.

White farmers in the early twentieth century identified prickly pear varieties largely by their cladodes – notably the doornblad, kaalblad and rondeblaar – because fodder was of particular importance to them. African people in the Eastern Cape tend to focus on the fruit. The most widespread, and the most important, is called *itolofiya yasendle emhlope* – wild, white prickly pear of the veld – or just *itolofiya yasendle*. This is *O. ficus-indica*, called doornblad in the early twentieth century and still referred to in Afrikaans as *doringblad*. The cladodes are longer and narrower than other wild types with many white thorns. Although the fruit is generally called white in Xhosa, it is usually light green when unripe and in Middledrift people specifically used the term that means light green. There is some variation in colour and the fruit acquires an orange tinge when very ripe. The pulp is also greenish-white. It ripens in summer from late December to March, depending on the district.

The oldest people that we interviewed recalled this variety as most common. R. Sokhaba (b. 1908), remembered 'the wild prickly pear with long leaves and long

---

XHOSA WORDS FOR DIFFERENT TYPES OF CACTUS

1. *itolofiya yasendle emhlope* or *itolofiya yasendle:* wild, white prickly pear of the veld. *O. ficus-indica*.
2. *ebomvu* or *isiqhamo esibomvu* or *ugazini:* red fruited prickly pear, called suurtjies. *Opuntia stricta* and/or *Opuntia lindheimeri*.
3. *itolofiya emthubi:* yellow-fruited prickly pear, probably descended from gymnocarpa or other spineless cactus and partly reverted to thorniness.
4. *itolofiya engenameva:* spineless cactus with different types of fruit (cultivated *O. ficus-indica*, occasionally called *itolofiya yabelungu*).
5. *ukatyi:* jointed cactus, *Opuntia aurantiaca*.
   There are no doubt other local names.

white thorns' and a 'white fruit (*isiqhamo esimhlophe*) that tastes very well indeed' from his childhood in Kamastone.[15] A.D. Sishuba (b. 1929) said that his grandfather spoke of it on African settlements and white farms south of Queenstown in the nineteenth century.[16] In Hewu, *itolofiya yasendle* thrived on slopes and rocky land. In Hankey, in the southern Cape, informants suggested that this plant did best in lowlands and river valleys. As we have noted, there were different patterns of dispersal, sometimes by flooding down rivers and sometimes by livestock, birds or wild animals.[17] Hankey, in the Gamtoos River Valley, was considered one of the worst infested areas in the first half of the twentieth century and one of the most difficult for biological control.

A second species of wild prickly pear had rounder leaves and was called *ebomvu* or *isiqhamo esibomvu* (red fruit) in Hewu. The spines are browner and shorter, and the reddish fruit, that ripens in autumn from March to May, is sour. Those that we interviewed in Hankey called this type *suurtjie* in Afrikaans and it is almost certainly the kind called rondeblaar in earlier decades. In the Amatola basin of Middledrift this, or a similar variety, is called *isidwedwe* or *ugazini* – red as blood.[18] These

Prickly pear in the veld in Hewu, 2008

plants are almost certainly derived either from the species *Opuntia stricta* or *Opuntia lindheimeri*, or both. The former, which was the main invader species in Australia, tends to have longer spines than those commonly described for the *ebomvu*; the latter was certainly recorded in the Eastern Cape and it can be variable in its shape and growth.[19] The fruits are not generally eaten but the central part of the pulp is sweeter and can be used. Informants in Fort Beaufort

Livestock grazing on an old prickly pear hedge in Hewu, 2010

called one variety with a reddish fruit *itolofiya yabelungu*, because they thought it was planted by whites more recently. This is very likely to be a variety of spineless cactus some of which, such as the tasty Algerian variety, have red fruits.

A third type, *emthubi* (yellow), also has long cladodes but a large, yellowish fruit with fewer thorns and fewer glochids on the fruit. The spines are short and brownish. It is also favoured for eating and, according to some informants, the fruit tastes even better than the wild, white prickly pear. Those interviewed in the northern part of Hewu around Kamastone and Bulhoek mentioned it as prevalent. While some thought that it had been present for a very long time, Sokhaba, the oldest informant in Kamastone, recalled that it had been brought from neighbouring white-owned farms in the 1920s and 1930s.[20] Former headman Matshoba mentioned that it was planted in his area around Bulhoek as well as on the neighbouring and formerly white-owned farms of Hayden Park, Tigerklip, Loudon and Thornhill. African landholders placed it along the borders of arable lands, but by the 1940s it spread along streams and valley bottoms on the Kamastone commonage.[21]

This was probably the Gymnocarpa variety of spineless cactus, which had partially reverted to the spiny form by reproduction from seed.[22] Some Burbank spineless cactus introduced into Australia in the early twentieth century did produce viable seed and some of the resulting plants became spiny invaders.[23] This appears to have been uncommon amongst the most widespread Burbank varieties in South Africa, although exceptions have been noted.[24] African informants thought that the *emthubi* was a hybrid of kinds. In Middledrift, they thought that similar plants, growing close together, could produce both yellowish and light-green fruits.

Emthubi was distinguished from, fourthly, spineless cactus (*itolofiya engenameva* – without thorns) of which a few types were mentioned. Interviewees associated this particularly with white-owned farms, including some that had been taken over in the territorial consolidation of the former Ciskei. Fifth, many could identify the jointed cactus (*ukatyi*), which became a major menace by the inter-war years and is still widespread. Lastly, some homestead owners in Hewu planted a cylindrical cactus along their residential boundaries, a species of cereus.

Most informants perceived wild prickly pear (*itolofiya yasendle*) to be declining. In former Ciskeian districts, this is sometimes attributed to changes in settlement patterns rather than the biological campaign. Before betterment (*phambi kwe Trusti*), people would transplant wild prickly pear to fence residential plots, gardens or even the boundaries of arable lands alongside their homesteads.[25] The hedges helped to keep out livestock as well as secure their crops against theft and wild animals. It was not always planted in sufficient density to form a secure fence. Spiny prickly pear could be grazed as it stood, especially by goats and cattle, and this also led to uneven growth. It did not always knit together at ground level, but even so prickly pear was useful to homestead heads to 'delineate their boundaries (*bazobe imida yabo*)' and also to 'control their space (*balawule indawo yabo*)'. There was the additional benefit of fruit and fodder close at hand.

Agave americana (*garingboom*), with its long, spiky leaves, was a better guarantee against damage to crops and vegetables by animals, although it could also grow unevenly unless carefully maintained. Occasionally both were planted together in hedges, especially around kraals, and this provided an additional fodder source. Indigenous aloe (*ikhala*) was also planted on boundaries for hedging, a practice reported from the early nineteenth century. It too was sometimes mixed with other plants.

The use of prickly pear in this way could be construed as what later became called agro-forestry, into which a great deal of development funding has poured over the last few decades.[26] Prickly pear is not usually mentioned in this context, although it is widespread as a multi-purpose plant, especially in north and north-east Africa. The major species advocated recently for agro-forestry in Africa have tended to be for fuelwood as much as fodder and some favoured acacia species do provide both.[27] In South Africa, African smallholders in the wet, east coast districts have grown black wattle on their plots for building, fencing materials and firewood. Prickly pear cladodes were dried for fuel in some South African districts, in much the same way as dung, but they are not ideal as they take too long to dry and they burn too quickly.

After homesteads were moved during betterment or the imposition of 'Trust' settlements, the hedges of prickly pear and other species were left on what became grazing commonage. We should explain briefly the term 'betterment'. From 1939, and especially between the 1950s and 1970s, many rural African communities on reserved land in South Africa were moved from their traditional, more scattered settlement patterns – where homesteads and their gardens were dispersed in the communal pasturages – into villages. The justification for this intervention, which triggered resistance in many districts, was multi-facetted. Officials believed that in the longer term, modernisation, services and facilities such as schools, electricity and water could be more effectively provided to villages. Perhaps the major argument for resettlement was to conserve the pasturages by developing fenced, rotatable camps in the African reserves. To this end, the settlements had to be separated from the pastures. Hundreds of thousands of African homesteads were moved. The scheme was later called rehabilitation and is widely known in Xhosa as the 'Trust' because this concentrated pattern of settlement was used on land acquired by the South African Native Trust after the 1936 Native Land and Trust Act to consolidate African reserves.

In the districts of the former Ciskei, then, the prickly pear that used to form part of hedges could no longer be protected and some of the plants around the old homesteads were destroyed by animals. In Middledrift, the Ciskeian government ordered the uprooting of prickly pear on old sites during betterment. Planners also instructed people to chop down and uproot opuntia and thorn bushes on the land being prepared for the new village sites.[28] After betterment 'it became fashionable to use wire (*ucingo*) as fencing'.[29] Households had to compete for the remaining prickly pear on the veld, which resulted in both a reduction of availability and of usage.[30] Resistance to the eradication campaign persisted in Middledrift in the 1940s and 1950s.[31] Agricultural officers organising eradication were denied entry to settlements and some of the plants around homesteads remained intact at that time, but most of these succumbed to insects or were destroyed during the imposition of betterment in the 1960s. There is an interesting parallel here in Israel. Prickly pear was used as hedging by Palestinian farmers, and when their villages were destroyed by Israeli forces, clumps of prickly pear were sometimes left. It became a symbol for the site of old settlements. (Both Israelis and Palestinians, like whites and blacks in South Africa, have at times shared an interest in the fruit.)

Widespread malnutrition was reported from the Ciskeian districts in the 1960s and 1970s.[32] There were clearly many factors at work, including the migrant labour system, disintegration of families, general rural poverty and the impact of forced removals from farms. Relatively few Ciskeian families were able to meet their subsistence needs from smallholder farming at this time; the betterment removals generally made it more difficult to farm. Also, we do not really know whether malnutrition increased at this time or whether it was just better reported. It is possible, however, that malnutrition was in some small part related to the reduction of prickly pear supplies. There is a coincidence in timing. Prickly pear provided a hidden resource to the rural poor, one that they had used for many decades, and which in some areas diminished quite suddenly. The fruit had long been particularly important in the season of dearth before the harvest in April to June. It is true that infants were most seriously affected, and the fruit was not of much significance for their nutrition. Nor did it have significant protein content. But for children as well as adults, and especially women, the fruit was a valuable source of vitamins, minerals and moisture.

Eradication did not preclude regrowth or replanting. The anthropologist Robin

Palmer heard that in Gwabeni village in Peddie during the 1960s, prickly pear was destroyed by 'an orange powder' sprayed over the area from an aeroplane.[33] The Tribal Authority ordered that one man from each household should participate in destruction. For a time this important resource was destroyed. Since then it has grown back, but insects control the plant at low densities. Prickly pear was still used by 43 per cent of households in this village when Palmer researched there in the 1990s. Poor, female-headed households were most dependent on it – for some it was the sole source of fruit. One of his informants mentioned 'of all the wild food resources in the environs of Gwabeni, the most desirable is probably the prickly pear.'

During the 1970s and 1980s, the Cape provincial Department of Nature Conservation bought a number of farms neighbouring Peddie to expand the Double Drift reserve, later called the Great Fish River Conservation Area. With additional donations of land, it reached 22,000 hectares by 1987.[34] One of the priorities in this new reserve was to eradicate alien species, particularly opuntia of all kinds. In 1978 alone, over 38,340 man hours (about 70 people working full time for a year) were expended on this task, plus large amounts of herbicide. Despite these attempts, villagers in Gwabeni thought that prickly pear was denser in the reserve than on their land. But Nature Conservation restricted access. As one informant commented to Palmer in disgust '[we] can't even get [that] prickly pear, they say it is for their baboons'.[35]

In 1995 Bantu Holomisa, Deputy Environmental Affairs Minister in Mandela's new government, spoke at the launch of the Inxuba Conservation and Economic Forum which was designed to incorporate local communities and other stakeholders into planning and development around this conservation area. By then the area had doubled in size again. Over a lunch of roast warthog, he was assailed with questions about the loss of grazing to the community. Nowait Ketya of Ngqaka village complained about the fencing of the reserve without consultation, 'resulting in deep resentment in the community'.[36] A journalist reported:

'The worst part of it was that we could not go in to retrieve our livestock, get water or pick up firewood – nature conservation officers patrolled both inside and outside the reserve, shooting dead our dogs,' she said.

'She said that the age-old practice of picking wild prickly pears as a source of food had also been regulated by a permit system imposed by reserve officials. Another representative added: "We had to walk 10 km to get to the officials for the permit, and another 10 km back and then go into the veld to pick the prickly pears.'

People surveyed in 2005 at Tidbury village in the Kat River Valley, immediately to the north of Fort Beaufort, also perceived that the density of prickly pear had declined and felt it was too low.[37] This area around Seymour, formerly Mpofu district, now in Nkonkobe, was once solidly covered with a variety of opuntia species. Most informants agreed that prickly pear provided an important resource and should be protected for people in the Kat River Valley. Some argued for higher densities to support poorer people. A number of informants said they were reluctant to allow prickly pear, and especially jointed cactus near their homes, because it was dangerous for livestock and even for barefoot children who tramped on fallen spines. But they would have liked more thickets of fruiting prickly pear on the mountain slopes for picking. While fruit was not sufficient for commercial use in the village where only four people sold in 2005, it remained valuable for subsistence, was widely bartered and helped to cement reciprocal social relations. Those surveyed collected fruit three to four times a month on average in the season. Villagers here also preferred prickly pear to other wild fruits as it was sweeter and 'gives us more energy'.[38] One man who planted it in his garden commented on its beauty.

Around the village of Machibini, south of the main road between Middledrift and Alice, a woman remembered that prickly pear had been so thick in her youth that they called it *ezitolofiyeni* (the place of prickly pear).[39] Now she had to pick fruit across the Tyume River, in Victoria East, on former white farms which were not so densely settled, and which had the remnants of spineless cactus planted before they were incorporated into the Ciskei.[40] As we mentioned in Chapter 1, the prickly pear at Apiesdraai (Drayini) location in Fort Beaufort was cleared after the settlement was forcibly removed under the Group Areas Act in the 1960s. Prickly pear was less suitable in the cramped conditions of the new township and was not encouraged. Occasional plants can be seen in Fort Beaufort, such as that in Nowinile's front yard, but they are not common.

By contrast, a greater proportion of people in Hewu, at least those who lived in a more rural context, replanted prickly pear or spineless cactus after they moved. They tended to have a few plants in gardens next to their homesteads along with other fruit trees such as figs, peaches and pears. Communities in this area had clearly been planting spineless cactus for decades. Sishuba remembered that his uncle obtained cladodes from a farmer and planted them at Upper Hukuwa in Hewu in the 1940s.[41]

This plot became a source for others. In the 1960s headman Matshoba at Bulhoek also planted spineless cactus in his garden after he had been required to move.

A former Ciskeian extension officer, Welsh Mxiki, recalled the drought of the mid-1960s when a number of households lost livestock: 'the winter months were so dry that there was hardly a blade of grass.'[42] They used wild prickly pear for fodder but this was:

> always a painstaking process. First one had to endure pruning thorny leaves from the trees and carrying them from the veld to home. Once picked and collected these leaves were brazed (*rhawula*) with fire in order to burn thorns. People were quite apprehensive about thorns spiking livestock on their mouths.

So people purchased cladodes of spineless cactus at about R2 per wagon from neighbouring white farmers.

> Mind you those days that was not regarded as cheap, and, in fact a number of villagers used to make a collective contribution. One would provide draught oxen, one would provide the wagon and maybe two households would provide the R2 for the load and once it was fetched it would be split up. We were so amazed with the density of spineless cactus and organisation of plantations on white-owned farms. The trees were fenced, arranged in linear rows and the pruning was well regulated.[43]

By the late 1960s it became fashionable to grow spineless cactus in this Hewu area of the northern Ciskei. In 2008 we returned briefly to Hewu and neighbouring parts of the former northern Ciskei. Along the road from Bulhoek to Thornhill, we saw prickly pear and spineless cactus in about one fifth of the gardens. Some of the plants were well-established and gave substantial quantities of fruit. There was far less prickly pear in Thornhill, the old dumping ground for people from Herschel, itself.

Nofezile Gcweka, who lived in Haytor (Sibonile), Zweledinga, told us that she had planted prickly pear in her garden in 1989, both round and long cladodes, which she got from a former white-owned farm which had been incorporated into the northern Ciskei.[44] Her neighbour had done the same. A rough count of households in Haytor in 2001 indicated that about one-third had prickly pear plants on new sites. In one interview, it transpired that young herders had planted *itolofiya yasendle*

145

from the veld onto a roadside homestead site. They did so for easier access to the fruit, but the plants grew very slowly because they were eaten by livestock.

Spineless cactus in gardens, on the Bulhoek-Thornhill road in 2008 showing different varieties of opuntia

In the Gamtoos Valley, around Hankey and Patensie, a different set of processes shaped the reduction of prickly pear. We met Christine Malan, who worked for some years as a librarian in Uitenhage, at the town's prickly pear festival (Chapter 8).[45] Her deceased father, George Malan, was a National Party MP who farmed in Patensie and wrote a book called *Die Brullende Leeu Getem* (*The Roaring Lion Tamed*, 1970; Gamtoos is a Khoikhoi word with this meaning). This tells the history of dams and irrigation in the valley. George Malan recalled playing hide and seek in the prickly pear as a child.

> *Daardie dae was die landerye nog nie so aanmekaar soos vandag nie – dit was sulke lappe tussen die doringbome en turksvye.* (In those days fields were not yet so contiguous as today – it was just strips in between the thorn bushes and prickly pear.) *Mens kan jou vandag amper nie voorstel hoeveel turksvy daar in ons vallei was nie . . . Feitlik deur 'n tonnel van turksvye en doringbome ry.* (Today people cannot comprehend how much prickly pear there was in our valley ... you literally went through a tunnel of prickly pear and thorn trees.)[46]

The family has an evocative photograph of a pyre of dried prickly pear cladodes being set on fire in 1952. The occasion was a memorial service for Tjaart van der Walt, a local Afrikaner hero from the early nineteenth century said to have met his death in the 1802 Khoikhoi rebellion.

When Christine Malan was a child in the 1950s and 1960s, farmers could still only use some low-lying lands, and much of the rest was covered with prickly pear. There, and in Hankey, prickly pear was cleared with heavy machinery

Dried prickly pear stems used for a fire beacon, Patensie, 1952

to open rich alluvial land in the valley bottoms for cultivation. The Paul Sauer or Kouga Dam, completed in the 1960s, not least through campaigning by George Malan, facilitated large-scale irrigation in the Gamtoos Valley for citrus, tobacco and vegetables.[47] Pumping technology enabled farmers to expand citrus plantations up the valley sides, and this provided a further incentive to clear opuntia.

In this area, prickly pear was seen as a host for false codling moth and fruit fly, which provided another incentive for eradication near the citrus plantations.[48] Not everyone took this view in earlier years. We did hear of cases of complementary use. Cladodes were dug into the soil around orange tree roots as fertilizer. In the Transvaal, some citrus farmers actually planted prickly pear which they believed would attract orange scale away from their trees. In Uitenhage in the 1930s, farmers thought that the overspill of ladybirds feasting on cochineal might help to control scale in their orchards.

Nadia Ferreira confirmed this narrative of clearance in the Gamtoos area. Born in 1929, she came to Hankey in 1952. Her husband worked on a farm in the Kleinrivier area near the town for over 50 years.[49] In 2002 they were living in Phillipsville, a coloured area in old Hankey. Kleinrivier was heavily infested with prickly pear when she arrived there. The thickets harboured wildlife. People 'hunted wild animals such as bushpigs, warthogs and baboons that enjoyed prickly pear fruit'; some people would live off the land, hunting and picking during the summer months. Many picked to sell, brew and produce syrup.

When she arrived in 1952, parts of Kleinrivier Valley were already planted with naartjies. Irrigation was supplied by water furrows. However, most of the uplands were still covered by prickly pear. After the Kouga Dam was completed in the late 1960s, sprinkler irrigation systems were installed and naartjies expanded onto the uplands. Kleinfontein was not totally cleared of prickly pear which survived on rocky slopes. People continued to pick 'as they used to do in the olden days'. But in the valley and nearer town, most of the plants had gone. Ferreira reminisced: 'even though we still crave the prickly pear fruit … areas which I used to walk to for picking the fruit here in Phillipsville, are now either part of the municipal park or are rugby and soccer fields … We are buying what we used to obtain freely.' The commonage at Hankey still has dense prickly pear, as does the Soetkloof pass to the south-west, but most plants around town succumbed to the expansion of townships (Centerton and Weston). She did acknowledge that tastes were changing and some preferred cheap citrus.

On Middledrift commonage, prickly pear was also perceived to have declined recently because of expanding house-building and the prison garden. However, two smallholders in the nearby Amathole basin were unsure of whether it was an overall retreat because of the complex ecological dynamics that they thought affected the incidence of prickly pear locally.[50] Prickly pear grew best amongst dense vegetation, especially around 'mimosa' (*umga* or *Acacia karoo*), possibly because livestock could not get at it when young. On the one hand, they suggested that it did not always out-compete indigenous species, and that it had been submerged in places by acacia and indigenous aloe (*ikhala*). On the other hand, people chopping acacia for firewood or aloes for medicine, 'often free the space for prickly pear to expand'. Firewood and fruit collectors often broke off cladodes which then took root.

The overall picture is clearly uneven, and different factors – biological agents, land clearance for agriculture, urban development and changing settlement patterns – all seem to have contributed to the decline of the wild prickly pear. In the largely white-owned farming districts of the eastern Karoo, the biological campaigns were particularly successful. It is possible that the subsequent re-growth of prickly pear has been inhibited not only by insects but by increased grass cover – a result of declining levels of livestock and better management. The inverse process of denudation was a factor in the spread of prickly pear in the early twentieth century.[51] In some of the post-betterment African villages, prickly pear and spineless cactus have been replanted, but they are not as widespread as they were before. On privately owned land in river valleys, prickly pear has largely been swept aside by intensive agriculture. Managers of conservation areas which have expanded significantly in the Eastern Cape have also tried to clear land of alien and invasive species. As we will explain (Chapter 9), this applies to private as well as public conservation areas. The perception that prickly pear incidence has declined over the last few decades is almost certainly correct.

CHANGING USAGE

As we have noted, a great variety of uses were evolved for prickly pear and spineless cactus by both whites and blacks. Many of these are reported from Mexico and the Mediterranean.[52] While some of this knowledge may have come with early imports of the plant to South Africa, or through international networks of information, some has certainly been locally developed. Prickly pear has grown in the midland and eastern Cape for over 200 years. Rural communities have clearly been highly adaptable in incorporating it into their lives and developing a local knowledge around the plant. It is worth emphasising that local knowledge is not restricted to indigenous plant species – most of the crops and food plants grown in the Eastern Cape have been introduced. Dold and Cocks have researched the medical as well as culinary uses found for many exotics.[53] Informants whom we interviewed did not generally distinguish between indigenous and exotic plants, nor did they see opuntia as an invader. There is a constant process of innovation around plant uses, and older practices are also sometimes discarded. We cannot provide a chronology for the origins of various usages as many were well-established by the time our informants were children. However, we can give some sense of the declining interest in the plant.

Many uses involved time-consuming preparation. Prickly pear was an ideal plant resource in communities where households manufactured their own products and where there was sufficient labour time for processing. Plant use is subject both to changing tastes and the availability of household labour.

We have described recent sales of fruit in Fort Beaufort (Chapter 1). This remains the most valuable contribution of prickly pear for African people. Wild prickly pear has a long season and it is free. Its disadvantage is that pickers have to be careful not only of the spiny cladodes but of the glochids. Mrs Ngundle in Hewu remembered:

> as young girls, we ate a lot of prickly pear on the move. Picking up fruit required good skill especially for the thorny, white, wild prickly pear. We used objects such as sticks to unhook or detach the fruit from its leaf. The difficult part was picking up the thorny fruit from the ground into a container. One has to cushion your hands with either a cloth or a plastic bag. It is trickier when one has to eat the fruit on the spot. Before [de]skinning or peeling off the cover, the fruit needs to be rubbed very hard on the grassy surface so that spikes are crushed. But even so in the process of dissecting the cover one expects to be needled .... A number of parents used to discourage children from eating the fruit on the move ... because they tended to finish skinning off the cover with their teeth and mouth .... In these circumstances they tended to be hurt.[54]

One man recalled that as youths they tried not to pick when it was windy as the glochids blew into their eyes. Clearance teams in the 1940s had enormous difficulties with glochids in the skin and eyes of workers. This was one reason why Italian prisoners of war, who were initially used for this purpose, went on strike.

Prickly pear fruit are part of childhood memories and associated with a certain freedom and adventure. This included contacts across racial boundaries that became more difficult in adulthood. Daphne le Roux, a white woman and graduate of Rhodes, recalled 'a number of occasions [when] we used to walk some distance with coloured children on our farm just to pick prickly pear and we used to be stung on our hands and our mouths because we ate the fruit as we moved along'.[55] Children would be prepared to walk long distances to get their favoured fruit. Mrs Ngundle recalled:

> Most of my friends including myself preferred the yellowish fruit even though it was a bit scarce and difficult to access from Mceula's veld. But we were always keen to move and gather wood from other areas around Kamastone where we knew we would get the yellow prickly pear. Most times this involved longer trips; fortunately we always had white prickly pear to fall back on.[56]

Kids enjoyed picking off the cochineal, covered by its dense white web, and pinching it, so that the reddish liquid was released.

The Malan family in Patensie picked prickly pear fruit with a long, bamboo reed, split at one end, and the fork separated by a stick or mealie cob.[57] The edges were then smoothed so that it did not damage the fruit or cut its skin. They fitted the stick around the fruit, twisted it off and then wiped it with leaves. They did not need to touch the fruit until it was free of glochids. Alta Malan recalled that her mother used a metal *hoepel* (hoop), though picking large quantities was still '*helse werk*'. African communities used various wire contraptions, called *amagwegwe*, to reach the higher fruits. Prickly pear fruit brought home in any quantity was soaked in water so that glochids detached themselves. The skin could then be wiped and peeled. Fridges enabled larger quantities of fruit to be stored and white consumers especially preferred prickly pear cold.

Many people that we spoke to mentioned that overconsumption of fruit produced constipation. Children were told not to eat too many '*as jy gaan vas sit*' (stick fast or *qhina* in Xhosa).[58] Constipation has been attributed to the high tannin content of the fruit and in more serious cases, to obstruction from the seeds.[59] Ferguson Miles thought that baboons did not suffer from the same complaint: 'they are skilled about how to pick and eat the fruit. For instance, they eat the fruit with the sub-cutaneous white flesh between the outer cover and the actual pulp to prevent constipation'.[60] Informants told us they were less likely to suffer from constipation if prickly pear was consumed with other food that contained roughage. A doctor who worked in

TURKSVYSTROOP, A SOUTH AFRICAN SYRUP

Syrup was apparently unique to South Africa, or at least it was not made in the same way in Mexico, home of the prickly pear. On the farms it was one of the most common products, widely made up to the 1950s.[61] Families from Hankey and Patensie would move for a month up the Koega Valley, into the Baviaanskloof, and camp around their ox-wagons, picking prickly pear and making syrup and soap.[62]

Five litres of fruit would produce about 750 ml of syrup. The fruit had to be peeled and boiled until it dissolved into a thickish, soup-like liquid. Fruit pips were then removed, honey and brown sugar could be added, and the mixture re-boiled for another hour, by which time it turned dark brown. It was then poured into containers and sealed. Christine Malan remembered that her mother's syrup was like honey.[63] Syrup was an Afrikaner delicacy used on a daily basis. Where insufficient was made at home it was bought from specialist producers who included black women. Children buttered their bread on one side, and then turned it over for the syrup. If syrup was poured on the butter, it would spill all over the plate, but if they turned it over the syrup would sink into the bread.

Keiskammahoek in the 1960s recalled frequent cases of constipation presented to her. The easiest method of dealing quickly with this problem involved the unpleasant task of spooning out the blockage. The Settlers Hospital in Grahamstown used to keep a large supply of laxative medicines on standby during prickly pear season to deal with the schoolchildren who over-consumed.

Prickly pear is still widely eaten by African people 'on the move', such as 'hunters (*abazingeli*), herders (*abelusi*) and firewood collectors'. Former Bulhoek headman Matshoba recalled that people from his area who were hunting and collecting prickly pear trespassed on neighbouring white-owned farms: 'like wildlife people who poached fruits such as prickly pear caused devastation and sometimes dragged leaves for long distances'.[64] Simon Kata, from Lower Shiloh, Hewu, and a member of the local farmers association was unusually hostile to prickly pear for this reason.

> I wish it could be uprooted. Our fence on that perimeter boundary has gone since prickly pear harvesters as well as hunters, who hunt wild animals such as baboons and bushpigs (*ingulube*), do not have respect for fences. You often see and hear hunters from either Sada or Langedraai with a pack of dogs proclaiming that they would be

hunting on the prickly pear hills (*ezintabeni zetolofiya*). It seems that prickly pear has made it convenient for them, as these wild animals tend to live around it. Unfortunately areas where there is still dense growth of prickly pear have also become graveyards for our livestock. If the livestock are not targeted by hunters themselves, they often become prey to renegade hunting dogs.[65]

Both the white, yellow and red wild fruits, and some spineless varieties, were suitable for making jams, syrups and preserves. Turksvystroop was taken up for commercial production on a farm near Hofmeyr in the 1990s.[66] They used the fruit from a plantation of spineless cactus established initially for drought fodder. During season, harvesters collected about a ton of fruit per day, which was dropped into boiling water to help remove the outer skin in the same way as a tomato.

Some African women made syrup but most preferred jam. Fezeka Mpendukana, who recalled her mother's jam manufacture near Kamastone so vividly, gave it up herself after betterment.

> When we moved into *etrustini* (betterment villages), a large amount of arable land on which the household prickly pear fruit grew was abandoned. Some trees that were around the new homestead grids were uprooted in the course of the realignment and the extension of the new residential areas.[67]

At her home in Kamastone now they had only a couple of plants. In earlier decades, jam was not only used in the household but sold at school concerts, as well as sports and church functions despite the perennial problem of finding sufficient glass containers. Afrikaner women in Patensie also sold syrup and jam at church bazaars.[68] Quince and prickly pear were used together in preserve making; their tastes and textures complemented each other. This

Prickly pear, Mpendukana's plot, Kamastone, 2008

was also done in Chile. In Hankey, prickly pear fruit was combined with blackberry, raspberry and peaches for a mixed fruit jam. More generally, Mpendukana explained: 'at that time prickly pear was part of people's lives because they lived around and used it. People rarely visited shops during those days; we would probably go to Queenstown once in two months.' Easier availability of transport, cash incomes, manufactured jams and canned fruit all contributed to the decline of homemade prickly pear jam.

In addition to brewing, prickly pear fruit was made into a non-alcoholic drink. Preparation time also militated against the survival of this beverage. Most people abandoned it for fizzy, bottled products or fruit squash such as 'Oros and Coco-pine from the shops' – to which, of course, they had only to add cold water.[69] One woman interviewed used the red-fruited variety like beetroot in a salad adding sugar, pepper, vinegar and salt. Because of the dressing, it tasted like beetroot salad, which was popular amongst middle-class African people.[70] Farm workers in the Karoo pickled the young cladodes and immature fruits; this was also a common recipe for Afrikaners.[71] In the African areas, young cladodes do not seem to have been eaten except in times of extreme need.[72]

Prickly pear plants are no longer used much for barriers and fencing. Other species of cactus including declared weeds, are, however, evident in former Ciskeian districts because they are not grazed like spineless cactus and prickly pear, and not poached and cut like wire fencing. We saw a cylindrical cactus, possibly *Cereus peruvianus* or 'Queen of the Night', grown as a barrier plant and an ornamental on account of its attractive white flower.[73] One informant at Kamastone noted that even former Ciskeian headmen, of whom he was one, were using this plant as fencing, though they knew it was illegal.[74] (The plant can also be seen on white-owned farms and in Karoo villages such as New Bethesda.) In addition to its other advantages, this 'knits from a very low height and does prevent passage.'[75] There is little enforcement of noxious

Cactus as fence, 2008

weeds legislation. Australian saltbush and indigenous spekboom are also found as hedging in and around the former Ciskei. We saw saltbush hedges in various places such as the old township at Adelaide.

Prickly pear leaves are still occasionally picked and brazed for fodder (Chapter 4). Goats, especially, eat wild prickly pear, nibbling away around the thorns.[76] This is one reason why the remnant plants around old homesteads in the former Ciskei have gone and goat numbers have probably increased in these districts during recent decades. One informant mentioned that most people do not bother to impart the skills of preparing the cladodes for fodder and the young people do not really want to learn. The barriers to transmitting local knowledge between generations came up in a few interviews.

The anthropologist Monica Hunter (Wilson), who was amongst the first to research on farms in the area around Fort Beaufort, found cladodes used as roofing in Adelaide district in the 1930s: 'huts in the prickly pear area show an interesting adaptation to environment, prickly pear "leaves" being used in place of grass for thatch'.[77] They were sewn together 'a la Xhosa'.[78] We have not seen or heard of such constructions in recent years.

As noted, cladodes were also important for soap manufacture, and here the wild, spiny *itolofiya yasendle* was preferred. Spineless cactus leaves were thought to be less effective because they did not carry the same type or strength of fluids. Cladodes were used for soap by both Afrikaners and Africans up to the 1960s. Sometimes the outer layer and spines of the cladodes were stripped off so that the inner softer tissue was laid bare before being mixed with fat (*amafuta*).[79]

Fezeka Mpendukana recalled how her mother boiled large quantities of fresh green cladodes (*amagqabi aluhlaza*) with animal fat in cast iron pots. 'When boiling, soda was added to the mixture [which was] allowed to simmer gently and then cooled down.' After a few days 'a hard crust will develop and that was cut with a sharp knife and each piece was used as a bar soap. My mother produced a lot of bar soap, used it at home and even sold it to other households'.[80] She remembered another cleaning product from opuntia.

> After I got married in the 1960s it became almost fashionable that wood-stoves were used in a number of households that were headed by either teachers, or by policemen or even migrant workers. These stoves led to the advent of shiny steel pots and kettles that were more difficult to clean. Some of the Zenzele women initiated a plan of mixing the

prickly pear bar-soap with egg shells and then grinding the mix so that it resulted in a yellowish, pot-washing powder (*umgubo wokuhlamba omthubi*) that was used to scrub off dirt or over-burn on the outer and inner surfaces of the kettles or pots. ... [Laughing] not exactly as strong as the Vim 99 was, but this powder soap could clean all enamel dishes, steel pots and kettles and we also used it on our three-legged, black pots and it worked very well.[81]

Matshoba noted, however, that 'in the long run, people opted to buy soap even though they could have continued producing it. My wife has always pointed out to me that it is cheaper anyway to buy bar soap and that does not cost much time'.[82]

Opuntia also features in home remedies (*amayeza asekhaya*) in the Eastern Cape. In general, we heard of it being processed at the household level, rather than manufactured and applied by a specialist herbalist (*ixhwele*). People used to come from as far afield as East London to prickly pear thickets in order to pick cladodes for this purpose. In Hewu, aloe (*ikhala, Aloe ferox*) was brewed with prickly pear leaves to produce a laxative stomach medicine (*iyeza lesisu* or *iyeza lokuhambisa*).[83] Prickly pear leaves, as we noted earlier, induced the runs or purging in animals if fed in too great a quantity. For the human remedy, the outer cover of the wild prickly pear was skinned, the leaf boiled for a long period, and the liquid then mixed with very bitter (*krakrayo*) green aloe juice. The mixture was re-boiled, simmered gently, filtered, cooled and bottled. Patients were advised to drink it cold.

Aloe leaves were used when young because they carried more juice, which was an important ingredient for a number of homemade remedies including worm medicine. In Peddie, there was an attempt to collect aloe commercially for medicinal purposes but the tappers developed allergies, including asthma, and it was abandoned.[84] There is a significant aloe industry on the south coast around Albertinia.

Other concoctions made by both Africans and Afrikaners out of a solution of boiled prickly pear leaves included an inhalant used for chest complaints and to clear the nasal passages. Fezeka Mpendukana noted that they used less water for this in order to retain the strength of the solution. When it was simmering, they placed a blanket around the patient's head to form a tent, so that the steamy vapours could be inhaled and the heat kept in. It was a typical household remedy which everyone knew and did not require a specialist to recommend it. Prickly pear was also made into cough mixtures and Winnie Louw published a recipe for 'emphysema trouble' in her cook book, which required only boiling of the cladodes (Chapter 8). She recommended that this solution should be drunk at breakfast. Such remedies were, apparently, used by the Voortrekkers and this may be another reason why they travelled with prickly pear. Afrikaners also used the inner section of the cladode mixed with turpentine to smear on varicose veins.[85]

A different recipe was used for a tonic associated with blood purification (*iyeza lokucoca igazi*). In this case, the prickly pear and aloe leaves were squashed and

---

PRICKLY PEAR CLADODES AND THE TREATMENT OF BOILS

The Mpendukanas in Hewu explained that:

> Xhosa people tend to agree that boils generally grow as a result of blood infection hence they treated them with the blood purification mixture. To precipitate the swelling (*ukudumba*) and outburst (*nokugqabhuka*) they treated with prickly pear cladode on the boil head directly. The outer layer of the cladode on the one side is skinned off so that the inner fluids are exposed. Then it is heated (not boiled) on a pan or directly on fire with the side with the skin off facing upwards. After some ten minutes of heating and when the fluid on the cladode starts bubbling, the skinned side of the cladode is then placed and bandaged firmly on the boil.[86]

Prickly pear fluid was seen to soften the tissue, hasten the bursting and clean out the dirt. This process was repeated until the boil was cured. The treatment was still being used in Hewu when we interviewed and only the wild white prickly pear which 'carries stronger fluids' could be used.[87] Inner jelly from baked leaves is applied to sores between toes and fingers caused by 'dirty blood'.[88]

---

boiled together with water and a small quantity of sea water or Epsom salts added. When sufficiently simmered after about two hours, the mixture (*umxube*) was filtered, cooled and it formed a gell (*ijeli*).[89] Informants suggested that medicinal products remained quite common. Unlike jams and syrups, these could fetch higher prices which made the labour involved worthwhile. They were clearly seen to be effective. In 2002, hawkers in Whittlesea sold 500 ml bottles of blood purifiers for between R10 and R15.[90] Recent scientific work suggests that opuntia does have value in regulating blood lipid levels and thus in reducing cardiovascular risk.[91] We heard in Patensie of a man who thought he had cured his diabetes by making a medicine from prickly pear leaves which grew on his farm.[92] Certainly opuntia is used for this purpose and also for high cholesterol levels in Mexico.

In Mexico opuntia cladodes are incorporated in skin lotions and we heard of similar practices in the Eastern Cape. A man in Mgwali said that he used the soft inner part of the cladode as a lotion for his face.[93] First, he grated off the outer layer until the whitish pulp was exposed. He dried this, crushed it into a browny-white powder, mixed it with boiled water and smeared the potion on his face and body. He believed that it cleansed the pores.

MARKETS AND SALE

Prickly pear fruits have been marketed through the southern, midland and eastern Cape for over a century. Transport routes and transport hubs, once a vector for the spread of prickly pear, became increasingly important as marketing sites. Increases in traffic and the congregation of people around taxi ranks and roadside stalls have all contributed to this change. In earlier decades, perhaps, marketing on roadsides was less significant. The problem then for rural households who wished to trade was not only finding labour on a sufficient scale to pick and clean the fruit, but transport. In Hewu in the 1950s and 1960s, villagers supplied the local general dealers or had informal stalls at church services or social events. In the 1960s fruits were sold for about 1 cent. Even so, 'if one picked a lot of fruit, washed and cleaned it, one stood a chance of accumulating some cash. Remember even the school fees were just about 10c a quarter those days and some of us did pay our annual school fees through prickly pear sales'.[94]

Mrs Ferreira outlined the recent history of marketing in Hankey. During the 1950s, coloured farm workers used to load and transport fruit by ox-wagon to Humansdorp and other towns. They supplied local agents who in turn sold the fruit at markets.[95] Returns would be split in half between the farmers and the workers who picked and transported the fruit; the workers would have to pay the agents out of their share. Sometimes, farm workers would stay with relatives in Humansdorp and sell the fruit themselves so that they did not have to pay the commission fee to the agent. They sold a 25 litre container with fruit for 10 shillings as a standard price. In the 1960s, the clearance of land and the absorption of workers into the new irrigation schemes diminished both the amount of prickly pear and labour for picking and preparing. In any case it was more difficult to get access to fruit and hence more time-consuming to pick. She suggested that some farm-worker families, and women in particular, bemoaned the loss of prickly pear income: 'naartjies and oranges are controlled by the ... white farmers but we felt with prickly pear that we had our own control ... we were initially livid because [citrus trees] were grown on prickly pear land.'

Africans in Weston, the Hankey township, took over the business. Weston was still surrounded by prickly pear and closer to the Soetkloof pass. Those with vans hired women fruit pickers and sold along the roads and in towns. The advent of taxis in the 1980s made it possible for a wider range of people to engage in trade, in that they could use them for transporting small quantities. In 2002, vehicle owners were still employing people to pick and load fruit in the Soetkloof pass where there are dense thickets. The fruit was sold in Hankey, Patensie, Jeffreys Bay, Humansdorp and Tsitsikamma. Hawkers kept stalls along some of the main roads. There was a fairly standardised set of measures: 5-, 10- and 20-litre containers. Prices were lower in early season when 5 litres were sold at between R6 and R10. When supply was at its height a 20-litre container fetched only R20. Late in the season, prices rose sharply to R15 for 5 litres in March.[96] Bulk purchases were sometimes made by shop owners or for syrup and chutney.

A white farmer in Cathcart, near Hewu district, also marketed prickly pear commercially up to the 1980s.[97] He recalled transporting bakkie loads to an East London fruit merchant who in turn supplied hawkers and supermarkets. Supermarkets could buy in bulk and sell at higher prices than hawkers. The problem for farmers was that labour costs were high and the fruit fragile. The wild fruit is scattered, delicate and does not last long. Picking, washing, packing and offloading had to be done by hand. Unlike citrus, economies of scale were harder to achieve and because of this prickly pear lends itself to handling on a smaller scale where families use their own labour. Fruit was also displayed and sold at agricultural shows in places such as Cathcart, Queenstown, Stutterheim and King William's Town. In some respects, the problems of large-scale picking and selling of prickly pear fruit has served, over the long term, to protect the smaller participants in the market.

As in Fort Beaufort, the farmer in Cathcart was reluctant to allow outsiders to pick and sell prickly pear because it disturbed work programmes and created 'disorder'.

> We could have a case of the usual harvesters assigning kids to pick up
> the fruit. Once that happens, kids would invite their friends, tree leaves

could be broken, and fruit would be peeled off and eaten on the spot. The last thing we need is uncontrolled growth. Moreover, the tendency is once you start allowing people free access to any protected resource our fences tend to go.[98]

In fact women interviewed on the R67 roadside in 2002, bordering Hewu and Cathcart, claimed that they did get fruit from farms and sold it at the weekends. They said it was their only chance to generate quick cash.

Two women who sold at Ngwenya on the R83 between Middledrift and Alice came from villages just south of the road (Macibini and Capo). In 2002, a particularly good season, they harvested enough to sell for three to four days a week from January to March.[99] The 2003 harvest was less bountiful but prices went up and they could sell 2.5 kilograms (18-20 fruits) at R4, mostly to passing motorists. Occasionally the owners of supermarkets and spaza shops in Alice and Middledrift bought larger quantities. They usually earned between R50 and R70 a day and claimed to have made about R2,000 together in January 2002. This is similar to the amounts we heard from successful sellers in Bhofolo a few years later. The Middledrift women claimed that they had to give some of the money to their husbands in recognition of the long periods they spent absent from household duties.

To earn on this scale involved considerable labour during hot weather. They walked a couple of kilometres to thickets on farms across the Tyume in Victoria East, picking in the afternoons and soaking the fruits overnight. They then had to carry them about five kilometres to the road in two 20-litre containers the next morning. Women from Middledrift and Alice also hired men or youths to transport bulk loads with donkey carts or bakkies.

Although there are some suggestions in the interviews of a decline in the availability and marketing of prickly pear fruit, a good deal was still being transported and sold in the Eastern Cape in the early years of the twenty-first century. It is interesting that prices were much the same in Hewu, Middledrift, Fort Beaufort and Hankey, up to 200 kilometres apart, suggesting a regional market of kinds. In earlier years, Hankey seemed to be a more important centre for the supply of towns and supermarkets. Fort Beaufort, Peddie, Grahamstown, Hewu and Middledrift have a larger local market for hawkers and brewers. The difficulties of bulk picking and the fragile nature of the wild fruit itself have clearly resulted in some space being maintained for harvesting and informal marketing by women.

Overall, the use of prickly pear as a multi-purpose plant appears to be declining, partly because it is less easily available and partly because of the labour time involved. Informants had largely given up processing for jam, syrup and soap by the 1960s and 1970s and felt that it was no longer cost effective. Most of the processing was done by women and, given the increasing demands on the time of many rural women, it is not surprising that they sought replacements. Taste, fashion and ideas of modernity also clearly play a part. But fruit selling, brewing and some small-scale medicinal use were still widespread in the Eastern Cape in the early twenty-first century.

———————————————

Edible Wild Fruit
Prickly pear

SCIENTISTS AND THE RE-EVALUATION OF CACTUS FOR FODDER AND FRUIT, 1960-2006

GROOTFONTEIN'S REVIVED ROLE

Gerhard de Kock started work at Grootfontein agricultural college and research station in 1957 and he stayed for four decades.[1] When we interviewed him in 2006, he was still living in Middelburg, the nearby Karoo town. Despite being retired, old and immobile, he had until recently driven regularly to Fort Hare to teach in the university's agriculture department. We talked on the stoep of his unostentatious bungalow in the bright, autumn Karoo sunlight. His ideas still lived with him. De Kock had experimented over a long period on finding the best spineless cactus plant for South African conditions and he remained fascinated by the history of opuntia. After he joined government service, he went to Stellenbosch to complete a Master's in plant breeding. When he came to Grootfontein there were only remnants of the great orchards of Thornton's day (Chapter 4), but seed samples of all of the varieties grown in earlier years were preserved. De Kock recalled that, 'interest had been lost, the cactus was seen as dangerous'. Agricultural experts tended to see 'no good in prickly pear'. It was 'the plant of the poor, a flag of misery', inconsistent with progress.[2] When de Kock started to research opuntia again as one of the drought-resistant fodder crops suitable for South Africa, his colleagues 'thought I was mad'.[3] He became an expert not only in prickly pear breeding but also in prickly pear brandy. His persistence gradually enthused others and had long-term outcomes.

Despite the eradication campaign, it is clear from the previous chapter that prickly pear survived and was widely used in subsequent decades. This chapter examines the scientific and official approach to the plant from the 1960s. We argue that there is a striking change in the views of some of the key specialists involved. Up to the 1970s, scientific work on prickly pear largely concentrated on its eradication. Entomologists were the leading figures in this quest because of the centrality of the biological campaign. The Department of Agriculture was also increasingly committed to poison dispensed by its weed inspectors. However, a few scientists such as de Kock remained interested in, even passionate about, the potential of opuntia species. We suggest that the shift in scientific ideas related to the changing balance of power and knowledge in South Africa. The homeland context provided a vehicle for state involvement in African agriculture, sometimes in surprisingly innovative ways. This was one context. More broadly, scientists began to pay more attention to issues of poverty and to the priorities of development. In view of the general critique of science in Africanist literature, it is important to understand the flexibility of scientific approaches.[4]

Perhaps the three most important and knowledgeable prickly pear men who participated in the rediscovery of opuntia in the Cape were de Kock, Helmuth Zimmermann and Marc O. (Marco) Brutsch. De Kock worked at Grootfontein, Brutsch at the University of Fort Hare and Zimmermann in Pretoria and in Uitenhage for the government Department of Agriculture. De Kock and Brutsch became protagonists especially for new varieties of spineless cactus, both for white farmers and African smallholders. Zimmermann was in some senses more radical. He, along with some other key scientists, accepted that wild prickly pear was more or less in balance with the introduced insects and was unlikely to become invasive again. He was an innovative ecological thinker and his research touched on broader environmental ideas. He, Brutsch and others located in the Eastern Cape also began to think about and experiment with use of the prickly pear. Scientific opinion was to some degree split. For most eradication remained the major goal, but the voices in favour of usage had increasing impact.

Spineless cactus was replanted in the late 1940s at Grootfontein following the destruction of most of their established stocks by the cochineal and cactoblastis. They used only the so-called blue-leafed (*bloublad*) varieties, especially Robusta, Chico and Monterrey which had thicker skins on their cladodes and some resistance to cochineal. Pettey had advocated replanting with these varieties. They were less palatable to livestock but not useless. Chico was especially resistant to cold and therefore suitable for higher altitudes. Farmers had also taken them up again and some began to plant large areas. Research continued on the properties of the plant. For example, agricultural officers calculated that three per cent of a farm surface in the Karoo should be planted with spineless cactus as an effective drought fodder bank. The implications were that a 3,000 hectare sheep farm should have 90 hectares of spineless cactus.[5] This was a very similar figure to that which Sidney Rubidge calculated in the 1930s (Chapter 4; 240 hectares for a 5,700 hectare farm). Perhaps more surprisingly the value of spiny prickly pear for combating soil erosion was still recognised and it was used along with other vegetation to control the huge gulleys at Vlekpoort in Hofmeyr district.

Thus de Kock had some small foundation to build on. He visited Uitenhage district to collect seed and cladodes because the insect parasites were less successful there. De Kock thought the wild *O. ficus-indica* found in different parts of South Africa was of the same species but had clear varieties in cladode shape, fruit and flower colour with various shadings of red, orange, yellow and white. While he recognised that soils and environmental conditions could affect colour and shape, the differences suggested a diverse genetic inheritance. Moreover, the wild prickly pear could cross-pollinate with spineless cultivars. He found some promising wild spineless varieties, possibly descendents of the old kaalblad. One of these he named Bakensklip – after a farm in Uitenhage. He then planted 20 hectares of different types and kept an eye out for the most successful and productive plants. In 1967 he visited the United States to study and collect material.

De Kock found the hard-coated seeds difficult to germinate in soil without treatment. He discovered that the best way to ensure germination was to feed them to a turkey and pick up the excreted pellets. He was replicating the process that had happened in nature in earlier years – the process that spread the prickly pear so widely (Chapter 2). The turkeys kept at Grootfontein for poultry demonstration and teaching were easy to work with. Sulphuric acid was also effective but the seeds germinated more unevenly. Many of the plants grown from seeds did revert to spiny varieties. He kept largely those plants that were spineless and identified 32 varieties which he evaluated in detail. Cochineal found its way into the new plantations but they washed it off with high-pressure water. De Kock also attempted to cross-pollinate in order to produce plants with the best characteristics. His former assistants described how they did this: 'Take the flower and insert pollen and then close so bees don't interfere'.[6] He was, in some respects, developing Burbank's experiments 70 years earlier.

Through the years, de Kock tried to breed for a number of purposes. In addition to productivity for fruit and fodder he crossed varieties to find resistance to cochineal. He sought combinations that would yield higher protein content in order to provide a more complete fodder. Like Burbank, he was encouraged by the small differences in various cultivars. He believed that he succeeded in pushing up the protein content in one variety by about one per cent. By crossing blue and green cladode types of spineless cactus he hoped to produce a non-fruiting or sterile plant which would not become invasive. De Kock also tried to develop varieties with more circular fruit for better handling and appearance, and hoped that he would breed this characteristic from the blue leafs, which tended to have rounder fruit, into the more upright green leafs, which tended to have sweeter and larger fruit. He was not very successful in improving spineless cactus for fodder but had better luck in selecting and improving fruit. His best plants yielded 30 tons of fruit per hectare in the dry climate of Middlelburg. Sileage made from pruned cladodes and lucerne was a valuable by-product. De Kock also supervised extraction of oil from seeds and produced compacted fodder blocks from dried cladodes. Some farmers

DE KOCK'S SPINELESS CACTUS VARIETIES

Gerhard de Kock found promising spineless cactus varieties in many places. He confirmed that the green cladode varieties of spineless cactus were more palatable and more productive. Just as in the early experiments from the 1910s, Fusicaulis came out as one of the best. In addition to those he revived or bred, he and others found some excellent cultivars for fruit. Skinners Court, named after the Agriculture Department's headquarters in Pretoria, and probably derived from very early introductions of kaalblad into the Transvaal, came to de Kock's attention by chance in Pretoria. Another, named Direkteurs, was found in the Grootfontein Director's garden.[7] He also looked near cattle kraals and old toilets on farms where interesting plants may have grown in dung from seed. One very tasty red-fruited variety was found along the road from Middelburg to Murraysburg. It was probably the remnant of a spineless cactus type introduced in the 1910s and he named it Roly-poly because it had a round, red fruit. Meyers, with a light-green fruit, was found in the back garden of a house in Middelburg. Marco Brutsch found the Zastron on a roadside when driving through that district in the Free State. It had a beautiful fruit, probably from a cross-pollinated hybrid. In addition to cross-pollination, spineless cactus was 'genetically very plastic' and varieties could adapt over the years to the environment.[8] Partly for this reason, de Kock could not easily test the cultivars that he was naming against those previously imported from the United States. (The advent of genetic finger printing – see Chapter 8 – makes this possible.)

in the Karoo mechanised this process. An opuntia fodder industry at last began to seem feasible.

Though de Kock did not have much support, and prickly pear was always the subject of scepticism and humour, Grootfontein again became a hive of innovative activity. Coinciding with his experiments, he was a propagandist for the plant and managed to transmit some of his enthusiasm to others.[9] We found a number of files in rickety, old, metal filing cabinets and wooden cupboards containing his correspondence with farmers all over the country. Partly due to his influence, the area under spineless cactus expanded again. By 1974, de Kock estimated that 26,000 hectares was established on commercial farms in the Karoo alone.[10] This was probably half as much as before the eradication campaign. He exported cladodes all over the country and to Namibia, which was beyond the reach of cochineal. He was by no means obsessive about spineless cactus alone; most of his published research dealt with lucerne, 'king of the fodder crops'.[11] But opuntia began to regain a place alongside lucerne which could now be purchased and railed around the country in quantity. He continued to supply cladodes at subsidised costs until the early 1980s when the Department decided that enough material had been dispersed around the country.

News of this revival reached officials in the Ciskei as well as academics at the University of Fort Hare. In 1972, Brian Court of the Faculty of Agriculture started a plantation of spineless cactus on the Fort Hare farm, using cladodes from Grootfontein. De Kock gave him a collection of fruiting varieties which he thought would be suitable for African rural areas. Although Court left in 1973, Brutsch, starting at Fort Hare in 1974 and Wessels in Pretoria, both young men at the beginning of their careers, 'thought they were on to something exciting'.[12] Fort Cox Agricultural College also established spineless cactus at this time. This agricultural college and experimental farm had long served the Ciskeian region, training African agricultural demonstrators. It was being developed as a major centre for agricultural education and extension work in the homeland era. De Kock visited Fort Hare and Fort Cox to advise on planting, managing and using spineless cactus. Grootfontein subsidised the cladodes sent to the Ciskei. Saltbush was also distributed to Ciskeian African farmers.

De Kock's interests stretched to culinary use of opuntia. The domestic science division at Grootfontein experimented with the fruit and they were well aware that there was a good deal of knowledge about usage on the farms. They published articles on cookery and preserving in *Landbouweekblad* – the most widely distributed, Afrikaans-language, agricultural magazine. De Kock supplied cactus fruit, plants and recipes to Winnie Louw who came from an Eastern Cape farming family at Middleton, on the Fish River irrigation project, where wild prickly pear had been rampant before eradication. Louw wrote a cookbook titled *Prickly Pear: Don't Abuse It, Use It* (1989), gave demonstrations and radio talks and promoted the Uitenhage festival (Chapter 8).[13] A connoisseur of cactus fruit brandy still produced in the Karoo, de Kock gave us the renowned spirit from Dwarsvlei to taste – about 40 per cent alcohol by volume.

Cover of prickly pear recipe book

ZIMMERMANN AND CHANGING VIEWS ON ERADICATION

When Pettey retired in 1954 his teams had been disbanded and active biological control ceased for a decade. David Annecke who joined the entomology division in the same year was the major force behind renewed interest. He was son of Dr Siegfried Annecke who was involved in successful malaria control with DDT after the Second World War in the lowveld of Mpumalanga and Limpopo. A prolific author, he became head of the Biological Control Section of the Plant Protection Institute for a decade after 1964. In the 1970s he rose to head the Institute. At a time when the Department had reverted to poison, Annecke started to re-examine the potential for entomological intervention. On a visit to Australia in 1967 he found that cochineal was still being used in Queensland to control jointed cactus – although herbicides were preferred in New South Wales, as in South Africa.[14]

One resulting initiative was a survey of 41 Karoo spineless plantations in 1969, which found all but one harboured cactoblastis moth larvae despite the fact that the oldest of them was planted only 20 years before.[15] Cactoblastis was clearly very widespread and had survived well beyond the period of the major biological campaign. Cochineal was found in 18 plantations, probably because it dispersed more poorly after the replanting.

In the Karoo, cactoblastis was now more injurious than cochineal. Over a two-year experimental period, it destroyed about one-third of the leaves of spineless cactus plants and greatly inhibited new cladode formation. Both insects could, however, be controlled with insecticides.[16] In 1972, Annecke organised experiments in four sites in the Eastern Cape which showed that cochineal still caused considerable mortality of jointed cactus (*O. aurantiaca*), especially in the drier districts.[17]

A second initiative was to send Helmuth Zimmermann, a new recruit, to Argentina. We interviewed Zimmermann (b. 1942) in 2008 at the Rietondale Plant Protection Research Station in Pretoria. He had retired from state service but remained a lively and engaged scientific consultant, a world authority on opuntia species, related insects and on bio-invasions in general.[18] He was brought up at Makotopong mission station in Limpopo province. This had thickets of prickly pear, 'a free fruit orchard' when he was a child in the 1940s, but 'cochineal took them out'. His father, from Germany, worked for the Berlin Mission Society. Some leading South African scientists and Native Affairs Department officials came from this background.

When Zimmermann joined the Department in 1968, jointed cactus was his first preoccupation. He travelled to Tucuman in northern Argentina for four years to find a solution.[19] He learnt Spanish, worked with a team of Argentinean scientists, and together they experimented with five species of insects that seemed to favour jointed cactus. They also examined why jointed cactus did not become invasive in Argentina. On his return in 1974, he was briefly based in Pretoria, headquarters of entomological work under Annecke. His other mentor was Cliff Moran, an ex-Zimbabwean and professor of entomology at Rhodes, who wrote with Annecke on opuntia and biological pest control. They were key figures in applied entomology in South Africa at this time and involved in a range of control campaigns. Annecke found the finance to improve the research facilities at the Uitenhage Weeds Laboratory (which had become part of the Plant Protection Research Institute) where Zimmermann, like Pettey before him, was stationed.

Jointed cactus remained both a technical and political issue. More money was being spent on its eradication than any other weed. From 1957 to 1972 the Department distributed millions of litres of 2,4,5-T, the hormone weedkiller and component of Agent Orange – which devastated the forests of Vietnam to remove the shelter for Viet Cong guerrillas. Headquarters was a poison depot in Fort Beaufort where the herbicide was mixed with paraffin and stored in distinctive, 200-litre, purple drums, before being transported. Government teams were available for spraying at half cost, but the Department encouraged farmers to apply the solution – supplied gratis – themselves. This was seen as a better long-term solution, as repeated spraying was necessary. From 1970 transport costs were also covered. At the same time, weed inspectors carefully monitored progress. In 1973 a new chemical was deployed; costs escalated and by 1977 to 1978, R1 million was being spent annually on jointed cactus and perhaps R2 million on weed eradication in general. By the late 1970s it was clear to Annecke and Moran that the areas infested with jointed cactus had increased rapidly, not decreased, during the years of most systematic herbicidal poisoning.[20] They suspected a relationship.

Zimmermann vividly recalled the context of his early years at Uitenhage. After the apparent failure of cochineal in the 1940s, jointed cactus was perceived to be spreading quickly again. He thought that 'farmers and the government panicked' in going back to chemical controls.[21] By the time he arrived 'farmers were desperate'. 'Tons of herbicide' were being 'thrown at the plant' and 'millions pumped into poison' but they were making little headway. John Bowker, based near Grahamstown, had been a vocal advocate of the earlier biological campaign and was determined to secure renewed state involvement. Farmers around Blinkwater, near Fort Beaufort, and in the Golden Valley near Cookhouse on the Fish River also had huge problems with jointed cactus and agitated for more effective engagement. Graaff-Reinet landowners were up in arms about the threat of prickly pear, which also seemed to be spreading again. These were mainly English-speaking and United Party farmers.

After a few years at Uitenhage, and in conversation with Annecke and others, Zimmerman became critical of chemical eradication. In 1979 he published an article on herbicidal control suggesting that it seemed to be killing the cochineal insects.[22] Jointed cactus, he noted, unlike prickly pear, was sterile and only reproduced by dislodged cladodes. To a greater extent than prickly pear it tended to become established in clumps. Chemical control focussed on these clumps and missed isolated plants. It killed the cochineal on the main clumps and diminished their capacity to breed and spread to isolated plants. His initial conclusions in this article were that areas of chemical and biological control should be separated. He thought that 'the decision to use either chemical or biological control procedures in any one area should be based on frequent assessments of jointed cactus and natural enemy population densities in the field',[23] but he soon came to the conclusion that the chemical campaign as a whole was eliminating cochineal and hence becoming counterproductive.

Zimmermann's views solidified by chance observations in the Ciskei. A number of farms around Alice and on the Fish River were bought out as Released Area 58 and transferred to the Ciskeian government in the 1970s, in an effort to enlarge and consolidate the homeland before it was given independence. Most of them were leased out to African farmers and smallholders. Money for weed control was given to the Ciskeian government, but it was not effectively distributed. Thus chemical control in this area declined. Zimmermann realised by the early 1980s that jointed cactus had retreated in this area where chemical control was largely abandoned, because cochineal were able to respond. More broadly, however, cochineal was failing to respond to re-growth of jointed cactus, because insect densities were too low. Cochineal tended to die out when the first victories were won against jointed cactus and it was slow to disperse again. He believed that 'cochineal could be effective but needed breeding up'. This he did by winning funds for the expansion of staff and breeding facilities in Uitenhage. Eventually up to five researchers and a number of technicians worked with him there.

Annecke and Moran's survey in 1978 confirmed the partial success of biological eradication of prickly pear – 'more by good fortune than by sound judgement'.[24] They noted continuing problems with beetle predation on cochineal and also wondered whether South African scientists – reliant as they were on Australian research – had introduced the best species of cochineal. Critcially, they suggested: 'it could be argued that at low densities prickly pear is a desirable plant'.[25]

Though not centrally concerned with prickly pear, Zimmermann was increasingly convinced that there was a cyclical pattern in the relation between the plants and insects. In wetter years, the plants tended to grow more quickly and to expand their range, but the insects always seemed to catch up. As noted above, cochineal does better in hot, dry seasons and years, so that its impact was related to climatic conditions. He concluded that 'a natural equilibrium has been achieved and the prickly pear will never again become a menace'.[26] Biological control rooted in ecological understanding could provide the solution, and they underpinned a less-interventionist view. There was no need to pursue eradiation any longer except through occasional boosting of the cochineal population.

P. W. Roux, Director of Grootfontein from 1978 to 1987, agreed with this analysis but added a further ecological dimension. He was convinced that prickly pear expansion was closely related to the overall state of the veld. We have argued (Chapter 3) that the decline of vegetation in the Karoo during the years of heaviest stocking facilitated invasion. Roux described this as a vegetation 'vacuum' from about 1910 to 1940 and believed that it was no coincidence that prickly pear invasion reached its height during the serious 1932 to 1933 drought. From the late 1940s when he first came to Grootfontein, the Karoo vegetation gradually recovered, or at least became denser.[27] The window for the invasion partly closed and he reckoned that opuntia would naturally have declined with the thickening of indigenous vegetation, even if there had not been a biological campaign.[28] 'Spiny cactus gets surges and then naturally goes down', he thought and this was related to climatic factors as well. He was also unconcerned about future invasions but emphasised the impact of better indigenous vegetation cover, rather than simply the effects of the insects.

While many African rural communities and some Afrikaners were still using prickly pear, Zimmermann found that most agricultural officials and white farmers were very negative. The earlier biological campaigns had clearly changed the consciousness about opuntia. They had a 'mental fear' and 'oversensitivity'.[29] Government strategy was still focussed on herbicides. The weed section, employing about 15 inspectors, was based in a different branch of the Department in Queenstown. They were largely Afrikaner officials who were unconvinced by his new arguments. Farmers were very reluctant to stop poisoning, which would result in them losing their subsidy.

In 1979 Brutsch published his article advocating utilisation and Zimmermann began to explore the possibilities as well. The 1982 drought stimulated the expansion of Ciskeian spineless cactus projects and a visit to Mexico gave him further ideas of using the plant for people. He thought: 'let's get people to eat prickly pear leaves' in the manner of Mexican nopalitos. His wife was working part-time as a teacher and together they began to talk to farmers; they published a pamphlet, held workshops and broadcast on the radio.[30] They advertised the cladodes as a 'nutritious vegetable' rich in protein and vitamins A and C with high levels of minerals such as potassium, calcium and phosphorous.

Zimmermann was particularly interested in expanding the use of tender cladodes amongst poor African communities to supplement food supplies. The young, fresh leaves, which did not have spines, appeared around September at a time when food was often short, and they continued until the end of the summer. The nopalitos season was therefore potentially longer than the fruiting season: 'if they are picked regularly, the plant can produce young leaves for nine months of the year.'[31] The Zimmermanns recommended it baked with a cheese sauce and bacon, or with an onion and tomato sauce. This was a personal rather than an official project although they did publish an article in the government journal, *Farming in South Africa*. They described preparation in detail: the cladodes should be scraped and cut across into thin slices. Zimmermann's initiatives had some outcome in the general revival of interest and launch of the Uitenhage prickly pear festival. Although he was not directly involved, he knew some of the residents who started it.

ZIMMERMANN AND COCHINEAL

A couple of failed attempts had been made in the nineteenth century to establish cochineal dye production at the Cape. Chemical dyes in the late nineteenth century diminished demand but there was still some market for natural dyes and Zimmermann was enthused by the potential of a cochineal industry in the 1980s.[32] With Moran, he set up a new breeding system in Uitenhage. Dye-producing cochineal (*Dactylopius coccus*) were specialised insects, difficult to establish and sensitive to rain and wind, even where opuntia grew abundantly. The climate in Uitenhage was not suitable for production outdoors so they tried under cover in plastic tunnels and large sheds. One of their key problems was that the best cochineal for dye production differed from the insect (*D. opuntiae*) that had become best established on the wild prickly pear. The wild cochineal got into the sheds and outbred the dye cochineal species – 'they could not survive'.[33] A similar problem inhibited dye production in India in the eighteenth and nineteenth centuries.[34] The costs of the project were becoming prohibitive and after a few years it was abandoned as uneconomical. Zimmermann was later involved in a much more successful rerun in Ethiopia.

Zimmerman was also interested in the value of the fruit to African communities in the Eastern Cape. He was well aware of the roadside sales, as well as markets in Uitenhage and Port Elizabeth, and explored the idea of improving sales and handling. Wiemeler, a German student who worked with him in the late 1980s, tried to produce some hard statistics for the actual volume and value of fruits.[35] Uitenhage district, and especially the town commonage, had the most plants left in the Eastern Cape. He counted about 1,000 wild prickly pear bushes per hectare over an estimated area of about 8,000 hectares or a possible 8 million in all. He also counted a yield of 211 fruits per tree, or 211,000 fruits per hectare giving a potential of over 1,600 million (1.6 billion fruits) per year. (We calculate this as enough for 53 fruits per person per year in the whole of South Africa at the time.) The average weight per fruit was 60 grams, or about 12.6 tons per hectare. Although the total area of dense infestation had been greatly reduced, this calculation suggested that there was no shortage of wild fruits, if only they could be effectively picked and marketed. While Wiemeler probably overestimated the number of bushes on the commonage, Uitenhage alone could have supplied the whole country with wild prickly pear.

Wiemeler also tried to work out the value of the fruit. Sellers on the streets were receiving 2 cents per fruit in Uitenhage and 3 cents in Port Elizabeth. If all the fruits on 8,000 hectares were picked, their value could be as high as R40 million. Clearly only a small portion of this area was exploited. His survey suggested that roughly 44 per cent of fruits were picked on selected trees that he observed, but he could not measure how many plants, or how much of the 8,000 hectare commonage, were utilised. An optimistic reading suggested a possible value of R1,812 per hectare and a total potential value of wild fruit in that area of R14.5 million with current harvesting practices. This was probably the first time that such surveys and calculations had been attempted. While the values were exaggerated, Zimmermann was certainly justified in thinking that fruit from wild prickly pear was worth 'millions of rands' – certianly if the Cape as a whole was included.[36]

The problem was that only a limited quantity of the wild fruit could be sold and that it fetched low prices. They felt that the future lay with improved marketing. They organised a trial picking of the best quality wild fruit, labelled it and named it Steinbeck, 'as a consumer conscious, quality product'.[37] Carefully packaged cartons were sent to shops including Pick n Pay, and sold at up to 11 cents per fruit – four or five times the value obtained on the streets. Wiemeler suggested that marketing should be aimed at older people of all communities who still consumed prickly pear, or had fond memories of doing so. He thought that they preferred the fruit while younger consumers were less wedded to it. Some farmers such as Ferguson Miles in Cathcart were in fact supplying urban supermarkets at the time but there was no major transition to sales through formal retail networks.

Zimmermann also became involved in a project with Gilbeys distillers. Farm-based distilling became illegal and dwindled in the early twentieth century though it did not disappear. Zimmermann initiated large-scale picking by African women around Uitenhage, collected 'mountains of fruit', stored it in the garages at the Weeds laboratory and trucked it to the Gilbeys factory in Stellenbosch. The drink was on the market for a few years as Baines Prickly Pear Liqueur – a cream liqueur, like Cape Velvet, Baileys or Amarula, at 17 per cent alcohol by volume. Another project involved employing workers to cut large quantities of cladodes, making silage and railing it to cattle feedlots in Vereeniging for the Johannesburg market. This worked for a while but the businessman involved 'got into trouble'. In the late 1990s, a German company explored collecting dried flowers for medicinal purposes. They were used in Sicily for enlarged prostrate and in North Africa for dysentery.

Zimmermann's German background, upbringing on a mission station and long period researching in Argentina gave him a broader perspective than many of those working in the Department of Agriculture. He was outside of the mainstream of Afrikaner agricultural officials and had a certain independence for 15 years as the head of a small research institute in the eastern Cape. When he left the eastern Cape in 1989, research activities dwindled partly because of his arguments about the relative stability of plants and insects making an impact, and partly because of the institutional turmoil around the political transition. Eradication was eventually taken over by the Working for Water Programme – a major attempt by the post-apartheid government to control invasive species, especially those seen as soaking up water and reducing the runoff (Chapter 9).

THE FORT HARE PLANTATIONS

During the 1980s both de Kock and Zimmermann worked with Marco Brutsch. Born in Lesotho in 1945, Brutsch's father, like Zimmermann's, was a missionary. We talked to him in his busy office on the Alice campus of Fort Hare where he was head of the Department of Agronomy. A quiet man overburdened by administrative and teaching responsibilities, he was no longer researching opuntia. However, his office was full of memorabilia from the time when he was more engaged with the plant: labels, bottles of syrup, pamphlets and a striking first day cover from the Ciskei.

Brutsch worked in the Department of Agriculture from 1971 and came to Fort Hare in 1974. A new plantation of spineless cactus had recently been established on the university farm with 13 fruiting varieties from Grootfontein. The university as a whole was in a difficult phase at the height of apartheid. On the one hand, it received generous, new state funding as a central Ciskeian institution. On the other hand, it was being ethnicised with Afrikaner staff and Xhosa-speaking students and struggled to attract good academics. The university's agriculture department, however, was to some extent an exception, maintaining a research culture and providing a home for some innovative thinkers such as Winston Trollope. Brutsch became involved in detailed trials to test the cultivars before they were offered to African smallholders.

Brutsch was convinced that spineless cactus was highly suited to the drier areas of the Ciskei. Over 40 per cent of the homeland's surface, largely classified as valley bushveld and thornveld, fell into this category. These sections of the Ciskei were marginal for most rain-fed crops and when they were cultivated by smallholders, mainly with maize, the yields were very low. He concluded that 'because of its hardiness, ease of cultivation, low establishment and maintenance cost, the prickly pear would seem to be an ideal crop for these semi-arid zones. In addition to providing fruit, it could be used as a hedge plant or low windbreak around home gardens and as a fodder bank for times of drought'.[38] Its value for soil-erosion control was well established.

Brutsch recognised that weeds legislation made it illegal to spread spiny prickly pear, but in addition to planting spineless cactus, he saw huge potential in finding selected clones of the best, wild varieties. Spineless varieties would require wire fencing to keep livestock at bay and this would be difficult to maintain on commonages in the Ciskei. Many of the wire fences constructed in implementing the betterment or rehabilitation policy during the 1950s and 1960s were partly dilapidated. There was also always the threat that spineless cactus varieties, if not carefully managed, might seed and revert or cross-pollinate, but he thought it very unlikely that plantations would get out of control and thus advocated 'production on subsistence level' for black smallholders.[39] Equally, he supported projects by

MARCO BRUTCH'S SPINELESS CACTUS TRIALS

The plants were spaced four metres apart in rows with five metres between them giving 500 per hectare – a considerably lower density than advocated by de Kock for fodder purposes.[40] They found that they needed a strict spraying programme to keep the cactoblastis and cochineal at bay. Yield data for two seasons (1977 to 1978) revealed that Muscatel, Fusicaulis and Blue Motto produced the biggest fruits. The average weight of fruits from all cultivars was 97 grams and the biggest, from Muscatel, 113 grams – twice the average of the wild prickly pear as measured in Uitenhage. Blue Motto, Gymnocarpa, Signal, Corfu and Guyaquil produced the highest percentage of marketable fruits (80 grams and above). Some varieties were susceptible to fruit splitting and skin blemishes. Fusicaulis, which was highly successful in the Karoo, was very susceptible to scab (probably *Phillosticta opuntiae*) at Fort Hare because of higher rainfall and atmospheric humidity.[41] Roly Poly was a good bearer but with too large a proportion of small fruits. The most promising all round cultivars included Algerian, Gymnocarpa, Malta and Blue Motto. The yield of fruit per plant was a little less than that of the wild prickly pear as measured in Uitenhage ten years later but the weight of fruit per plant was about twice as much. (Given that Wiemeler counted about 1,000 wild plants per hectare, the yield in weight for a similar area was much the same.)

government or development corporations on a commercial scale. He even envisaged urban and export markets. The Fort Hare plantation supplied planting material to Namibia, Lesotho and Kiribati.[42] By this time, the Ciskei National Development Corporation had started commercial production of pineapples and citrus. In later years, Brutsch experimented with the Italian technique (*scozzolatura*) of extending the growing season by removing the first bloom of flowers. Fort Hare trials showed that certain cultivars could produce excellent fruits six to eight weeks later than the usual cropping period – thus extending the season.[43]

De Kock, Zimmermann and Brutsch were increasingly plugged into international networks and developments. Despite the isolation of South African scientists in the apartheid years, prickly pear conferences were not high on the agenda of anti-apartheid activists. They all travelled, contributed to conference publications and included comparative material in their writing and observations. At the international level, an intriguing assortment of scientists specialised in the plant and its insect predators. They came mainly from the countries where it was most prevalent: Mexico, Chile, Brazil, Argentina, the United States, Italy, Morocco, Algeria, Tunisia, Ethiopia and Israel. In 1979 Brutsch visited the United States, Mexico and Brazil. Later he went to Ethiopia and Tunisia. His travel was facilitated by a Swiss passport.

During the 1980s, Brutsch and Zimmermann concluded that a concerted effort was needed to remove spiny prickly pear (*O. ficus-indica*) from the list of declared weeds because they felt that it no longer posed a major invasive threat.[44] This would also resolve the status of spineless varieties which could revert back to spiny forms. 'Full commercial exploitation of the fruit', they argued, 'on an organised basis is only possible if the Agricultural Resources Act no 43 of 1983 is amended to allow the use of the countrywide marketing system'.[45] *O. ficus-indica* had been controlled and the populations were relatively stable and they felt it 'could now be reclassified from weed to economic plant'.[46]

But just as they were arguing this view, the most successful programme for utilisation in the Eastern Cape was biting the dust.

CISKEI PLANTATIONS: FROM HOMELAND ENTERPRISE TO POPULAR RESISTANCE

These various scientific and agricultural enterprises around prickly pear came to fruition in a major government programme to establish plantations in the former Ciskei homeland. As we noted (Chapter 6), some African smallholders were planting spineless cactus themselves in the 1960s and 1970s. Former agricultural officer Lesson

Ngoma remembered the introduction of spineless cactus in government projects in the early 1970s.[47] He came to Whittlesea in 1968 at the time the Ciskei was establishing government departments, and joined the expanding bureaucracy. He later joined the Soil Conservancy Unit from 1979 to the late 1980s. In some areas, spineless cactus was planted, along with agave and saltbush, at the same time that betterment and rotational grazing were introduced. Every Ciskei land use plan had a fodder plot in it, and spineless cactus had occasionally been used.

During the 1970s, major population movements were taking place in the Ciskei.[48] Farm workers were pushed off, or voluntarily left white-owned farms and crowded into dense, rural villages and temporary camps. Sites had to be found for those shunted off the so-called black spots in white-owned, farming districts. Tens of thousands of people migrated into the northern Ciskei from Glen Grey and Herschel districts in order to avoid incorporation into the Transkei which was given formal independence in 1976. Many found themselves in the dumping grounds of Thornhill, Zweledinga, as well as Sada, near the old mission station of Shiloh. Simultaneously, tens of thousands of hectares purchased from white owners were added to the northern Ciskeian districts of Hewu and Nthabathemba. Much of this land was carefully planned for new agricultural settlements and fodder plots were provided in the resettlement sites.

A former Shiloh irrigation extension worker, Welsh Mxiki, recalled that spineless cactus plantations of about two hectares were established in Bulhoek and Nqobokweni in the early 1970s. Ox-drawn ploughs were used, supplied by local residents who received a small payment. The plants were watered once and fenced for protection. Most of this was done by volunteers who received cladodes to plant on their own land in return. The department only subsidised the rangers who controlled access and fencing. A government nursery in Peddie was the main distribution source in the Ciskei at this stage. They favoured a round-leafed variety with big, light-green fruits, popularly known in Xhosa as *indyumba* because they were more watery and less sweet than the wild fruit. A long-leaf type with red-coloured fruit (*ugazini*) was also distributed. Plantations were designed partly as a soil conservation (*ulondolozo mhlaba*) measure and partly for fodder.

In the early 1980s, spineless cactus plantations became part of more ambitious rural development and drought relief programmes. A small group of interconnected Ciskeian officials had significant power to mobilise resources. The research at Fort Hare was encouraging. Ciskei livestock owners lost an estimated 100,000 head of cattle in the 1982 to 1983 drought.[49] The Surplus People's Project report on forced removals and rural poverty noted that in some areas the remnants of prickly pear were all that remained for grazing. In South Africa, the government gave individual farmer subsidies for drought control and enforced stock limitation, which was difficult in the Ciskei. Drought fodder was an alternative. Ciskei officials also, perhaps for the first time in South Africa, touted prickly pear fruit as effective against human malnutrition.

Areas that suffered from particularly severe erosion were prioritised. Ralph Norman, who trained at Grootfontein and worked as an agricultural officer in the Ciskei for many years, supervised the extension of the spineless cactus plantations after the drought.[50] He was inundated with requests from Ciskeian tribal authorities and by the mid-1980s trial plots had been established in 35 of 43 administrative areas.[51] Cladodes were rapidly procured from Fort Hare, Grootfontein and from a former white-owned farm in the Blinkwater Valley near Fort Beaufort. Spineless cactus was placed inbetween rows of *Agave americana* planted along the contour. Norman and his assistants added saltbush, lucerne and spekboom. They arranged a series of lectures and demonstrations at each tribal authority and started garden projects at schools. The South African government provided direct funding through the Ciskei Employment Assistance Program (CEAP) from 1984 to 1990. This was considered a model scheme and the Ciskei government released a set of stamps in recognition of the plant and its success.

Optimism proved to be misplaced as the scheme was battered by many of the same problems that bedeviled rural development projects in the apartheid era more generally. Up to 1981, in the early phases of implementation, the spineless cactus plantations were widely regarded as community enterprises, but after Ciskeian 'independence' in that year and the rapid expansion of the plots, the Department controlled the projects more directly.[52] Spineless cactus was increasingly considered as a government development project (*iinkqubo zophuhliso zikarhulumente*).[53] Departmental tractors replaced draught oxen. Workers were paid – the Ciskeian government was keen to create employment through public works and received the South African aid for this purpose. Increasingly 'the department subsidised the operation of the entire project' and 'the output was under the control of the respective tribal authorities'.[54] They were responsible for selecting the workers, distributing the excess cladodes to livestock owners (for a small payment) and also for access to fruit. An agriculture officer recalled that 'the politics of it was not really understood by the department' – which was accustomed to work through the tribal authorities.[55] Moreover, the pilot plots were too small to cope with demand so that there was competition for limited resources.

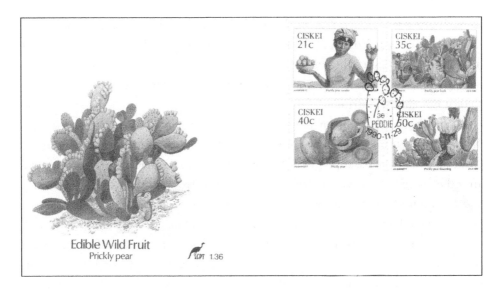

Ciskeian First Day Cover; the 21c stamp features a rural prickly pear vendor, the 35c stamp a row of spineless cactus plants with a young boy picking, the 40c stamp has fruit cut open and the 50c stamp a flower. Copy from Marco Brutsch

As the political position polarised in the mid-1980s, and as tribal authority supporters gained disproportionate advantage, hostility grew and black extension officers heard 'muffled objections' (*imihumzelo* – a word mimicking the murmuring) about the 'government's prickly pear' (*itolofiya karhulumente*).[56] Ngoma, who had been involved in the earlier phases, was upset about this reaction to what he felt had initially been a popular project. As another informant recalled, 'during fruiting seasons, the rangers and some Tribal Authority members would pick fruit ... [that] was sold on the open market.'[57] They made some quick cash out of it.[58] One woman in Hewu noted 'women like us did not benefit from the Ciskei spineless cactus plantations. While they were there we had to continue picking fruit from the wild prickly pear on the veld.'[59] By 1985 when the national insurrection reached the Ciskei and radical local Residents Associations were openly aligned with the UDF, many people disdained any project related to the government and the tribal authorities.

We went to Bhisho, administrative capital of the post-apartheid Eastern Cape, in search of archives on the history of the Ciskei spineless cactus plantations and the conflicts that arose over them. The new government still uses the old Ciskeian buildings, a depressing high-rise assemblage, isolated on a hill outside King William's Town. We could find no systematic record, but there were a number of interesting old agricultural planning reports in an office in the Department of Agriculture. These were stacked high, precariously hanging onto rickety bookshelves that could fall inward at any moment. They are a potentially valuable source should they ever be sorted and deposited in an archive.

By chance, we found some of Norman's correspondence. In 1986, he wrote that there were still 'numerous requests' from tribal authorities for drought fodder plots.[60] By 1987, 60 trial plots had been started and 2,595 casual workers were being employed.[61] But his letters at this time also reveal increasing levels of 'vandalism' aimed at the plots by opponents of the regime. Violence aimed at headmen and tribal authorities found targets in dipping tanks and government vehicles as well as fodder plots. Rangers were assaulted by comrades (*amaqabane*). Fences were cut, livestock grazed on plantations and fruit was stolen. Occasionally, livestock were impounded and people arrested for taking cladodes and fruit. This only exacerbated the problem and it became difficult to maintain the plantations.

By 1990 Norman reached the end of his tether. In an angry and upset letter, he summarised the position at many of the trial plots.[62] 'Millions of rands' were being wasted and 'excellent work' was being destroyed. At Zweledinga, and a number of other sites in the northern Ciskei and at Alice, the spineless cactus had been levelled by fence cutting and continuous grazing. The Bulhoek plot was partly burnt although the headman had re-asserted authority. At Shiloh the plot was burnt when the Department refused authority for grazing on the plants and at Balfour the whole project was burnt down. At Ngcangeni, near Alice, the new Residents Association said they did not want the plot because the tribal authority had approved it. Elsewhere, he thought that communities had agreed to trial plots in order to gain the income from paid employment, but when employment ceased 'the community destroys everything'. In the few places where plots survived, communities would not give voluntary labour for maintenance and harvesting.

Sebe was deposed in 1990 and the Ciskeian state was in disarray.[63] In the Tyume Valley, headmen were killed or challenged and spineless cactus disappeared in that context. The serious drought in 1991 to 1992 intensified fodder demand and most of the rest of the plots were grazed to their roots by then. The Bulhoek plot was one of the few that survived, but only until the mid-1990s.[64] Agave plants, which could not be grazed directly by livestock and which sent out long stalks, remained in rows with large gaps between them as beacons of the old fodder plantations.[65] For this reason it is still possible to detect the sites of these schemes, but instead of spineless cactus only grass grows between agave.

AFTER THE PLANTATIONS

The plantations on communal land were an innovative idea that should not be forgotten but the intense conflicts of the political transition undermined them – much to the disappointment of the agriculturalists, white and black, who were involved. In the late 1980s evidence was accumulating about more successful enterprises. Agrikor in Bophuthatswana established a large, commercial spineless cactus orchard. A retired vet farming near Pretoria launched one of the first private fruit plantations and during season supplied 600 cases daily to Pretoria and Johannesburg markets. Wholesale prices were over R500 per metric ton, higher than oranges and about the same as apples.[66] Although the quantity produced was comparatively small, less than 0.5% of apples and oranges, 400 metric tons of fruit were marketed by 1990.[67] In these Gauteng markets, spineless cactus was close to being a luxury fruit. The fruits sold were about twice the size of the wild variety and some types had a lower quantity of seeds which made them more attractive for wealthier, urban purchasers. If the quantities reported are correct, then formal internal markets were absorbing perhaps 3 million fruits, which suggests that a significant number of South Africans were tasting.

By contrast there was very little demand in the Eastern Cape for upmarket, spineless, cactus fruits. The availability of cheap, informally marketed prickly pear undermined the potential for commercial production. Many people in the Eastern Cape preferred the wild variety. For this reason, almost all of the new commercial spineless cactus plantations were located in the north of South Africa – especially in subtropical parts of Mpumalanga and Limpopo. Scientific and extension work was increasingly centred in these provinces.

Researchers and protagonists in the Eastern Cape had to recognise that wild prickly pear was likely to take precedence and Brutsch started more socially oriented research on this theme in 1996.[68] It was not published but he gave us some questionnaire forms to illustrate the information gathered. He wanted to get a sense of total volume of sales in the Eastern Cape, the value of the sales and their significance in household incomes. Like Zimmermann in the 1980s, he was also keen to explore the possibility of adding value in sales of wild prickly pear. We have his questionnaire results from two weekends in March 1996 when he spoke to eight roadside hawkers around Grahamstown. All of them were women and it is interesting to note that four of them were under the age of 40. His random interviews indicated that participation in sales included a new generation.

At that time, the women were still able to pick on three white-owned farms near Grahamstown. They had paid R5 a day for the privilege and R10 return for the 10 kilometre bakkie journey. The material confirmed his view that fruit sales provided an important income supplement for poor women. Mavis Fulani who lived in Grahamstown sold roughly 2,000 fruits a week at 5 cents each which gave her R85 a week for the three months of the fruiting season. This compared favourably with the R300 a month that she could earn as a domestic worker, working for two days a week.[69] A woman who lived on a farm was able to make R50 to R70 per week (R280 a month) by selling fruit on the road near the farm gate. She harvested the fruit for free on her employer's land. Her husband received only R285 a month in cash as a farm worker so we can again see the significance of income from fruit at this time of year. She also made *iqhilika* and her family ate about 30 fruits a day. She insisted that they did not get constipated if they ate the fruit with other food.[70] Others reported earning between R10 and R30 a day although they did not necessarily sell every day. Vendors on the Grahamstown to Peddie road combined prickly pear with pineapple fruit sales.

The information from Brutsch's interviews is very similar to that we heard in Fort Beaufort and in other parts of the Eastern Cape, five to ten years later. It is clear that the informal market for prickly pear fruit was being sustained. Brutsch thought it was actually expanding although our informants were not all of the same opinion. Neither his nor our research was able to form an overview of the total scale of income for poor women. Wiemeler's estimates for the value of Uitenhage's fruit in 1988 at R14.5 million was certainly too high because by no means could all of the 8,000 hectares be picked and sold, but Zimmermann was clearly correct that the plant brought in millions of rands to poor people in the province as a whole.

Brutsch was clearly impressed with the scale of sales but less optimistic about the capacity of women to improve the quality of fruit for urban markets. He pursued one particularly promising avenue for adding value to the fruit through drying.[71] This technique used the thicker, fleshy, inner part of the peel to make 'dates'. Usually this part of the fruit was discarded. Date manufacture was not only an excellent way of preserving the fruit for up to five months, but ensured that more of each fruit was used. He and colleagues at Fort Hare developed a cheap, solar drying box.

Meanwhile, at Grootfontein, the spineless cactus plantations deteriorated again after de Kock retired. We visited in 2003 and found an enthusiastic protagonist in a new agricultural officer, Strydom Schoonraad.[72] He was closely in touch with the South African Cactus Network, now with its centre of gravity in Bloemfontein and Pretoria, where he met Zimmermann. They agreed that there was no potential in further crossing and hybridisation. Zimmermann advised: 'destroy as they will contaminate'. Schoonraad therefore uprooted the hybrid plants developed by de Kock because of their unpredictability. He preserved 'originals' such as Robusta, Monterrey and Chico and replanted the best-known and most successful cultivars in order to preserve the genetic material. 'De Kock won't like it', he confided in us. There were also problems in that cochineal had become established in the old orchards and the plants were weak.

Schoonraad showed us around the new plantations with pride. (He retained a few of the old hybrids for interest). He was keenest on Robusta in the Karoo for its all-round properties and was trying a variety of Fusicaulis, obtained from a local farmer, which seemed more insect resistant. Grootfontein has to control cactoblastis and cochineal with chemicals (ultracide) in March and November and they also destroyed cactoblastis eggs by hand. He was finding, like those before him, that spineless cactus could be a relatively labour-intensive crop.

De Kock's former assistants, August Wenaar and Isak Abels, still working at Grootfontein, were a mine of information. They told us that livestock always eat Fusicaulis first, that Chico reverts to the spiny form more frequently and Robusta not only has the best fruit of the blue-leaved varieties but reverts less.[73] Schoonraad obtained his new stock from Limpopo province where 70 cultivars were kept on a government farm. 'Currently there is a huge demand for fruit cultivars,' he said. Grootfontein was again selling cladodes in the early twenty-first century. Although Karoo farmers

The two photographs show old and new plantations at Grootfontein in 2003 with August Wenaar, Isak Abels and Strydom Schoonraad

were not planting a great deal for fruit, there was increasing interest in the dry districts of the Northern Cape where cochineal was less well established. We were struck, driving recently from Upington to Augrabies National Park, and then to the Fish River Canyon in southern Namibia, by how many farmhouses had spineless cactus as hedges or in small plantations. At Grootfontein, after 1994, members of the local community came onto the farm to collect fruit annually, and the agricultural officers could no longer exclude them. They did not destroy the plants.

When the government experimental station at Cradock decided to establish 16 cultivars of spineless cactus in 2003, they also got their plants from Limpopo rather than Grootfontein, because the latter were not seen to be in the best condition.[74] Schoonraad had become acting Director in 2005 and could no longer devote as much attention to the plantation. Goats had also escaped from the smallholder demonstration plot and damaged a number of the new plants.

In some senses we could say that the scientific work to promote opuntia that flourished from the 1970s to the 1990s failed to stimulate major new developments in the eastern Cape. Cultivated fruit, mass consumption of napolitos and dye production were not effectively introduced and many landowners still prefer to eradicate prickly pear. The Ciskei plantations were destroyed and the Fort Hare plantation was neglected, then uprooted in 2003 to 2004. The main new ventures on the university's farm were dairy production, using irrigated pastures and lucerne fodder, and the development of an all-purpose indigenous Nguni cattle herd adapted to the local vegetation and conditions.

Yet, in other ways, the scientists left a significant legacy. It was a fertile period of experimentation, and in other political circumstances, more of the initiatives may have matured. State-sponsored eradication ebbed and in the 1990s the government excluded spineless cactus (but not prickly pear) from its list of declared weeds. This encouraged planting. There is abundant information on the characteristics of spineless cactus varieties. Grootfontein retains its plantation, a number of individual growers have taken up spineless cactus and the memory of the centrality of prickly pear in Afrikaner society has been revived in the Uitenhage prickly pear festival (Chapter 8). Moreover, as we discuss in the next chapter, a new generation of scientists, also part of an international network, has emerged with ever more ambitious plans. Picking and brewing of fruit by African communities remained healthy in the early twenty-first century – and we can see that this partly undermined the development of plantations in the Eastern Cape.

AFRIKANERS AND THE CULTURAL REVIVAL OF PRICKLY PEAR

As Afrikaans-speaking people moved to the urban areas, and as farming became more specialised, so their use of opuntia waned. The number of poor white people in the rural areas declined as did interest in prickly pear amongst wealthier livestock farmers. The eradication campaigns soured opinions of the wild plant, which was increasingly seen as a weed and pest. Yet spineless cactus was still planted on some farms and the memory of prickly pear did not entirely fade away, nor did the skills in processing it. In 2005 and 2006 we attended two events which showed considerable awareness, and even curiosity, about opuntia among different constituencies. One occasion was the Uitenhage prickly pear festival and the other an international scientific conference in Bloemfontein.

The Uitenhage festival was launched in 1987, initially growing from local interest in Afrikaner heritage. It preceded the major Afrikaans-language arts festival, the Klein Karoo Nasionale Kunstefees in Oudtshoorn (established in 1995). The latter had ambitions to be a national cultural event, and its organisers distanced it from the old idea of a politically construed 'volksfees'.[1] They saw it as part of a new South Africa and a means to help forge a broader, Afrikaans-language cultural nexus that would rid Afrikaans of some of its political baggage. Uitenhage started as a local event, with more modest ambitions. During a time of rapid social change and increasing wealth for most Afrikaners, Danelle van Zyl has argued that some looked back with nostalgia to farm-based and rural activities.[2] Uitenhage was not specifically focussed on opuntia, but it drew on the plant as one, sometime humorous, element in local cultural expression and identity.

While the festival largely functioned as a cultural event, the conference was scientific and academic. South African participants were largely Afrikaner in origin and there was clearly some sense of maintaining an earlier tradition of scientific and popular interest. Many of the papers had a direct bearing on expanding commercial cactus pear production. With the exception of our paper (a draft for Chapter 1 in this book) and a few on North-East Africa, conference presentations focussed on spineless cactus.

THE UITENHAGE PRICKLY PEAR FESTIVAL

A variety of people and ideas set the festival in motion: scientists, museum staff and those associated with the Friends of the Uitenhage Museum. When de Kock and the Zimmermanns began to stimulate renewed interest in opuntia, and to publicise recipes and usage in the 1970s and 1980s, there were still many people who had first-hand experience of picking and processing. De Kock was in touch with Winnie Louw in 1987 and forwarded leaflets and recipes.[3] He also sent material for articles in *Landbouweekblad* and the popular Afrikaans magazine *Rooi Rose*. The latter was entitled '*Lekkerye* (sweets) uit *Turksvye*' and included '*turksvy en appel botter*', '*jong vruggies in suikerstroop*', *konfyt* and *stroop*.[4] Charles Howell, the vet who started commercial fruit production near Pretoria, visited Grootfontein and the Cuyler Museum at Uitenhage in the mid-1980s. He recommended that they start some celebration of the plant.

The Cuyler Manor Museum is an old Cape Dutch house, which served as the farmhouse of the first *landdrost* or official in this eastern Cape district. Uitenhage, founded in 1804, and named after Commissioner Uitenhage de Mist, was the second administrative centre established in the eastern Cape after Graaff-Reinet.[5] Jacob Glen Cuyler, an American of Dutch descent whose father was a British loyalist in the American war of independence, joined the British army in 1799. He was sent to the Cape and appointed *landdrost* in Uitenhage by the new British colonial government in 1806. He built his manor in Cape Dutch style after acquiring the land in 1814 and he retired there to farm in 1827. Cuyler supervised the arrival of the 1820 settlers, and was a key figure in early settler agricultural development.

In the early decades of the twentieth century, Uitenhage's white population was largely English-speaking. When Pettey the entomologist lived there in a house in the centre of town, it had a distinct, English-speaking elite, clustered around businesses, the schools, the race course, sports clubs, professional activity and the amateur dramatic society.[6] But the growth of the railways and factories brought in large numbers of Afrikaner as well as African workers. It became an increasingly industrial town by the mid-twentieth century, home of Goodyear Tyres and the Volkswagen motor works, one of the biggest car assembly plants in South Africa. Uitenhage's factories produced two of the most popular cars nationally: the VW beetle, which was overtaken in 1988 around the time that the festival was started, by the Golf. [7] Despite intense political tensions in this decade in the eastern Cape, the city's industries survived. By the early twenty-first century, Uitenhage and neighbouring Despatch housed a largely Afrikaans-speaking white population of roughly 25,000 and a total population of about 225,000.

In 1987 the director of the three local museums, Gerrit Swanepoel, decided to hold an open day in order to increase attendance and visibility, to raise funds and provide a tourist attraction.[8] The widely known Grahamstown festival had started in the 1970s and various eastern Cape towns were looking for cultural events to boost their profile. Offerings – some more commercial and some more cultural – now range from the smaller-scale biltong festival in Somerset East to the Kirkwood wildlife festival.

The Uitenhage museums catered largely to the local white population and this initiative was conceived primarily as a white cultural event. A major purpose of the open day was to demonstrate Afrikaner home industries at the Cuyler Manor Museum, which still had a nineteenth-century working kitchen. During the first open day, there were exhibitions of butter making, goose plucking, sheep shearing, spinning and weaving, soap and candle making, meat smoking and bread baking. A *kruie* tannie demonstrated medicinal herbs.[9] Melktert was made over an open fire and meat was braaied. There was a *potjiekos* (stew in a three-legged cast iron pot) competition, kettle shooting, a *klei-os* competition, a tug of war, horse riding and a traditional *boereorkes* playing Afrikaner music (as well as less traditional drum majorettes). Those demonstrating old skills used implements from the museum and wore period clothes.[10] Amongst the exhibitions were *turksvy* or prickly pear products, including a demonstration of prickly pear syrup production.[11] Both the commonage and a number of local farms retained plentiful thickets of wild prickly pear. In an effort at inclusion, members of leading coloured families in town were also invited.

Howell gave an opening address in 1987 at which de Kock was present. The prickly pear exhibits, drawing on Alta Hayman's knowledge of old skills, were popular. Winnie Louw, who lived in Despatch, also participated in the first open day.[12] In 1988 she was featured as 'the Prickly Pear Lady' in the newspapers and on television. Her cookbook was published for the 1990 event.[13] A network of people from different backgrounds, incorporating the museum, opuntia specialists and local women, saw some potential in this cultural revival.

In 1988 the open day became a festival, staged to coincide with the national Diaz festival, celebrating the 500th anniversary of the rounding of the Cape by the Portuguese mariner. It was named the Turksvyfees – a day on which not only Diaz but prickly pear was 'specially honoured'.[14] There was in fact a distant historical link between the two: opuntia had been transported around the world by the early Spanish and Portuguese mariners (though not by Diaz). The oldest Portuguese resident in town was guest of honour. This time, prickly pear products were not only demonstrated but enough was produced to market some of them. They were sold out by midday. In 1989, prickly pear fruit alcohol (*witblits*) was distilled at the museum.

The prickly pear festival became an annual event. It changed in focus through time and the demonstration of traditional skills gradually fell away, but every year prickly pear products were produced and sold, which provided a symbolic heart to what was increasingly an eclectic, low-brow, largely Afrikaner gathering. The first open day attracted about 4,000 people and the first prickly pear festival in 1988 about 8,000. By the late 1990s and early 2000s, numbers were sometimes estimated at over 20,000, with 22,000 in 2004 (the bicentenary of the Uitenhage foundation).[15]

The *Sunday Times*, a national newspaper, sent a reporter in 2000 who gave a rollicking boost to the festival. Comparing numbers and atmosphere favourably to similar events, he quoted a hard-pressed policeman saying: 'Nee, this is it, I'm telling you. Cactus pears is very big here.' An organiser told him 'this is a working-class thing'.[16] The reporter ranked it, with some hyperbole, as 'one of the country's major celebrations of boere culture'. 'Afrikaans kultuur is back in fashion,' he noted, but his use of culture was ironic. Sculptor Anton Momberg was quoted, clutching a bottle of 'liquid lightning': 'the flavour and the smoothness are excellent – maybe better even than marula witblits … but it's the effect that's the most distinctive thing about this stuff. For instance, I'm hallucinating right now'. Reports of the festival often contain an element of humour, even parody, along with fascination about its combination of family entertainment, music and alcohol.

In the wake of Afrikaner political fragmentation, the festival offered a relatively apolitical, locally-generated activity around which families and visitors could congregate.[17] This kind of event is a product of the late-apartheid and post-apartheid years. It is very different from the Klein Karoo festival in Oudtshoorn which features the latest developments in Afrikaans-language drama, literature and arts. The organisers were drawn from the museum's trustees, and more broadly from the committee of the Friends of the Uitenhage Museum. By 2005, when we attended, there were about 500 museum friends and they clearly formed a significant local association. Up to 400 helped voluntarily at the festival.[18] Most of them lived in Uitenhage and Despatch. Increasingly, the event became a fundraiser for the museum in order to keep its activities going at a time when provincial subsidies were declining. This applied especially to museums which focused on white society and culture.

THE FESTIVAL IN 2005

On 26 February 2005, about 15,000 people descended on the Cuyler Manor Museum. Perhaps 80 to 90 per cent of them were white, and most of these were Afrikaans-speaking. Although it adjoins factories and also houses the police dog training facility, the manor still has its own grounds and some open farmland around it. One of the fields was covered with about 4,000 cars.

The festival was sponsored by *Die Burger*, the leading Cape, Afrikaans-language newspaper. Jan Kleynhans, who, with his wife Mathilda, has been at the centre of the festival organisation since the late-1980s, and who also acted as the manager of the museum grounds and farm, explained his motives for keeping the festival going. He said that museums are important for memory and identity. In turn, the festival gave the town, and the local Afrikaner community, some profile, and prickly pear gave the festival

Festival, T-shirt and braaivleis, Uitenhage, 2005

a special identity. That was why they chose to focus it around this theme, although it was by no means the only or even main attraction.

The bulk of those present seemed to be attracted by a general cultural affinity and sense of heritage rather than any specific focus on Afrikaner identity. An English-speaker running the huge braaivleis operation told us: 'people need this kind of thing, people are hungry for this kind of thing, it's people's culture'.[19] He meant the festival rather than the meat, but equally, braaivleis is an important general expression of South Africanism. As well as boerewors, chops and steak, he was cooking about 1,000 *skilpaadjies* (little tortoises) - highly seasoned sheep livers cooked in intestines or bacon which are tasty but rich. As he emphasised, this only happens once a year.

During the morning of the festival in 2005, Dr Otto Terblanche, senior lecturer in History at the Nelson Mandela Metropolitan University (formerly University of Port Elizabeth), gave an opening speech in Afrikaans. He sustained a lengthy analogy between Uitenhage and the prickly pear which drew laughter throughout. Uitenhage was like the prickly pear fruit, he said, in that it did not look attractive from the outside, but this was misleading. Just as people get to like prickly pear – once they know it – so it was with the town. '*Turksvy* has many facets and uses', he continued, 'fruit, *stroop* and *witblits*, and so it is with the town – it is many facetted and in addition to the factories, has its beauty spots such as lovely Cuyler Manor'. Just like *turksvy*, few people outside the Eastern Cape knew about Uitenhage – it was a local town. And he thought that *turksvy* could be used as a '*magtige marksmiddel*' (mighty marketing device) so that Uitenhage and prickly pear could get on the tourist map together. He concluded by emphasising the excellence and honest qualities (*deugde*) of both town and plant.

Terblanche was clearly making an ironic assertion of civic pride. Uitenhage suffers not only from its lack of wider profile but is also overshadowed by nearby Port Elizabeth, little more than half an hour away by car. Those who can afford to, especially amongst whites, often shop and find their entertainment in the larger city. Perhaps he was also alluding to analogies between Afrikaners and prickly pear. Israeli-born Jews, as we noted, called themselves *sabra* after the local name for the fruit – prickly on the outside but sweet inside. (This saying is widely cited in literature both on Israel and on prickly pear, although it is also suggested in some sources that the term was initially more disparaging, used by new Zionist immigrants about the older Jewish peasant inhabitants who – like Palestinians – lived behind prickly pear hedges.)

Terblanche was editor of *Uitenhage 2004, The Garden Town*, published to celebrate the bicentenary.[20] In 2005, he manned a stall selling this substantial book, and introduced us to people who could talk about the town's history. It should be emphasised that the publication is in English and has an extended and well-researched section on black protest by Janet Cherry. The volume was clearly an attempt to record a racially inclusive and integrated version of Uitenhage's past. Terblanche ended his talk with a joking admonition: '*stadig met daardie witblits*' (go easy with that witblits).

A traditional outdoor still was installed at the museum by 1989 and distilling of prickly pear spirits or witblits has since been a significant feature of the festival. For the last ten years, operations have been overseen by Vasie de Kock, from the Worcester Museum, who specialises in such equipment.[21] The production of spirits is now highly centralised in the hands of major manufacturers in South Africa and home distilling is illegal, but the Uitenhage museum, along with some others, has managed to obtain an annual license for the festival.

About 20 people, mostly Afrikaans-speakers from the Friends of the Museum committee, were involved in the process, helped by African workers and fruit pickers. A huge quantity of prickly pear fruit – sixteen 200-litre drums – was collected for distilling.[22] Picking began about two weeks before on a section of the Amanzi estates farm (formerly owned by Sir Percy Fitzpatrick), close to town on the road north-east to Motherwell and Addo. African women, mostly farm workers, were hired at R60 per 200-litre drum. They picked over three days, earning about R1,000 in all. In addition to the 16 drums picked for the witblits, 18 were used for the produce, perhaps six tons in all. Amanzi farm has a great deal of prickly pear and unlike the farms near Fort Beaufort, the owner was more open to pickers even outside the festival period. She charges women from KwaNobuhle (the Uitenhage township) and Motherwell R3 for entry and they sell to bakkie drivers who transport and market as far afield as New Brighton in Port Elizabeth.

Far more fruit is required for spirits than for an equivalent quantity of beer, so distilling is a labour-intensive process although less work is required in preparing the fruit. For witblits, the ripe fruit is not peeled but roughly churned in a motorised, steel drum. It is then placed in open containers for eight to ten days to ferment. Sugar and yeast can be added to speed the process and control it, but the fruits have sufficient of both to ferment by themselves. By the time we visited, on the day before the festival, the fermenting liquor was emitting powerful fumes.

Much of the distilling and bottling took place on the day before the event. This was a highly social and informal process, analogous to brewing in Fort Beaufort.

WITBLITS PRODUCTION AT UITENHAGE FESTIVAL

Vasie de Kock supervised the transfer of the fermented mixture into the still's large kettle where it was heated over a wood fire. The alcohol boils off first and the steam is captured in a copper hood (or *helm* in Afrikaans). The fire cannot be too hot or the water boils through as well. The steam liquefies as it flows down a spiral of copper piping immersed in cold water. The first distillation was a little murky, bitter in taste and about 20 per cent alcohol by volume. This went back into the kettle and was heated again to produce the clear liquor collected from the copper piping in an aluminium bucket. The product was 62 per cent alcohol by volume, measured with

a hydrometer. The first liquid that comes through, the *voorloop*, cannot be used nor can the last, the *naloop*. These can contain too much dangerous methanol. Although the process at Uitenhage was not being regulated, de Kock had great experience with this simple distilling process and he also sent a sample of the witblits to be tested in Stellenbosch in case there was too much methanol. About 3,200 litres of fruit produced 200 litres of alcohol.

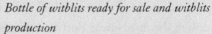

Bottle of witblits ready for sale and witblits production

Participants, a few of whom had camped in tents, were listening to Afrikaans popular music, including Marching to Pretoria. (Interestingly, the same song *Siyaya Epitoli*, or 'we are going to Pretoria', with different words, was also part of black insurrectionary popular culture in the 1980s. This was one of the most popular songs in the townships.)

During bottling, one of the museum friends set the witblits alight in a metal tray to demonstrate its strength. Generally, liquor with more than 50 per cent alcohol by volume will burn when lit by a match. The witblits flamed up suddenly and burnt so hot that no one could put it out. Spirits made in this way are colourless; they are coloured by additives or, in the case of brandy, by storage in wooden vats. At Uitenhage, fruit syrups such as aniseed, green fig and strawberry were added to some of the batch. Once the witblits was prepared and tested, it went through an informal production line. The liquid was poured into bottles, screw tops were fixed using an old, hand-worked machine and pre-printed labels attached.

About 500 bottles (350 ml) of clear witblits were produced and sold for R30 each and a smaller number of flavoured bottles (200 ml) for R20. The latter were particularly popular. The witblits went on sale at nine in the morning on the day of the festival and was sold out by midday fetching about R20,000 in all. As in the production of *iqhilika*, distilling draws on and preserves old skills in a process of collective and socially reinforcing work. The sales were attended by a great deal of joking about the drink and its strength. Many people came to try out small quantities, especially of the flavoured product. Someone had produced a homemade sign: '*Salig op die tong*' (heavenly on the tongue). The spirit is too strong to be heavenly or smooth, but it does have a distinctive flavour, rather like grappa with a hint of caramel. In the latter respect there is some similarity to the taste of beer. Two members of

the customs service (both white) visited to keep an eye on events. One said '*ek is nou nie op diens nie*' (I am not on duty now), 'we are just here for the *mampoer*.' Black members of the police force also came to check proceedings.

Witblits was not the only element in alcoholic sales at the festival. Far

Homemade poster advertising witblits at the festival

more was sold at a busy beer tent. Live music was played there throughout the day, including a traditional *boereorkes* and a rock and roll band which gave renditions of old classics. A number of people danced. In addition, an old, taciturn man from Despatch ran a stall signposted '*Oom Jopie's se Heuningbier*', selling homemade honey beer (as well as honey). He said that he still used '*moer*' or '*bossie*' (bush) roots, dried and ground fine and that he was the only Afrikaner still making honey beer for sale in this area. (He was well aware of African production in Grahamstown.)

We asked Vasie de Kock why prickly pear witblits, which clearly had a ready market, was not produced commercially. He thought that the main problem was one of secure supply – it was difficult to get hold of good quality fruit over a long period. Someone else noted that a large quantity of the fruit was needed and it was very labour intensive. The problems, however, are not fundamentally different from those faced in production of most fruit-based spirits. A tequila factory was established in Graaff-Reinet in the 1990s. This uses the heart of agave plants, but a different species had to be planted from the common *Agave americana*, widespread in South Africa. There had been disease in Mexico's agave plantations and South Africans spotted a gap in the market. The drink could not be called tequila but was sold under the brand 'Agava'. Production ceased

Labels for Napolitos and Witblits

in 2008.[23] Perhaps witblits could take its place but the competition in production of cheap spirits in South Africa is fierce.

Moving from the still to the kitchen, we came across a different world of household production. In addition to its nineteenth-century, cooking facilities, the Cuyler Museum has a modern dormitory annexe with a kitchen. This was once in demand for school parties and youth groups such as the Voortrekkers, Scouts and Guides. Whereas production of witblits was largely a white, male community affair, that of prickly pear preserves drew on a more mixed group of women. Up until recently, Alta Hayman took charge but due to illness Sannie Carelse replaced her in 2005. Carelse was a warm, loquacious member of the Friends, at the same time sharing some of the older language of white South Africans and mixing readily with black kitchen staff and overseas visitors. 'Steal with your eyes', she said, as we praised the cakes.[24]

Although she had been involved in assisting for some years, Carelse had limited experience of directing mass production and relied on the permanent kitchen staff at the museum, headed by the formidable Rosie Nonkululeko Rula. Carelse, Rula and their team, including both white and black women, worked closely together to produce, bottle and label a wide range of prickly pear products. Clearly the racial hierarchies have not dissolved, but black women had some authority in the kitchen and Rula, who has worked there for 18 years, and learnt the recipes from Hayman and Louw, interacted comfortably with Carelse. Rula and the other African helpers made prickly pear produce for themselves as well as the festival.[25]

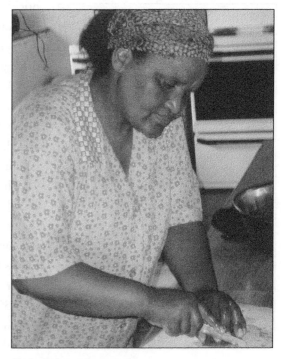

The produce was very largely sold out on the day of the festival. 500 gram jars sold for R16 in 2005, which was not inexpensive in South African terms. People joked while they bought; '*is dit vol doringtjies?*' (is it full of thorns?). There is novelty as well as a half-remembered familiarity with

Rosie Rula cutting nopalitos

PRODUCE AT THE PRICKLY PEAR FESTIVAL, UITENHAGE 2005

Over 1,000 items made from the fruit were on sale – almost all sold:

- 211 bottles of smooth jam
- 156 of jam with whole fruit, some red
- 204 of *skilletjies* or seedless segments in syrup
- 70 of chutney
- 44 of atjar or highly spiced chutney
- 81 *suurtjies*, or very young fruits, marinated in vinegar
- 135 packets of *dadels* or 'dates' – the inner peel dried and rolled
- 122 cakes with liquidised prickly pear fruit.

In addition, 322 jars of nopalitos were made from young cladodes, tasting something like pickled gherkins. They also sold over 500 bottles of syrup made in Cradock. Prickly pear syrup was historically perhaps the most popular product on the farms and is still used on bread and ice cream, as well as flavouring for cakes and puddings.

Cuyler Museum, Uitenhage, 2005

prickly pear products. The total sales amounted to about R25,000. Sales of 600 litres of non-alcoholic ginger beer from dried ginger and sugar brought the total to R30,000. Costs are relatively low, as Rula and some of the black workers are permanently employed at the museum, and the white women contributed their labour for free.

The organisers could not depend on prickly pear products alone to attract the crowds nor to provide most of their income: at about R50,000, these brought in less than 15 per cent of takings. The major element in their total income of R350,000 to R400,000 came from entrance fees. Liquor and braaivleis sales brought additional amounts. Strangely, only one store sold fresh prickly pear fruit, peeled, cut into segments, cooled and marketed in plastic trays. There were a couple of black sellers with small quantities outside the festival grounds. One was the son of a man who looks after the cattle at the museum farm. The failure to incorporate a more significant presence of street sellers was striking.

In addition to the beer tent music, bands played throughout the day on a stage, interspersed with a car raffle and children's fashion show. The audience sat on attractive rows of rectangular straw bales, golden on the green grass. The music added to the strong sense of an Afrikaner gathering. Proceedings started with the Klipspatch Orkes – a regular at the *fees* – singing John Denver's nostalgic 'Back home again'. The chorus runs: 'Hey it's good to be back home again, sometimes this old farm is like a long lost friend'. There has long been a close relationship between American country music and Afrikaans ballads. They soon swung into what they announced as a *'lekker Afrikaanse nommertjie'* – *Bloed*, followed by *Pampoen* and well-known local hits such as *Rooirokbokkie* (red-dress sweetheart). Subsequent groups included a traditionally dressed song and dance team, who went over the edge in some of their lyrics about *'die Boesman vat my land'*, and a group of black Christian rappers. The high point was the versatile Dozie, a major Afrikaans popular music figure, who cost R34,000 to hire for a two-hour stint at the festival. In the year before, the festival featured Steve Hofmeyr, a more strident and ubiquitous Afrikaner actor and musician, of similar popularity (for R30,000). There is no doubt that the music, as much as the prickly pear, drew in the crowds.

Volkswagen sponsored a raffle for a new Golf. Ten shortlisted contestants were each given a key and in turn tried it in the car door. If the key fitted, they could drive the car away. The competition was won by Charmaine Douglas amidst high excitement. She claimed: *'ek het 'n voorbode gehad'* (I had a premonition). The other nine received R500 each. A fashion show followed in which girls and a few boys from three upwards flounced and posed uncomfortably in skimpy clothes to pop music. Tiffany van der Merwe was chosen as Miss Hofstede 2005. Standing model-like with one leg bent in front of the other, she was rewarded with a tiara, sash and bunch of flowers. Marketing of women also starts early in South Africa, even at events such as the Uitenhage festival. Beauty and fashion shows are popular in both white and black communities. In the background, a recording played *'Dis my girl, die girl met die* ponytail'. The mood was relaxed, participatory and cross-generational with perhaps 15 per cent black people in the main audience.

The stalls were very diverse, selling everything from clothes and leather goods to plants. One stocked guns and knives. One purchaser loaded three rifles into a bag.

Slap (soft) chips were sold in the beer garden. As in the case of *iqhilika* brewing, there were some more general economic benefits for a range of businesses in Uitenhage – accommodation, shops, butchers. Eleven sheep and seven pigs used for meat came from the museum farm. Some money found its way back to museum employees and the African farm workers who picked the fruit. The festival was largely an Afrikaner and white-run affair, but it was not exclusive, and there was certainly space for others. The income it generated largely went to the museums. Uitenhage's festival used prickly pear as an emblem of the town and married a civic event, supporting a museum focussing largely on the history of local white society, with contemporary popular Afrikaner culture.

INTERNATIONAL CACTUS PEAR CONFERENCE, BLOEMFONTEIN, 2006

From the 1990s, scientific work on opuntia in South Africa increasingly focussed on spineless cactus, or cactus pear. Commercial fruit production on privately owned farms was at the heart of this new interest but there were other offshoots. Research agendas were also influenced by international networks, which coalesced at regular international conferences sponsored by the FAO International Technical Co-operation Network on Cactus Pear (CactusNet). Meetings were held in the early twenty-first century in such diverse locations as Tunisia, Mexico, Argentina and Brazil. In 2006, South Africa hosted a convention at the University of the Free State in Bloemfontein. The initiative was also connected to the International Year of Deserts and Desertification with which the national Department of Environmental Affairs was engaged. South Africans gave most of the papers but amongst the 72 presenters (of 43 papers) there was a significant sprinkling from Mexico, Chile, Ethiopia, Eritrea, Italy, Morocco, Turkey, Namibia and Nigeria.

The conference was particularly interesting because of the connections that were made around South African opuntia research – both social and international. The proceedings and conversations with participants gave us a taste of some recent research, as well as an insight into thinking about the future of opuntia as a commercial crop and industrial product. Papers from north-east African participants were especially valuable for insights into discussions about opuntia as a plant for the rural poor.

In the introductory presentations, cactus pear research and promotion was linked to soil conservation, poverty alleviation, food security, rural development and environmental sustainability. The conference organisers, such as Wijnand Swart of Plant Sciences at the University of the Free State, argued that opuntia was now, despite its chequered history in the country, underutilised in South Africa. Scientists working on cactus pear clearly wished to reposition approaches to opuntia, taking up the legacy of Zimmermann (who attended), de Kock and Brutsch, and – drawing on a global and local rhetoric of development – strongly emphasising the social and ecological benefits of the plant in a new South Africa. The key local university department which specialises in plant health, trains students from all over Africa.

Protagonists such as Johan Potgieter of the Limpopo Department of Agriculture promoted cactus pear as a plant that would come of age in an era of global warming and climate change. As landowners moved out of grains in marginal areas, he suggested that opuntia could provide an alternative, especially on degraded soils. Land degradation threatened one-third of the earth's surface, and one billion people. Opuntia could offer benefits both to soils and to poor people. In the words of one presenter, cactus pear was potentially the 'ultimate multi-purpose new crop'.[26] Both the South African Department of Agriculture and many poor, rural people thought the same 100 years ago. To those who know something about the tangled history of opuntia in South Africa, this might seem over-optimistic, but it captured the mood of the conference.

South African participants were very largely from an Afrikaner background. While the University has greatly diversified its student intake, its ambience was still that of an Afrikaner institution. The conference was held in the C.R. Swart foyer, named after the former National Party President (1961 to 1967) and conservative son of the Free State. Not all of the proceedings, particularly not the speaker at the conference dinner, were as politically astute as the introductory talks. The proceedings, however, were in English, without any interpretation, reflecting the international presence.

A strong delegation from Mexico included the ambassador, the rector of Mexico's largest agricultural university at Chapingo (a Native American) and Dr C. Mondragon-Jacobo, a global authority on the plant and consultant for the FAO. The Mexican ambassador saw prickly pear as a significant link between the countries. He praised Zimmermann, 'king of cactus pear in South Africa', as a scientific ambassador. Opuntia, he emphasised, was part of Mexican national identity. The coat of arms, drawn from Aztec mythology and embedded in the flag, features an eagle grasping a snake on top of an opuntia plant.

The emblem on the Mexican flag has an eagle and opuntia on it

A memorandum of agreement was signed with documents passed in the manner of an international treaty. The event, recorded on video, was reported on television and radio. One of the objects of the agreement is for South Africa to help in research on the control of the cactoblastis moth, which has attacked plants in central America. Opuntia may not be a sufficient basis for major summitry but the symbolism and intent were patent.

The conference focussed largely on cultivated spineless types, with papers exploring such issues as cultivation, plant health, breeding and genetics, marketing and usage. A special section was devoted to indigenous systems and knowledge (in which our paper was included). Despite the rhetoric and reorientation, most of the papers addressed issues that – while they had relevance to all growers – were of most immediate concern to those producing fruit on a commercial scale.

Mondragon-Jacobo explicitly and ambitiously sought to 'reposition cactus pear as a world-class product'.[27] For him, productivity was no longer a key issue – this compared well with other types of fruit. The major problem for commercial production was to find a fruit that could be more effectively marketed. In Mexico, where the retail sales were well-established, there was competition between producers, including those from Chile and Argentina, to sell the best quality and to expand the variety of fruits. Mexican growers, with more than 50,000 hectares under opuntia, overproduced during the height of fruiting season, so that research was prioritising an extension of the season.

In countries where the fruit had a long history, he argued, people tended to accept it as it was. Elsewhere cactus pear was a niche, tropical product. The great variety of fruit types and colours bred over the last century were potentially an advantage for marketing, but in many countries, the seeds or stones (about 300 per fruit), short-shelf life and residual glochids presented the major barrier to more widespread consumption. Mondragon-Jacobo argued that global expansion depended on breeding fruits that were larger, with more juice and fewer seeds. Cactus pear was often compared to Kiwi fruit, which, although it was smaller, had fewer and softer seeds. Dragon fruits were also competitors that were easier to peel and consume. International markets, he thought, required user-friendly fruits. In this context, the name change, from prickly pear to cactus pear, though it started in the scientific literature, is significant.

A central problem for breeders is that the fruit needs seeds for pulp development and varieties with fewer seeds tended also to have smaller fruits. Experimental breeding had reduced seed content and seed weight by more than half, but in both Israel and Eritrea, where such types were bred, they were smaller with a thicker peel. Mondragon-Jacobo saw this as a central dilemma. By 2006, genetic modification techniques had not been used on spineless cactus. Breeders considered this a dangerous option because they perceived that wildness and natural qualities were advantageous in marketing. In any case, large private corporations involved in genetic modification had not yet seen a sufficient economic advantage to take up opuntia.

South African commercial fruit growers made particularly interesting contributions. We had come across one of them, Douglas Reed, before. Around 2004, a Zimbabwean expatriate opened a grocery store in Rose Hill, Oxford. On a chance visit to the shop we found a large box of prickly pear from Reed's farm in South Africa. The fruits cost 50p each – the same as 5 litres or 30 wild fruits in South Africa. We contacted him for an interview and were eventually able to meet him at the conference.

A South African Cactus Pear Growers Association was formed in 1991 and worked with the horticulture section of the Department of Agriculture. Terence Unterpertinger, a landowner near Haenertsburg, Limpopo province, tried cactus pear after he saw wild opuntia thriving in the drought of the early 1990s. He planted 17 varieties on 35 hectares and after five years decided to concentrate on Morado, Gymnocarpa and Algeria. Working with the Department, he experimented with deep ploughing, fertilizer, manure and irrigation. He found that the fruits needed to be large for successful marketing, so thinning of fruits on each cladode and irrigation at critical moments was essential. Spineless cactus absorbs water effectively and quickly because the root systems are shallow – mostly less than 100 millimetres deep. The plant can take up water rapidly from light rain and showers and it transfers water to its fruits very quickly. Within three years, his plantation was yielding ten tons per hectare. This is about the same amount that Brutsch was getting at Fort Hare. Plants come to full yield after about five years and by 2005 he had doubled productivity.

Unterpertinger found that north-south rows worked best, enabling the plants to receive maximum heat more evenly spread through the day. Heavy pruning of cladodes was crucial not least to keep the plants low for picking and this produced 80 tons per hectare annually for cattle feed. It is now well-established that the protein content of younger cladodes is higher so that regular cutting of growth that is relatively fresh is advantageous for fodder (and for human consumption). Unterpertinger used a machine modeled on a biltong slicer to cut the cladodes and mixed them with chicken litter for additional protein. The cladodes provided his cattle with fodder for seven months a year and the herds in turn provided manure for the cactus fields at close to ten tons per hectare. He developed an integrated cycle of production with spineless cactus and cattle on a small area of land which was highly labour intensive but very effective. At seasonal peaks in the main fruiting season, from mid-December to mid-February, 220 people were employed to work the 30 hectare plantation. In 2005, when he produced about 22 tons of fruit per hectare, he exported 318 tons, sold 222 locally and sent 112 for juicing. Prices were highly variable, especially on local markets, but the turnover from the fruit was over R4 million. Livestock sales provided additional income.

Commercial production on this model is challenging. South African growers are advantaged because the southern hemisphere seasons enabled them to sell in Europe at a different time from Mexican, European and North African producers.[28] Also, the labour intensity of cactus pear is likely to rule out competition from Australia and Argentina, but such operations require capital, careful organisation and there are major risks. Growers have to produce a variety of fruit types because in Europe, red and yellow are favoured but many South Africans still prefer light green. Export is important because the local market is saturated at the height of the South African summer, when prices could be a quarter of those of the peak export prices. But exports depend on maintaining quality. Heavy investment in sanitary pack houses is also essential. South African producers are plagued by a high percentage of small fruits, cracked fruits and blemishes. Harvesting is done in pairs, one worker cutting and one stacking in baskets so as to minimise bruising. Fruit are cut together with a section of cladode to avoid damaging them at the joint, and they have to be trimmed in the packing houses.

In 2006, there was a larger than average harvest but of lower quality. Pest problems were hitting exports to Europe.[29] Free State scientists were trying to looking holistically at the ecology and pests of different varieties.[30] Aside from the introduced insects, cactus pear is vulnerable to vinegar flies, fruit flies and sap beetles – all potentially major vectors of pathogens. Researchers and growers are beginning to identify the most resistant species in different contexts. Swart's team has also shown that fallen fruits and cladodes can increase disease susceptibility and that grass in between plants can be a vehicle for some pathogens. As a result they advocate clean cultivation and regular collection of windfalls. So far, the limited size of commercial plantations and the fact that they are widely dispersed has helped to control the spread of pests. But aside from capital costs of establishing spineless cultivars on any scale, this susceptibility to pests, as well as ecological problems, are significant barriers and present formidable problems for smallholders.

The crops also have to be protected from cochineal and cactoblastis. Unterpertinger introduced bats for cochineal control – they were also being used for mosquito control in the Kruger National Park (where wild opuntia has become a small but troublesome invader). Plantation growers favour lower, bush-type varieties with smaller cladodes and a tendency to spread outwards for fruit growing. Aside from yields and ease of picking, open plants facilitate cochineal control. Regular pruning is therefore also essential to combat insect damage.

There is a further problem for Limpopo commercial growers, graphically described by Douglas Reed. He farmed 87 hectares of cactus pear and has 50 per cent more production than Unterpertinger, employing 200 workers at the height of the season. His yields were not, however, as high. One reason was that baboons, monkeys and warthogs ate the fruit. When he started producing in 1991 there were few baboons, 'now there are whole troops of 30 to 40 which come right into the fields'. The plantations have created 'a kind of ecological honey pot'.[31] Monkeys, Reed noted, take one fruit and run off with it so are not too damaging. Baboons sit on top of the plants, eat a number and break cladodes, destroying other fruit. He

POTGIETER'S RECENT LIMPOPO EXPERIMENTS

J.P. Potgieter launched trials at three sites in the early twenty-first century. He found milder, mid-altitude zones were best for fruit and hotter, low-altitude zones for cladode production. His mid-altitude site was at Gillemberg, a well-known citrus estate near Polokwane. This cooler zone also tended to produce spreading, rather than upright plants which were an advantage for fruit growers. Good fruit yields required at least 300 millimetrers of rainfall and suitable soil. Potgieter found that Zastron variety (white fruit, early-season fruiting) emerged as the most adaptable. Some of the well-known types grown over a long period such as Algerian (pink, mid-season), Gymnocarpa (orange, mid-season), Malta (orange, mid-season) and Morado (white, mid-season) did well in both the hot and mild sites. Nudosa (red, late-season) could be added in cooler, mid-altitude sites. Zastron, Nudosa and American Giant did best at the cooler, high-altitude sites. By chance, this mix gave a particularly good diversity of fruit colour and fruiting times for diverse marketing strategies. Old Karoo favourites such as Fusicaulis, Direkteurs and Skinners Court were not suitable for fruit production in Limpopo.

was reluctant to poison baboons – though it was a common enough strategy amongst fruit farmers – because this might have wider environmental repercussions. So he tried, with only limited success, to control them by occasional shooting. Warthogs were also attracted into the fields and fed on low and fallen fruit. They have also adapted to eat cladodes. (This may be another reason why they multiplied in the Fish and Koonap River Basins in the Eastern Cape, where wild prickly pear proliferated.) Most scientific studies, Reed felt, were of disease, plant breeding and usage but the ecological problems could be just as important in the future of commercial production.

Potgieter placed particular emphasis on finding the right cultivar for specific environmental conditions.[32] While climate change, water shortages and constraints on irrigation all pointed to cactus pear as an ideal crop, varieties have to be carefully chosen for maximum value. Much of the research on specific varieties has been done at Grootfontein or elsewhere in the Cape and most had been concerned with fodder as much as fruit. But in the early twenty-first century, most of the area (about 1,500 hectares) under intensive fruit production was in Limpopo.

A good deal is now known about the practicalities of plantation production of spineless cactus fruit in South Africa. It is fascinating that the new scientific work barely mentions the central issue for South Africans in the past: the tendency for opuntia to become invasive. Nor does there seem to be much concern that the spineless cultivars might produce spiny offspring by seeding – although scientists recognise that this can happen. It is certainly likely to happen if baboons are eating a great deal of ripe fruit, but scientists such as Zimmermann argue that the introduced insects will keep these young plants under control.

GENETIC RESEARCH, SMALLHOLDERS AND INSECTS

Part of the new research effort concerns identifying spineless cactus types and their genetic characteristics. Some of the original types imported into South Africa may have hybridised and some were not always clearly named – especially after they left Grootfontein. Genetic mapping provides one way forward. Potgieter established a research farm near Makhado in an area with about 450 mm rainfall, and planted about 70 varieties on a nine hectare trial plot.[33] The research station is aiming to collect all the available varieties in South Africa as the basis for a germplasm bank. Recently established experimental plantations in the Free State, and at Grootfontein, Cradock and Oudtshoorn, add to this stock.

A doctoral student at the University of the Free State, Barbara Mashope, analysed

> ## MASHOPE'S GENETIC GROUPING OF SOUTH AFRICAN SPINELESS VARIETIES
>
> Barbara Mashope found spineless varieties clustered into four main groups. Interestingly, Algerian and Malta were closely related suggesting that they were similar introductions from the Mediterranean. Some of the most important Burbank varieties with upright growth and long, heavy cladodes, such as Fusicaulis, Direkteurs and Blue Motto were also closely related. More surprisingly, Gymnocarpa was grouped with them, despite its different cladode shape. If Burbank did succeed in hybridising cultivars then such relationships can be expected.
>
> Mashope also analysed different aspects of fruit and cladode quality, focusing on 22 different varieties and trying to relate these to genetic characteristics. She found that Skinners Court and Zastron had the highest fruit-sugar content, and that the preferred varieties in Limpopo plantations tended to sacrifice sweetness for size, yield and reliability. Malta and Gymnocarpa had the highest protein content in their cladodes, while Algerian – despite genetic similarity to Malta – was low. Gymnocarpa was also amongst the most productive biomass producer. Protein content is significant for those farmers who wish to integrate fruit and fodder operations. Mashope found differences in resistance to fungal infections – and this may help to shape decisions about large scale plantings.

the genotypes of spineless cactus varieties acquired from the Limpopo bank.[34] She tested 42 spineless varieties, all but four from southern Africa, but strangely no wild plants nor the three major blue, spineless Karoo fodder varieties – Chico, Monterrey and Robusta.

Mashope's research is a first step in developing exact genetic records of all the varieties found in South Africa, which will also allow for international comparisons. Mexican researchers are more advanced and have identified over 1,000 varieties. South African scientists are attempting to match live, planted examples, photographic illustrations and DNA records for all of those they could find locally. This research has a direct relation to expansion of plantations. Most commercial growers of fruit in South Africa use six varieties so that it is important to understand their advantages and weaknesses, their suitability for different areas and possible alternatives. The varieties that have survived in South Africa, some for nearly a century, and those that have hybridised, may possess particularly valuable properties if these can be clearly identified. The new generation of scientists are keen to maintain agro-ecological diversity. A record of genetic identity and its relationship to some key fruit and cladode characteristics is beginning to emerge.

South Africa has one of the largest pools of genetic diversity amongst recorded cultivars after Mexico, but there may be an even greater variety in gardens in north-east Africa. Many have not yet been scientifically recorded. Tesfay Alemseged, from Ethiopia, noted that about 40 types were found in smallholder gardens during research sponsored by the FAO in 2002.[35] Opuntia has been grown there for perhaps 150 years without the introduction of much new plant material, without much government intervention and without a biological eradication campaign. One type produced a fruit of 360 grams – bigger than any found in South Africa. There is clearly potential for transferring varieties bred and grown by smallholders in Ethiopia and Eritrea to South Africa. It is quite likely that long-term, local breeding, coupled with the plasticity of plants and hybridisation, has led to greater diversity on smallholdings in north-east Africa than in South Africa.

There does appear to be a significant contrast between the history of prickly pear in Ethiopia and South Africa. Ethiopian smallholders have systematically cultivated and bred prickly pear varieties in walled, garden plots. African communities in South Africa have tended to use the wild, spiny *itolofiya*. It may be that there were (before the eradication campaign), and even are, unrecorded and valuable hybrid cultivars in Eastern Cape gardens. Eastern Cape smallholder gardens have not yet been explored by scientists looking for agro-ecological diversity. In our visits to African homesteads, especially around Hewu, we saw different types grown in gardens and in interviews heard that there was some process of selection involved when people used plant material from the veld or from white-owned farms. But we heard no evidence of breeding and interviews suggested that engagement with prickly pear as a cultivated garden or hedging plant diminished after the biological campaign and betterment. The similarity of wild *O. ficus-indica* through most of the Cape suggests that it has very largely reproduced itself with limited human intervention.

BIO-CONTROL

Discussions at the conference also opened fertile ground for comparative approaches to bio-control of wild, spiny opuntia in Africa. North-eastern African countries are facing a dilemma in this regard.[36] In some parts of Ethiopia and Eritrea, rural communities depend heavily on opuntia. It was a central resource during the devastating Ethiopian drought and famine of 1984 to 1985 when an estimated one million people died. Death rates may have been higher without this plant resource in Tigray and Eritrea. As in South Africa, the fruit ripens in mid-summer, from July to September in that area, before the grain crops are available, so that it helps to fill an important gap in the annual food cycle.[37] A survey in 2002 found that in these months, prickly pear contributed about 55 per cent of the total per capita calorie intake of some eastern Tigrayan rural communities. This is almost certainly higher than any past South African usage – though it is impossible to compare with impoverished, eastern Cape communities in the early twentieth century.

Opuntia spread particularly quickly after the 1984 to 1985 drought and the spiny cactus – though very useful – became invasive in some areas. In Tigray an estimated 36,000 hectares has been planted, mostly in homestead gardens. Some of this is spineless and is protected by stone walls, but beyond the gardens, wild prickly pear is expanding and it has taken over areas of fertile land that were devoted to other food crops. A survey of peasant households showed that while 74 per cent saw prickly pear as essential, 26 per cent noted its disadvantages. As in South Africa, it was spread by wild animals and seen to harbour them as well as to damage livestock. Some sites had 70 to 100 per cent cover. In Baringo in Kenya, rural communities in the early twenty-first century used a large, spiny prickly pear with an inedible red fruit for fencing homestead sites. This also threatened to become invasive.

There are some advocates of biological control in north-east Africa. One variety of cochineal has been introduced into Ethiopia for dye production. However, Zimmermann argued that further releases of cactoblastis and cochineal should be avoided.[38] He is not opposed to biological control in general, but he is increasingly concerned about the potential costs. In the Caribbean and on the American mainland, the insects threaten indigenous biodiversity. In north-east Africa they may have a major impact on the livelihoods of poor people. By chance, the release of cactoblastis and cochineal in Australia and South Africa was contained within these regions in the twentieth century. If insects are released in north-east Africa to control invasive spiny opuntia, they may not only cause hardship, but have the potential to spread throughout the Mediterranean basin and destroy plantations as well as smallholders gardens.

In many respects, north-east African countries face the same issues that South Africa confronted in the early decades of the twentieth century, but, in the absence of significant settler, or large, commercial, agrarian interests, the state may consider the interests of smallholders as more central. Further releases of insects even in small areas of Africa could have serious, unpredictable and economically ruinous outcomes. Zimmermann, who spent much of his earlier career studying bio-control, is now particularly cautious about this strategy in relation to opuntia.

THE INVASION OF NORTH AMERICA BY CACTOBLASTIS FROM SOUTH AMERICA VIA SOUTH AFRICA

South Africa is recognised as one of the research leaders on biological control. About 35 insect species were introduced into the country during the twentieth century in order to control invasive plant species, and this strategy has been successful in a number of cases.[39] However, they can have unexpected outcomes – as noted in relation to ladybirds in Chapter 5.[40] Zimmermann is involved in researching a troubling case of counter-invasion in the United States. Following the Australian and South African success with cactoblastis, the British authorities in Nevis, a small island in the Caribbean, introduced the moth there from South Africa in 1957. They hoped to contain expanding native spiny opuntia species that were being used for hedging but were running out of control (partly because of denudation). As in Australia, the moth was highly effective – so much so that it threatened to wipe out some native opuntia species.

Cactoblastis, originally from Argentina but not endemic to Central America, gradually spread to other islands and to the American mainland.[41] It was able to adapt to a range of opuntia species, more so than the different cochineals, and by the 1990s threatened indigenous prickly pears in their native territories. At one point, the moth's frontiers were moving at an estimated 150 km a year, facilitated on occasion by hurricanes. It spread through Florida to Alabama and South Carolina and was nearing the boundaries of Mexico. South African scientists have assisted in dealing with the invasion. Aside from insecticides, one technique involved the release of sterile insects following similar experiments on tsetse in Africa. A pheromone trap to attract and destroy the males was tested at New Bethesda in the Eastern Cape. There was also an attempt to create an insect-free barrier at the leading edge of expansion. Zimmermann believed that the more varied and sophisticated approaches to cactoblastis control deployed in American invasion could lead to more effective and localised strategies in South Africa. This would certainly help any localised expansion of spineless cactus.

Aside from deliberate insect introductions, a barely regulated nursery trade is taking cactus plants all over the world for gardeners and plant lovers. In the nineteenth century, such plant transfers were the basis for invasions: the jointed cactus is a case in point. Now the trade may also spread cochineal and cactoblastis. By coincidence, one of South Africa's largest and most successful ornamental cactus dealers, with species from all over the world, is based in Graaff-Reinet. It is quite possible that this could be the source of new invasions.

The Bloemfontein cactus pear conference highlighted innovative South African research and located it in an international context. A group of largely Afrikaner scientists, drawing on a long heritage of South African work, are reinvigorating interest in opuntia – especially the spineless cactus. Research is spinning off in a number of new directions, including work on the oil content of the seeds, the potential of opuntia for biofuels and for fruit juice, cosmetics and natural medicines. A German pharmaceutical company has been exploring the use of opuntia flowers for medicinal uses. New work on nopalitos, the young cladodes used for food, shows that they have a significantly higher protein content in the early stages of growth. While it was recognised in Mexico that young cladodes made the best food, this information could be valuable in promoting nutritional uses – always at the margins in South Africa. Fodder research is also taking innovative directions.

While the bulk of recent South African research, as reflected in the Bloemfontein conference and other work, has a particular eye on the development of large-scale, commercial fruit production, some of it is generic in kind, and has some relevance to the potential of smallholder engagement. Expanding academic linkages with Mexico and north-east Africa may help to reorient the focus of South African research. There is scope to follow up the issues raised in the attempts by Brutsch, and the former Ciskeian government, amongst others, to expand cultivation of spineless cactus in African areas. Recent surveys demonstrate the remaining value of wild prickly pear, together with other relatively free natural resources, to poor communities.[42]

Concerns about renewed invasions by opuntia species have not entirely disappeared and critics of alien vegetation remain uneasy about them. All of the wild opuntia are still listed as weeds and eradication continues, as will be illustrated in the final chapter. But popular interest in the shape of heritage-related festivals helped to expand the scope for innovative thinking about the plant and the fruit. The Uitenhage festival was primarily a celebration of Afrikaner popular culture. It folded after 20 years in 2007 because of increased costs, reduced profits and diminishing museum staff to prepare for such a large event. A new cookbook, *Prickly Pears and Pomegranates*, celebrating local Karoo food from English-speaking families, has given the fruit some additional profile in culinary constituencies.[43] To our knowledge, this kind of cultural renewal has not yet been espoused by black communities who are still interested in the plant.

Nowinile Ngcengele on a trip to find mula

CONCLUSION

BACK TO THE BREWERS

O ur history has centred on the relationship between people and prickly pear, and on the tension between the plant's value and danger. We have also explored the plasticity of plants. Running wild, on the one hand, or domestication and breeding, on the other, can change a species' characteristics, impact and the attitudes towards it. The history of prickly pear in South Africa shows that categories of alien, bio-invader, weed, useful plant and crop are rather fluid. Much has been written on the blight – both environmental and economic – that bio-invaders can bring. There are certainly many such cases and the South African research is particularly rich in this field. Yet we have, in part, an inverse case. Part of the story consists in successful bio-suppression. Opuntia extirpation campaigns in South Africa have again altered ecological balances in different parts of the country.

We have argued that wild prickly pear has been, and remains, of some significance to poor rural communities in the Eastern Cape. It is still part of everyday life and has left a cultural legacy for whites as well as blacks. By chance rather than intention, the biological campaign, while it greatly diminished prickly pear, did not entirely eradicate it. The fruit can be found in some quantity. However, some opuntia species can still be invasive, compete with indigenous plant species, hurt livestock and also some wildlife. All wild cactus species remain declared weeds and the state is still formally committed to their destruction. Strictly speaking, it is illegal to spread or deal in prickly pear in South Africa.

Is there a route out of this dilemma? Ideally, spineless cactus and prickly pear should be grown as horticultural crops in gardens and agricultural plots, and cleared from all other areas. In this way, those who wish to use the plants – or market their products – could do so, at the same time as natural biodiversity is protected. The government has moved some way down this route by removing spineless cactus cultivars from the list of weeds. At present, however, this scenario is unlikely to be achieved. Many poor people do not have the land on which to grow opuntia or the labour to manage it. Even if they could grow spineless cactus, they would face the task of protecting it against livestock. At the same time, wild prickly pear is available as a free or relatively cheap resource and the costs of clearing it completely would be very high.

Nowinile Ngcengele being interviewed

In this context, we concur with Brutsch and Zimmermann who have argued that wild *O. ficus-indica*, but not the other opuntia species, should be removed from the list of weeds. With the exception of jointed cactus, the dangers of rampant invasion, especially in the Eastern Cape, seem to be over. There are only a few areas, such as Uitenhage, Hankey and parts of Makana and Peddie, where dense stands can be found. There are some pockets of renewed invasion, but overall *O. ficus-indica* ceased to be a major threat in the late twentieth century. The evidence suggests that areas of prickly pear expand and contract, as do the cochineal and cactoblastis, depending on environmental and climatic conditions. Cochineal infestation can be boosted by new releases where necessary. Managers of land, both state and private, continue to clear opuntia mechanically and with herbicides. Legalising prickly pear does not imply protecting it.

In this conclusion, we will revisit the concerns of two different stakeholders in the future of prickly pear: Nowinile Ngcengele, the brewer in Fort Beaufort, and a landowner who is eradicating in Uitenhage. We will also explore the rather contradictory and ambiguous position of the government on the suppression of prickly pear and suggest, in more detail, what can be done. Our argument also has some implications for approaches to biodiversity.

BACK TO THE BREWERS

We returned to Bhofolo and met Nowinile Ngcengele on a few occasions after our main interviews with the brewers in 2004 and 2005. In 2006 we told her and a couple of her group about our interviews with local farmers and their explanations as to why Danckwerts and others closed their farms to picking.[1] We suggested that some farmers may be open to negotiation and asked if they would be prepared to pay a guard to go with them and ensure that only a limited number of women pickers entered farms. Nowinile found this a difficult idea – she felt that they were not the problem and much would depend on the cost of a guard. She was animated in stating that they were not going to 'mess' at Danckwerts' place.

In any case, they felt that the prickly pear on Danckwerts' farm near the road had diminished and it would be harvested very quickly in any season. It would not last long enough to supply all of them. They seemed resigned to the fact that farm workers were in a better position to harvest on the local farms. So while access near to Fort Beaufort would be valuable, the brewers would in any case have to go to the Grahamstown farms. In 2006 they put up the price of fruit by another rand to R8 for a 5-litre container, but the bakkie owners were also charging more – R50 each per round trip to Grahamstown, or at least R300 in total. Some bakkie owners were trying to go twice a day, which put pressure on the women to pick quickly. It was essential for them that Makana municipality maintained relatively free access to the farms that are overgrown with prickly pear.

Nowinile and Nositile Lungisa took us to Adelaide to look for mula on the farm Grenoble where she had lived and where some of her family still lives. She clearly keeps this network active and she took us there because she knew both the people and terrain. The mula was not flowering so it took a little time to find the plants, but we were guided to a clump within a few minutes. The roots were small as it has been dry. The farm workers mentioned that the smaller roots of this Bushman's mula, peeled, dipped in honey and then dried and ground, worked particularly quickly and well. They also noted that the plant cannot be used without peeling and the peel, if shredded into the mula, can cause an upset stomach. Sidney Rafa, on the farm, sold mula for R50 a cup, dried and shredded. He insisted that it was a lot of work to prepare mula. Nowinile dug some mula for herself.

We dug and paid for a whole plant, but this was not for making beer. We took it to Tony Dold at the Schonland herbarium, Rhodes University, for identification. It had not yet flowered at the time of writing, and it is difficult to distinguish definitively between the trichodiadema species before they flower – so we are still uncertain which species it may be. Nowinile and Nositile were on the lookout for other plants too. They picked some *yakayakama*, for stomach ailments and *isicakati*, the root of which is boiled and used by women in childbirth – or according to Kropf 'for opening the bowels of a newly born infant'. A trip to find mula thus became a multi-herb gathering expedition.

On this and earlier visits we talked about possible organisation by the women. They did not seem sufficiently confident to explore this idea – at least not with us. We also discussed possible approaches to the municipality or the farmers' association to negotiate access to the farms, or find land for a spineless cactus plantation so that they could grow their own fruit. Our impression was that they felt more comfortable with their informal operations and were uneasy about such negotiations. They would need to find an intermediary whom they trusted. The critical point for them was access to the wild fruit.

In 2009 we found Nowinile still active at the age of, perhaps, 82.[2] Nositile Lungisa had sadly passed away. We enquired specifically whether a new generation of younger women was involved with prickly pear. She maintained with conviction that they were – and gave us examples from her own experience. Knowledge of prickly pear, she said, was carried in families and younger women were absorbed into the picking and brewing groups. For example, her granddaughter on the farm Grenoble was involved. Julia Khamande's daughter married a farm worker and helped to pick and process mula. Younger women quite often sell fruit, sometimes for their mothers or older relatives, even if school or paid work make it difficult for them to find time to pick. Groups of schoolgirls congregate around fruit stands in the afternoons after school or during weekends. However, Nowinile and some of her younger associates suggested that it is mainly the older women who still brew. Frequent and systematic collection on a scale sufficient for sales and brewing also requires patience. Younger women, she felt, 'are more interested in employment and wages'. The citrus pack houses – KATCO and Riverside – are amongst the most attractive local employers. KATCO in particular has promoted youth employment of local school leavers.

Nowinile continued to pick at the Grahamstown farms and was convinced that there were, if anything, more pickers and more sales than usual in the 2009 season. The price of a 5-litre container had risen to between R13.50 and R15, but the bakkie rides had also nearly doubled to around R80 per return trip.

ERADICATION ON WILDLIFE FARMS

O. ficus-indica and all the other wild opuntia species in South Africa were listed as weeds in the Conservation of Agricultural Resources Act (1983).[3] This was an ambitious measure, designed to maintain 'the production potential of land' that combined a variety of older laws on soil conservation, water resources and control of weeds and bio-invasions. Under the original Act, opuntia species made up ten of the 47 declared weeds.[4] (An additional nine alien invader plants, mostly acacia trees from Australia, were named.) There does not seem to have been a great deal of debate at the time; opuntia species were incorporated because they had long been on the lists promulgated under the four previous Weeds Acts, starting in 1937. They were still the object of state-sponsored eradication. It was illegal to 'sell, agree to sell or offer, advertise, keep, exhibit, transmit, send, convey or deliver for sale, or exchange for anything or dispose of to any person in any manner for a consideration, any weed' or 'in any other manner whatsoever disperse or cause or permit the dispersal of any weed from any place in the Republic to any other place in the Republic'.

After the 2001 amendment to the Act, the list of 'declared weeds and invader plants' was expanded to over 200 species. Opuntias were classified as Category 1, which were amongst the most dangerous (later Category 1b). The rules governing any propagation, translocation, sale, donation or acquisition were tightened. Landowners are legally bound to eradicate these species. After 1994, all this legislation applied fully to the former homeland areas as well.

It is clear that in addition to the uncertain legality of brewing, many people have been living in an uncertain state of legality with regard to handling wild prickly pear. In most respects, this aspect of the Act is a dead letter. To our knowledge, picking and selling of opuntia fruit has not been tested legally in a court case under the Act. In fact, the state does not seem to prosecute for prickly pear fruit sales.

Subsequent to our mula hunting trip in 2006, we visited the remains of the government weeds station near Uitenhage on the Jansenville road. While some branches of the Department of Agriculture are making a renewed effort to distribute spineless cactus, this station, now focused on the Working for Water Programme, was still more concerned with eradication of wild prickly pear. They had four long tables of opuntia plants growing in pots in a greenhouse, each nurturing some cochineal. These were supplied free in relatively small quantities to landowners who were encouraged to breed themselves. Although the station no longer operated a proactive policy, there was still some demand for cochineal and in 2005 they sent out 50 batches of about 15,000 insects each. Sometimes these were sent by the post. The insects were largely destined for release on troublesome jointed cactus in wildlife reserves such as the Great Fish River Conservation Area and the upmarket private Shamwari game reserve near Addo. Weed inspectors, so active 20 years ago, are now few and far between so that there is not much government pressure on landowners. The station had a deserted feeling about it, with only one inspector left. The main local office of the Working for Water Programme is in Port Elizabeth.

Wildlife farming has become a major enterprise in the Eastern Cape over the last few decades. It is a diverse sector with different landowners concentrating in varying degrees on venison production, on ecotourism and viewing and on hunting and trophies. Some run wildlife and livestock on the same farm. Those who have switched from livestock to wildlife, most of whom are relatively wealthy, rely largely on their own resources for environmental management. They have significant incentives to clear weeds. Some are committed to regenerating indigenous biodiversity. Others believe that highly visible, exotic species such as prickly pear are bad for ecotourism. Texans, one farmer mentioned, might recognise prickly pears as alien. The two positions are not mutually exclusive. Eradication could also facilitate the process of accessing government subsidies by declaring land a private conservation area. If they met government conditions, such as clearing weeds, subsidies were available for expensive, two-metre high game fences and other resources. Once the fences are in place, hunting could take place throughout the year. The rapid increase of wildlife farming is certainly contributing to diminished access to prickly pear on farms.

We travelled with the weed inspector to Rietfontein farm, owned by Cois Dorfling, north-west of Uitenhage.[5] Like Danckwerts in Fort Beaufort, he had switched his farm to wildlife (Iliwa Hunting Safaris) and was eradicating opuntia. Dorfling, in his sixties and brought up on Rietfontein, was nevertheless fascinated by prickly pear and he had vivid memories of its prevalence in his youth. The area around Wolwefontein and Kleinpoort, where his farm is located, was renowned for prickly pear in earlier years and he too told stories about his family cutting through dense growth to make wagon tracks when he was a child. The plant grew very quickly in this area and the fruit sugar content was reputed to be very rich, especially at higher elevations. People used to come from Uitenhage town to pick this fruit. 'If you asked the local black people where to pick', he said, they answered '*bo teen die berg*' (high on the mountain).

Dorfling was well-attuned to the ecological issues around prickly pear. He thought that it was particularly effective in taking root and out-competing other plants on bare ground. It took water from them – a central argument of the Working for Water Programme. (In fact we have found few scientific studies which examine in any detail the displacement by prickly pear of other species.) He noticed that when the prickly pear diminished there was more grass and argued that this was better for most livestock. At the same time, he recognised that angora goats loved prickly pear and that it was very difficult to calculate whether it actually diminished carrying capacity. Much depended on the overall farming strategy.

Dorfling was convinced that aside from the other advantages of clearing prickly pear, this was the best strategy for wildlife farmers – and especially for the well-being of browsers such as kudu. Kudu first came onto the farm in the 1960s. In 1978 they put up game fences which restricted their mobility. They therefore had to survive on the farm's resources. In the 1982 to 1983 drought he thought that as many as 70 per cent of the antelope died directly from food shortage or indirectly from prickly pear spines and glochids. Kudu were particularly partial to the fruit and hence to damage. Unlike baboons they could not peel fruit or avoid the glochids. In 2001 the fruit stayed on the prickly pear plants for longer than usual and this created an additional hazard. Fruits were not being picked on this farm for human consumption. Once heavy picking stops, then the danger to animals increases and the incentive to clear becomes more urgent.

Dorfling recalled that 'the pattern began to form when they saw the response to drought and they had to do something'. Although prickly pear was relatively stable in the area it covered, it was the plant's impact on wildlife, especially kudu – which ate both fruit and cladodes – that prompted him to clear more actively. He was not confident about the capacity of cochineal, which made some impact in hot seasons, but lost ground in wetter years. Some of the plants on his land were five metres high, their stems impenetrable to the insect. He thought also that cochineal did better on plants growing on stony soil and north-facing sunny slopes. So he felt that he had little alternative but to use mechanical and chemical strategies partly subsidised by the state. Extirpation also provided employment at the minimum wage for women on the farm.

AMBIGUITIES AND UNCERTAINTIES IN GOVERNMENT POLICY

By far the most active branch of the state confronting South Africa's invasive species is the Working for Water Programme in the Department for Water Affairs and Forestry. This innovative programme, driven by Guy Preston since its launch in 1995, and espoused by Kader Asmal and successive ministers, highlighted the environmental dangers presented by many invasive species.[6] Their argument focused especially on water supplies in the country and the effects of invasives such as eucalypts (gum trees) and acacias (wattles) on soaking up valuable water. The programme has been particularly attractive to ANC governments because it created employment – 32,000 jobs by 2005 – especially in poor, rural communities. Working for Water has attracted committed managers and considerable national and global attention. It has helped to expand national environmental awareness.

It may seem that Working for Water would be the final nail in the coffin of prickly pear, a Category 1 listed weed. The programme commissioned a wide-ranging study (completed in 2004) to identify and evaluate the ever-growing number of invaders. Opuntia species ranked high amongst those judged environmentally damaging.[7] Somewhat to our surprise, however, key policy makers in Working for Water did not see prickly pear as a major problem. Guy Preston and Ahmed Khan felt that the bio-controls were reasonably adequate – despite reports of some spread.[8] Although they were ambivalent about the harvesting of invasive plants in general, they accepted such practices where they did not actively assist bio-invasion. They also accepted that many alien species were in South Africa to stay, that harvesting was difficult to control and that Working for Water should work with communities that used such plants. On these points, if not in the definition of weeds, Zimmermann's arguments seem, to some degree, to have been accepted.

Working for Water has focused especially on Australian acacias and eucalypts (wattles and gums), American prosopis (mesquite) and the attractive American lantana. The only cactus on which significant amounts of money and labour were spent was the cereus species, or queen of the night. This was cleared over a wide area of the country with reasonable success but was not sufficiently dense in many places to require huge expenditure. Our impression is that Working for Water is relatively pragmatic in its approach to different exotic species which have some use, but they were less keen on a change of legislation that would take prickly pear off the list of weeds and officially make harvesting and hawking legal. If opuntia later became a problem, Preston and Khan suggested, it might be very difficult to restore legislative controls.

A key scientist in this area, Brian van Wilgen, who tended to be more rigorous in advocating control, noted that there is little research which quantifies the loss of income from eradication of 'conflict of interest species' such as prickly pear.[9] And in some cases, such as black wattle (*Acacia mearnsii*), which is also of great value to poor communities in the wetter, east-coast districts of South Africa, the plant is spreading more quickly than it can be used. (There is some evidence that black wattle is no longer so heavily used for firewood as rural electrification spreads, nor in new buildings, as styles and materials change.) Active eradication was, therefore, justified and it was unlikely to impinge on local use unless it was spectacularly successful. Environmental judgements, conservationists would argue, also need to look to the future. As in the case of prickly pear in the early twentieth century, or climate change now, any delay in action could lead to even greater expense in the future.

Our research does not entirely resolve the problem, although we have indicated something of the scale of income that accrues to poor families in the Eastern Cape from opuntia. Quantifying costs and benefits is very complex. Attempts have been made to reach clear conclusions about black wattle, but these are flawed.[10] The problem question is often: who loses if a plant is eradicated? In both these cases, it is poor individuals and communities who stand to lose most. They may find it difficult to replace small amounts of supplementary income or resources that accrue through alien or invasive plants. So even if it is possible to calculate that the overall economic and ecological benefit to society of clearance is greater in quantitative terms than the loss of the plant, this does not clinch the argument. The state is unlikely to supplement such losses directly to poor people.

Our interviews with officials concerned with these issues in the Eastern Cape showed perhaps an even greater tolerance of prickly pear. There is now a significant and experienced cadre of black environmental and conservation managers at the highest echelons of provincial and municipal government. Some of them grew up with prickly pear and were fully aware of its social value.

Phumla Mzazi-Geja was director of the Biodiversity and Coastal Management Unit of the Provincial Department of Environmental Affairs when we interviewed her in 2009.[11] She began as a receptionist in that former Ciskei's Tsolwana game reserve in 1986 and this experience inspired her to study at Fort Cox for a three-year diploma in nature conservation. She worked from 1991 at Double Drift (the Great Fish River Conservation Area) and had first-hand experience of dealing with prickly pear. Mzazi-Geja had previously understood prickly pear, which she knew as a child from Glen Grey, to be 'an indigenous plant or fruit' and she insisted that most of her colleagues at Double Drift then thought the same. One of her duties was to issue permits to people coming onto the reserve to pick fruit during the summer months. Park officers found it very difficult to regulate entry effectively: guards were bribed or extended favours to their friends and relatives. Punitive measures soured relationships with surrounding communities who were already unhappy about exclusion from a range of resources (Chapter 6). 'The bottom line', she recalled, 'was that the harvesting or fruit-picking regulations created some enemies for the Double Drift reserve'.

In the early and mid-1990s, politicised communities in the Eastern Cape occupied some state land and nature reserves. Given the unhappy history of forced removals in the apartheid era, the new government was not prepared to act against them. Through such experiences, Mzazi-Geja and her colleagues in government after

1994 tried to find ways of working with communities. She moved to SANParks for four years to manage the Cradock Mountain Zebra National Park (2001 to 2005) where political pressure was less intense because its boundaries were largely private farms, but since returning to the Eastern Cape government, Mzazi-Geja has had to engage fully with such environmental politics again. While her department is still trying to eradicate opuntia in areas reserved for conservation, and no longer allows access by permit for harvesting, they have maintained a 'positive' attitude to *itolofiya* elsewhere. In effect, they are not prioritising control outside of reserved land. Even so, issues of access on reserved land remain troubled. In 2007 a man was killed by elephants when going to pick prickly pear in one of the Addo National Park extensions.

Gwen Sgwabe articulated a similar position.[12] She was brought up in Keiskammahoek district and as a child collected prickly pear when out fetching firewood and water. Like many other people we interviewed, she recalled the excitement of the fruiting season. Her parents were not involved in sales and discouraged her – she picked just because she 'craved the fruit' despite sometimes getting 'stung' (*hlatywa*) by the glochids. In her family, she had to 'bear the "prick pains" silently' so that she was not chided. Sgwabe trained at Fort Cox as a forester and was one of the few African women to enter into this branch of government in the early 1990s. Her first post involved managing indigenous forests in her home district and when the forestry staff harvested prickly pear fruit in season, they too were not aware that prickly pear was an exotic. It was only when she did a degree in forestry at Stellenbosch from 1996 that she learnt otherwise.

In 2000 Sgwabe was appointed to a senior role managing indigenous forests in the Eastern Cape. For the first time she had to confront the decision about whether to do anything about wild prickly pear in and near the forests. Those in her department involved locally in Working for Water saw it as a plant that consumed water, and therefore a target for clearance. They worked with the local Department of Agriculture, which still had the duty of enforcing the 1983 Act and subsequent legislation such as the National Environmental Management Biodiversity Act (2004). Sgwabe and her colleagues, however, tended to see prickly pear in the same way as the spineless cactus, as essentially a horticultural plant. An NGO called the Mvula Trust was commissioned by the Department in 2008 to manage the rehabilitation of some Eastern Cape forests. While part of their brief is to clear invasive species, and this still includes, officially, prickly pear, they are particularly committed to develop community-based forestry projects and to consult with local users.

In some ways, Ndumiso Nongwe is even more strategically located for the future of prickly pear in the Eastern Cape. He grew up on the farm Mayfield near Grahamstown where his father worked. The farm is now part of the urban zone. Even in the 1970s, 'there were certain sections of the farm where you did not have to look or hunt for the fruit, it was always there to pick and we young boys and my mother often picked it and packed it in bags'.[13] His mother sold fruit in Grahamstown and to brewers in Rini. The income helped to pay for their primary school fees. He thought that his mother's control of some of the household cash through this source was particularly important for their education.

Nongwe joked that prickly pear had indirectly played a role in the fate of Mayfield farm. As Rini township and informal settlements expanded in the 1980s, so people cut fences of neighbouring farms to get at the prickly pear and other natural resources. Unable to control his farm boundaries, the owner sold it to the municipality. Nongwe studied at Fort Hare in the early 1990s and then did Geography honours at Rhodes. This took him into the Eastern Cape Agricultural Research Project, a local NGO, which was directly involved in planning settlements on Grahamstown's expanding peripheries, including Mayfield. The prickly pear close to town was by then largely destroyed by formal and informal settlements. During this time, Nongwe learnt about the prickly pear on the farms north of Grahamstown acquired by the Makana municipality. He was aware that they were becoming the busiest picking spot in the region. In 2005 he started a masters at UCT and simultaneously worked for the Eastern Cape Parks Board as a liaison officer. He found himself at the heart of conflicts between conservation authorities and local communities. Thus he started his post as Environmental Manager of Makana municipality in 2008 with considerable experience of the local context and of environmental politics. He is now one of the key people in charge of the prickly pear picking fields on the municipal farms (called Fourie's farm), north of Grahamstown.

Makana municipality is bound by national legislation to remove alien species. Working for Water has been active in clearing wattle around Grahamstown. Environmentalists are particularly concerned about rehabilitating the bushveld in the Fish River Valley, where opuntia still has some foothold. But he has found that in a municipality preoccupied by economic development and employment creation, prickly pear eradication is not a priority. 'In fact,' he mused, 'I would not be far from exaggerating to say there would be war if Makana municipality attempted to bulldoze *itolofiya* from spots such as Fourie's farm. We just need to apply common sense and not antagonise poor people. *Itolofiya* is one of the few resources they have managed to generate livelihoods from.'

ACCEPTANCE OF ALIENS AND THE IMPLICATIONS FOR APPROACHES TO BIODIVERSITY

Our overall argument for acceptance of plants such as prickly pear creates thorny problems for concepts of biodiversity and related policy issues. Nativist or purist concepts of biodiversity have limited spatial applicability. They fail to cater for the actual diversity of plant species in most inhabited regions of the world which have been transformed by plant transfers, settlement and agriculture over a long period. In this sense such approaches often lack a historical dimension. Much of the literature on ecosystems and biodiversity focuses on the value of relatively undisturbed environments. For example, in his recent article in *Nature*, Pavan Sukhdev, lead author of the recent UN report on biodiversity, makes a renewed argument that the benefits of biodiversity (and 'ecosystem services') are greatest for poor people, especially in relation to their access to public or common goods.[14] But there is little sense in his discussion that poor people also use, and rely on, non-native species. In fact, he also puts bio-invasions at the heart of his discussion of degradation and environmental costs. It is not entirely clear whether his view of biodiversity includes only indigenous plants or whether it can cater for transfers and crops. This is potentially a fundamental problem. We cannot assume that, historically speaking, poor people favoured indigenous plants. As we noted, African people have adopted a wide range of new plants, especially from the Americas.

Clearly bio-invasions can damage the diversity of native plants and even lead to extinctions. But Michael Soule argued some years ago that 'a policy of blanket opposition to exotics will become more expensive, more irrational, and finally counterproductive as the trickle becomes a flood. Only the most offensive exotics will be eliminated in the future'.[15] The implication is that even if policy is aimed at protecting and restoring native plants, the idea of biodiversity will have to include some of the thousands of species that have been transferred to South Africa. We are in favour of attempts to eradicate the worst invasive species that threaten sensitive indigenous natural ecosystems and cause extinctions. There is a very strong case for reserved areas in which attempts can be made to protect something approaching native biomes, such as fynbos. But for much of the country there may be little choice but to 'concentrate on managing and co-existing with exotics and controlling the worst cases of invasiveness.'

Officials to some degree recognise what Michelle Cocks calls 'cultural values of biodiversity' or the importance of 'bio-cultural diversity'.[16] Our argument for the significance of prickly pear in the cultural landscape of South Africa has something in common with hers. We recognise, however, that culturally and economically valuable alien plants can and do become invasive, and threaten indigenous biodiversity. Utility cannot be the only criteria of value. Moreover, cultural values can change. Fynbos is now correctly championed against the invasive species of the Western Cape but it has taken a century of education and campaigning to generate widespread popular support for this unique biome. Many Capetonians used to admire the pines and gums of the peninsula and some, both rich and poor, are still ambivalent about the naturalised aliens.

It is difficult to arrive at an overview of recent eradication strategies. Government departments and Working for Water have given more attention to eradication within national and provincial parks and other land reserved for natural resources. A recent invasion of the Kruger National Park by *Opuntia stricta*, which is not widespread in the Eastern Cape, has prompted new releases of cactoblastis and cochineal. As in the Eastern Cape, initial introduction of cactoblastis had limited effect.[17] With regard to privately owned land, interviews suggest that concerted efforts are being made to clear opuntia from wildlife farms and these have expanded in area over the last couple of decades. But there may well be less activity on smaller livestock farms, where weed control has diminished. State subsidy for herbicides has diminished, the costs of labour increased and government agencies are not enforcing legislation.[18] Few African communities on land held in customary tenure have much incentive to eradicate unless they are directly paid to do so by Working for Water.

Our interviews as a whole (Chapter 6) suggested that prickly pear is stable or declining on municipal commonages and in districts largely occupied by African communities. But in some communal grazing areas, such as around Tamboekiesvlei in the Kat River Valley, the rondeblaar (probably *O. lindheimeri*) is spreading again. The overall picture is uneven. Jointed cactus is not effectively under control.

THE FUTURE

The century-old dilemma over opuntia in South Africa continues to play itself out. Some people wish to maintain access to prickly pear and some wish to eradicate. The change in government in South Africa after 1994 has not made a major difference. Although the legislation on opuntia is tough and the state, in the shape of Working for Water, is more committed to dealing with alien species, government has not prioritised

Rondeblaar at Tamboekiesvlei, Kat River Valley, 2008

prickly pear. There is no significant public debate or open conflict about this issue in the Eastern Cape, but people hold strong opinions. Opuntia is well-embedded in eastern- and midland-Cape society and many, especially poorer people, still have the skills to use and market its products.

How should we think about the future of this naturalised alien? It would be a pity if prickly pear in South Africa was consigned to the history books. From the vantage point of the women brewers in Fort Beaufort, the most valuable intervention would be for local government or NGOs to broker deals between them and landowners on whose farms there are thickets of prickly pear. When we interviewed them the women were not sufficiently organised and confident to do so themselves, and had no access to the farmers. The disparity in economic power, and of course in landholding, between these largely white farmers and the township prickly pear pickers is wide. Conversely, the farmers, who do have a local farmers association, prefer to deal with official bodies or their own farm workers. Yet local and provincial government and their agents run consultations of stakeholders (to use the common South African term) on many issues, including land reform. It would surely be possible to establish a Fort Beaufort prickly pear forum.

Informal economic activities in South Africa often involve hawking mass-produced

PRICKLY PEAR IN POPULAR DISCOURSE

Prickly pear turns up unpredictably in public discourse. When dissident communities challenged Lucas Mangope, President of Bophuthatswana, in 1989, he warned them: 'Bophuthatswana is like a prickly pear, very strong, tasty, but it is also dangerous .... Do not play games with me. If you do I will prick and pierce you like the prickly pear.[19] A Black Sash pamphlet on the homeland was entitled 'Grasping the Prickly Pear'. When Congress of the People (COPE) leader Mosiuoa Terror Lekota spoke to hundreds of supporters in Umlazi in 2009, he likened his party to a prickly pear.

> If you take the leaf of the prickly pear, there where the leaf lands it develops roots and grows, and after a while people will eat from the pear. The reason why Cope will go anywhere and everywhere is because we are like the prickly pear. Everywhere we land, we will grow there.[20]

This did not prove to be an accurate description of COPE, but the metaphor was interesting. Elsewhere, especially in the Afrikaans media, the plant is used to indicate a thorny or difficult problem. An Afrikaner commentator called land reform a 'turksvy met baie dorings' (a prickly pear with many thorns). More generally in the global media and literature we see references to the plant associated jokingly with discomfort or with spiky opinions. In Latin America there is generally a more benign view. A wine in Argentina has been named after the plant, apparently because opuntia grows amongst the vineyards.

goods. In the case of prickly pear, women engage in a wider range of tasks, from picking and brewing to selling. Although they are not actually growing the plant, they are adding value to it and reproducing old skills in a more commercialised context. The level of skills required for entry into such activities is not high, and access to the market does not depend on formal education, but the women are also accumulating and transmitting knowledge about processing, brewing and markets. This is a sphere of activity that is worth encouraging and supporting.

There is certainly scope for women in Fort Beaufort townships to acquire land on which they could grow opuntia and produce fruit for sale. Those who we interviewed could not easily envisage this, they would need assistance from government or an NGO. Some of the women who we interviewed had received state grants for housing and spent these on upgrading their township accommodation. Nowinile used hers to supplement her shack with an RDP house on the same plot. Others added rooms to their houses. Acquisition of agricultural land was not their priority. Yet there is plenty of suitable space on the local commonage which abuts the township for a cactus plantation. It still covers thousands of hectares, and at present is used for municipal projects, for expanding settlements, as a rubbish dump, as a place to which initiates are sent or for township cattle and goats. It would be entirely feasible for local government or other organisations to emulate the former Ciskeian experiment and develop plots of a few hectares of cactus.

While wild *itolofiya* cannot be planted legally, a carefully monitored, experimental plot would surely be justified. This would be preferred by local pickers and brewers. Spineless cactus would be suitable for fruit sales if not for brewing. It may also be possible for private landowners on smallholdings near town to enter into partnerships in which they grew fruit locally for picking, selling and brewing by township women. Spineless cactus and prickly pear are grown on a small scale in fenced, garden plots in the former Ciskeian districts (Chapter 6). These could be a promising place for expanding plantations and fruit supply.

Effectively managed plantations of spineless cactus require a good deal of capital and organisation. They have to be securely fenced, protected, systematically pruned and kept free of cochineal and cactoblastis. Some expertise would be required because, for example, pruning regimes are different for fodder production (where younger cladodes are best) and fruit production (where sufficient older cladodes must be left). It is difficult to envisage this outside of a guarded project or privately owned land which is situated at sufficient distance from the township to deter opportunistic picking or poach grazing. The decline in arable production on communal lands in former Ciskeian districts has frequently been noted in recent research. As one former agricultural officer, Welsh Mxiki, said: 'You probably know that a number of people are no longer cultivating their fields because they cannot keep out animals and their fences are either cut or are disappearing on a regular basis. I can imagine it would be even more difficult to control a communal [prickly pear] project'.[21] Yet in a suitable location, such as on the neglected irrigation schemes of the Eastern Cape, small-scale plantations could be manageable and beneficial at relatively low cost. Both fruit and cladodes could be sold and might kick-start some more ambitious enterprise.

From an ecological point of view, the gradual demise of wild prickly pear, *itolofiya yasendle*, and most other opuntia species can be considered a success. But in other respects, some of the African occupied districts of the Eastern Cape have the worst of both worlds. The most dangerous species, jointed cactus, is relatively uncontrolled and presents an environmental threat, while the most valuable prickly pear and spineless cactus plants are in short supply. There is a strong argument for changing the status quo and taking *O. ficus-indica* off the list of weeds and invasive plants. State efforts should focus on discouraging those species that are ecologically most dangerous and economically insignificant.

There is also scope for expanding sales of alcohol. Garth Cambray launched a commercial honey beer plant at the old power station in Grahamstown after he completed a doctorate in chemistry at Rhodes.[22] He has an encyclopaedic knowledge of the chemical processes involved as well as the history of honey beer and mead. We were intrigued to learn from him that by grinding the mula the yeast cells split and when rehydrated it works more quickly. Local knowledge had evolved a chemically effective strategy. Large-scale honey beer production is linked to bee-keeping projects in African communities in the Eastern Cape, so that its advantages spread beyond the factory (though people find that their beehives are stolen for informal *iqhilika* brewing). The product is sold as a relatively expensive, filtered, bottled mead and does not compete with locally produced *iqhilika*. This initiative suggests that there is also potential in large-scale, commercial brewing of prickly pear for urban markets. The capital involved would be prohibitive for the Fort Beaufort brewers, but such an enterprise could give some profile to the drink amongst a new clientele.

Any interventions in the informal marketing of fruits and home brewing would be difficult. At present, these activities undercut more expensive fruits and alcoholic products. The danger in attempting to create larger enterprises or formalise and regulate such supplies might be to exclude those poor, rural women for whom prickly pear provides a valuable income. The crux for them is access to fruit, and to secure legal status for selling, propagating and brewing. Open access to roadsides, both in towns and in the countryside, is vital for sales, and the roadsides throughout South Africa are not only a conduit for vehicles and people, but important trading sites.

The cost of full legalisation of brewing may be a system of inspection to monitor the quality of their product, but it is unlikely that this would be extensively implemented. Handling of wild fruit could be improved and inexpensive systems devised for brushing and cleaning. Surely there is a case for advertising prickly pear fruit, both wild and cultivated, as interesting and organic produce? There is also surely an opportunity for further linking of rural and small-town communities with urban markets, supermarkets and events such as the prickly pear festival.

APPENDIX

RECIPES ADAPTED FROM
WINNIE LOUW, *PRICKLY PEAR: DON'T ABUSE IT, USE IT*

Be careful when handling any part of the prickly pear. Pick fruit with gloves, put them on the grass or cloth, brush the glochids off the fruits, then soak them in water. If you are eating them fresh, top and tail then cut into quarters and peel back the skin, preferably with a knife. Do not put the fruit to your mouth until it is properly peeled. Use gloves and a knife to scrape and cut the young cladodes for nopalitos.

You can grow prickly pear as a pot plant in northern Europe and it can be taken out of doors for the summer months. It will supply a few small cladodes for salad, but these do not grow as quickly or as big as in semi-arid or Mediterranean climates. It is unlikely to fruit indoors.

WINNIE LOUW ON PRICKLY PEAR

'The prickly pear has always fascinated me, even since I was a child. I grew up in the Graaff-Reinet area, where the prickly pear grew in abundance. As children, staying far away from town, there was no shop to buy sweets and we had to look [to it] amongst other things ... to supply us with that something to chew during the long, cold winter months. We [made] all our pocket money by selling prickly pears, which we picked ourselves, and polished them with a soft cloth till they shone like apples. ... We, as children, got our share of fruit to peel for ourselves for "dates", our own sweets for the winter. When my mum [Margaret Turner] had enough syrup ready we could make our dates'.

For the book she 'used recipes my mum used, and also received some from other people'. She thanked Zimmermann: 'he did wonders for the prickly pear, trying to bring it home to people that it is food and not a weed'.

PRICKLY PEAR CAKE

(a version of this was made for the Uitenhage festival, 2005)

Ingredients

250 ml white flour (or put in 20 per cent wholemeal)

5 ml mixed spice or cinnamon

10 ml baking powder

Pinch of salt

3 eggs

150 ml sugar (or less if you don't like it too sweet)

50 ml cooking oil or margarine

30 ml water

lemon or vanilla essence

30 ml chopped nuts

250 ml chopped prickly pear fruit. If you can take out some or all of the pips this will improve the eating, but this is time consuming and the Uitenhage festival version left the pips in.

Method

Mix the flour, spices, nuts and baking powder. Pour the water on the sugar, beat and then add the oil. Beat until smooth. Add eggs one by one, beating as you go. Add essence and prickly pear and mix well with the dry ingredients. Spoon the mix into two greased circular cake tins and bake for about 40 mins at 180°C. Leave to cool before turning out on a cake rack or board. Use jam or icing with cream cheese and nuts between the two layers of the cake. It can also be made in bread tins.

PRICKLY PEAR JAM

Ingredients

1 kg peeled and chopped prickly pear

375 gm sugar (or less if you prefer it less sweet)

250 ml water

Juice of one lemon or half a lemon finely chopped.

One teaspoon chopped fresh ginger (optional).

Method

Cook prickly pear in a little water (you can do without the water as long as you start it very slowly and are careful not to burn it) in a large covered saucepan for about 30 minutes. Take off heat. Add sugar, lemon and ginger if using. Stir to ensure sugar is dissolved, then turn up heat and boil for about 15-20 minutes until it thickens, the fruit looks clear and it gels when you place a drop on a cool plate.

Chutneys can be made using similar recipes to apple chutney.

PRICKLY PEAR BEER (WITHOUT MULA)
Ingredients and method
Peel fruit and add 100 ml of water to 1 kg of fruit. Cook for an hour until it is a pulp, then strain through a muslin cloth or sieve. Add 25 gm sugar and a teaspoon of fresh yeast for one litre of juice. Leave in a covered bowl until it starts to ferment. Bottle and cool it in the fridge. Drink soon.

NOPALITOS SALAD
Use only fresh small cladodes before the glochids and spines have formed. Scrape any buds off and lightly scrape the whole cladode. Slice thinly and blanch for a couple of minutes in boiling water, wash under cold water then blanch again and wash again. This diminishes the rather glutinous quality of the moisture in the cladodes. Marinade for a couple of hours in a mix of 2 tablespoons wine vinegar, 2 tablespoons water, 1 teaspoon sugar, a pinch of salt, dry mustard, pepper, finely sliced red onion or shallot and finely chopped garlic. (Best of all, crush the garlic, dry mustard, pepper and salt together with a spoon into a paste first, then mix well with the vinegar and add the other ingredients.)

Add one sliced tomato, half a red pepper, a sliced apple and oil. Add green leaves, cucumber and roasted nuts such as walnuts if desired.

Fruits as well as nopalitos can be added to a very wide range of savory and sweet salads. You can buy preserved, bottled nopalitos which are not dissimilar to bottled gherkins.

NOPALITOS COOKED IN SAUCE
Clean, cut and blanch napolitos as above.

Saute onions (and chopped bacon if desired), add nopalitos (and optionally lightly boiled potatoes) and cook for a couple of minutes. Place in a baking dish. To make a cheese sauce, melt margarine or butter over a low heat and add a small amount of flour stirring continuously. Have some milk, water or stock on hand to add immediately, stirring all the time to get a smooth sauce. Add dry mustard, salt and pepper and grated cheese and when it is amalgamated and off the heat, some yoghurt. Pour over the nopalitos, add some breadcrumbs and bake.

Onion and tomato sauce with nopalitos is also tasty.

ENDNOTES

INTRODUCTION

1   Park S. Nobel, *Remarkable Agaves and Cacti* (Oxford University Press, New York, 1994); Park
     S. Nobel, *Environmental Biology of Agaves and Cacti* (Cambridge University Press, Cambridge,
     1988); Arthur C. Gibson and Park S. Nobel, *The Cactus Primer* (Harvard University Press,
     Cambridge, Mass., 1986).

2   R.A. Donkin, *Spanish Red: An Ethnogeographical Study of Cochineal and the Opuntia Cactus*
     (American Philosophical Society, Philadelphia, 1977).

3   Xhosa has many loan words from Afrikaans and they are sometimes adaptations rather than
     very close renditions. A. Kropf and R. Godfrey, *A Kafir-English Dictionary* (Lovedale Mission
     Press, Lovedale, 1915), which is by far the best dictionary for this period, records *itolofiya*
     (plural *iitolofiya*) as a translation of *turksvy*. This link is also made in the earlier 1899 edition
     (Lovedale Mission Press, 1899), p. 396 and in I. Bud-Mbelle, *A Kafir Scholar's Companion*
     (Lovedale, 1903), p. 34. It is worth pointing out, however, that the Xhosa noun *utolo* (class 5)
     means an arrow and another noun *umtolo* (class 6) refers to a type of indigenous thorny acacia.
     There may have been some cross-referencing to these words when the plant was first named.

4   National Archives, Pretoria, Department of Agriculture (LDB) 1711, R2846, vol. II, F.W. Pettey
     to Chief: Division of Plant Industry, 4.7.1932, 'Report of Tour of Inspection of Jointed Cactus and
     Prickly Pear Areas in the Cape Province Eastern Districts, June 5-19, 1932'.

5   William Beinart, *The Rise of Conservation in South Africa: Settlers, Livestock and the
     Environment, 1770-1950* (Oxford University Press, Oxford, 2003).

6   F.W. Pettey, 'The Biological Control of Prickly Pears in South Africa', *Union of South Africa,
     Department of Agriculture and Forestry, Scientific Bulletin*, 271 (Government Printer, Pretoria, 1948)
     is an extended analysis by the key entomologist involved. D.P. Annecke and V.C. Moran, 'Critical
     reviews of biological pest control in South Africa: 2. The Prickly Pear, *Opuntia ficus-indica* (L.)
     Miller', *Journal of the Entomological Society of South Africa*, 41, 2 (1978), pp. 161-88.

7   Marc O. Brutsch and Helmuth G. Zimmermann, 'The Prickly Pear (Opuntia Ficus-Indica
     [Cactaceae]) in South Africa: Utilization of the Naturalized Weed, and of the Cultivated
     Plant', *Economic Botany*, 47, 2 (1993), pp. 154-62.

8   David M. Richardson and Brian W. van Wilgen, 'Invasive Alien Plants in South Africa: How
     Well Do We Understand the Ecological Impacts?' *South African Journal of Science*, 100 (2004),
     p. 45.

9   Peter Coates, *American Perceptions of Immigrant and Invasive Species: Strangers on the Land*
     (University of California Press, Berkeley, 2007) for a lively discussion of cultural perceptions of
     invasive species.

10   James McCann, *Maize and Grace: Africa's Encounter with a New World Crop 1500-2000*
     (Harvard University Press, Cambridge, Mass., 2005).

11   Peter Coates, *American Perceptions of Immigrant and Invasive Species: Strangers on the Land*
     (University of California Press, Berkeley, 2006).

12   A.P. Dold and M.L. Cocks, 'The Medicinal Use of Some Weeds, Problem and Alien Plants
     in the Grahamstown and Peddie Districts of the Eastern Cape, South Africa', *South African
     Journal of Science*, 96 (2000), pp. 467-73.

13   M.P. de Wit, D.J. Crookes and B.W. van Wilgen, 'Conflicts of interest in environmental management: estimating the costs and benefits of a tree invasion', *Biological Invasions*, 3 (2001), pp. 167-78.

14   A. de Neergaard, C. Saarnak, T. Hill, M. Khanyile, A.M. Berzosa and T. Birch-Thomsen, 'Australian wattle species in the Drakensberg region of South Africa – an invasive alien or a natural resource?', *Agricultural Systems*, 85, 3 (2005), pp. 216-233.

15   Karen Middleton, 'The Ironies of Plant Transfer: The Case of Prickly Pear in Madagascar', in W. Beinart and J. McGregor (eds.), *Social History and African Environments* (James Currey, Oxford, 2003), pp. 43-59; W. Beinart and K. Middleton, 'Plant Transfers in Historical Perspective: A Review Article', *Environment and History*, 10, 1 (2004), pp. 3-29.

16   Brutsch and Zimmermann, 'The Prickly Pear (Opuntia Ficus-Indica [Cactaceae]) in South Africa'.

17   Nobel, *Remarkable Agaves and Cacti*.

18   Amy Butler Greenfield, *A Perfect Red: Empire, Espionage and the Quest for the Colour of Desire* (Black Swan, London, 2006).

19   Michelle Cocks, *Wild Resources and Cultural Practices in Rural and Urban Households in South Africa* (Institute of Social and Economic Research, Rhodes University, Grahamstown, 2006).

CHAPTER I

1   Recent estimates of population are between about 60,000 and 78,000. In view of the scale of building of new RDP houses, the population may be higher. The 2001 census gave 128,619 for Nkonkobe municipality as a whole.

2   We first interviewed Nowinile Ngcengele together for a few hours on 16 April 2004 at Bhofolo, Fort Beaufort. We returned in 2005 and visited again in subsequent years.

3   Anders Sparrman, *A Voyage to the Cape of Good Hope towards the Antarctic Polar Circle Round the World and to the Country of the Hottentots and the Caffres from the Year 1772-1776*, edited by V.S. Forbes (van Riebeeck Society, Cape Town, 1977), vol. 2, p. 260.

4   Kenneth Wyndham Smith, 'From Frontier to Midlands: A History of the Graaff-Reinet District, 1786-1910', Occasional Paper, no. 20, Institute of Social and Economic Research, Rhodes University (Grahamstown, 1976), p. 188.

5   Cape of Good Hope, Parliamentary Papers, A.9-1891, *Report of the Select Committee on the Prickly Pear*, p. 20ff.; A.C. MacDonald, 'Prickly Pear in South Africa', reprinted in the *Agricultural Journal of the Cape of Good Hope*, 30.7.1891.

6   Cape of Good Hope, Parliamentary Papers, G.3-1894, *Labour Commission, vol. II, Minutes of Evidence and Proceedings*, evidence of J.H. Smith, MLA Graaff-Reinet, 16.12.1893, 670, 22543. Thanks to Anne Mager for directing us to this source.

7   Ibid., evidence of P.B. Botha, 2.12.1893, 506, 19512.

8   C.F. Juritz, 'Kafir Beers: Their Nature and Composition', *Agricultural Journal of the Cape of Good Hope*, 28 (1906), pp. 35-47 and *The Prickly Pear (Opuntia). Possibilities of its Utilization* (Government Printer, Pretoria, 1920), Industrial Bulletin Series, 65, reprinted from the *South African Journal of Industries* (August and September, 1920).

9   A. Kropf, *A Kafir-English Dictionary*, second edition, edited by Robert Godfrey (Lovedale Mission Press, Lovedale, 1915). Juritz recorded other spellings and pronounciations such as *dante, dande, dantie* and *dyante*. The origins of this word are unclear; Kropf and Godfrey usually state whether a word is borrowed from English or Afrikaans/Dutch.

10   Interview with Nosakhumzi and Velile Jacobs, Bhofolo, 7 March 2005.

11   Monica Hunter, *Reaction to Conquest: Effects of Contact with Europeans on the Pondo of South Africa* (Oxford University Press, London, 1936, 1964) p. 523; University of Cape Town Archives, Godfrey and Monica Wilson papers, BC880, additional box 3, files entitled Farms, 2 and 3.

12   Monica Hunter, 'The Bantu on European-owned Farms' in Isaac Schapera (ed.), *The Bantu-Speaking Tribes of South Africa* (Routledge and Kegan Paul, London, 1937), pp. 389-404.

13   Margaret Roberts, *Labour in the Farm Economy* (South African Institute of Race Relations, Johannesburg, 1958), p. 72.

14   Interview Nothobile Ludziya, 17 April 2004, Bhofolo, Fort Beaufort.

15   Interview Nowinile Ngcengele, 16 April 2004, Bhofolo, Fort Beaufort.

16   Interview Jacobs; Interview Ngcengele.

17   Interview Nomphumelelo Lolwana and Nothobile Ludziya, 17 April 2004, Bhofolo, Fort Beaufort.

18   Interview, John Mildenhall, 6 March 2005, Fort Beaufort.

19   Interview, Andre Danckwerts, Kluklu farm, 26 March 2006, Fort Beaufort.

20   Interview, P. le Roux, Koedoeskloof farm, 25 March 2006, Fort Beaufort.

21   Interview, Rob Sparks, 8 March 2005, Fort Beaufort.

22   The farm is a municipal property called Uniondale.

23   Interview, Ngcengele.

24   Interview, Mildenhall.

25   Interview and picking trip, Nowinile Ngcengele and others, 3 March 2005.

26   Interview and picking trip, Ngcengele and others.

27   Interview, Nowinile Ngcengele and Nositile Lungisa, 16 April 2004.

28   Although they used a particular species, Kropf and Godfrey gives the meaning of this word as 'small twigs with green leaves', or 'herbs' suggesting that it could be a variety of different species. The term is also used more broadly to refer to the branches picked from any suitable plant for sweeping.

29   Interview, Ngcengele and Lungisa, 16 April 2004.

30   One mentioned R200 if all the fruits were undamaged.

31   Interview, Alice Ningiza and Nocingile Platyi, 22 and 23 June 2003, Bhofolo, Fort Beaufort.

32   Interview and observation, brewing party, 4 March 2005, Bhofolo township.

33   We heard from Ludzila and Lolwana that they did not peel the fruits first, but chopped them.

34   At present we don't know which specific species was being used in Fort Beaufort. Tony Dold, Michelle Cocks and Patricia Kralo, 'Iqilika: Mesmb beer of the Eastern Cape', *Aloe*, 36, 2&3 (1999), pp. 52-4 record four species being used for honey beer in Grahamstown area: *Trichodiadema barbatum, T. stellatum, T. stelligerum* and *T. intonsum*.

35   Juritz, 'Kafir Beers', pp. 45-6.

36   Interview, Garth Cambray, Old Power Station mead factory, Grahamstown, 6 June 2006.

37   Gerrit Harinck, 'Interaction between Xhosa and Khoi: Emphasis on the Period 1620-1750' in L. Thompson (ed.), *African Societies in Southern Africa* (Heinemann, London, 1969), pp. 145-70; J.B. Peires, *The House of Phalo: A History of the Xhosa People in the Days of their Independence* (Ravan Press, Johannesburg, 1981).

38   Interview, Jikela Ndikila, Rietfontein farm, Fort Beaufort, 30 August 2006; thanks to Andre Danckwerts for the introduction. Interview Zintombi Zabo, Grahamstown, 6 April 2006.

39   Interview, Nosakela Mbovane, brewing party, 4 March 2005, Bhofolo township.

40   Interview, Nolast Mkhontwane, Merino farm, 28 September 2005, Fort Beaufort.

41   Trip to Adelaide with Nowinile Ngcengele and Nositile Lungisa, 2 April 2006.

42   Interview, Mbovane.

43   Interview, Ndikile.

44   Interview, Mbovane.

45   Interview, Zabo.

46   Juritz, 'Kafir Beers'; Ben-Erik van Wyk and Nigel Gericke, *People's Plants: A Guide to Useful Plants of Southern Africa* (Briza, Pretoria, 2000).

47   Interview, Nowinile Ngcengele and others, Fort Beaufort, 5 March 2005. The term *ivanya* appears in Kropf to mean the dregs of beer with water added so it has clearly been in use for a century.

48   Interview, Zabo.

49   Interview, Ndikila.

50   Interview, Ningiza and Platyi.

51   Interview, Ngcengele, 16 April 2004.

52   Dold, Cocks and Kralo, 'Iqilika: Mesmb beer of the Eastern Cape'; Interview, Zabo.

53   Participant observation of brewing, and interview with Nowinile Ngcengele and Nosakela Mbovane, 1 April 2006.

54   Interview, Cambray.

55   Interview, Sergeant Khanyisa Memani, Fort Beaufort Police Station, 14 November 2006.

56   Interview, Ningiza and Platyi.

57   Interview, Ningiza and Platyi.

58   Interview, Memani.

59   Interview, Memani.

60   Interview, Zabo.

61   David Kirby, 'Invasive Alien Plants – Friend or Foe: A Study Investigating the Contribution of the Prickly Pear (*Opuntia ficus-indica*) trade to Community Livelihoods in Makana Municipality, South Africa', unpublished honours dissertation, Rhodes University (2005).

62   Interview, Mildenhall.

63   Kirby, 'Invasive Alien Plants'.

64   Interview, Mncedisi Tsotsa, Fort Beaufort, 8 March 2005.

65   Interview Mbovane.

66   Interview, Tsotsa.

67   Interview, Sparks.

68   Interview, N. Mkhontwane.

69   Interview M. Mkhontwane, Merino farm, Fort Beaufort, 28 September 2005.

CHAPTER 2

1   I.A.W. Macdonald, F.J. Kruger and A.A. Ferrar (eds.), *The Ecology and Management of Biological Invasions in Southern Africa* (Oxford University Press, Cape Town, 1986); Lance van Sittert, '"The Seed Blows about in Every Breeze": Noxious Weed Eradication in the Cape Colony, 1860-1909', *Journal of South African Studies*, 26, 4 (2000), pp. 655-74.

2   A. Appel, 'Die Geskiedenis van Houtvoorsiening aan die Kaap, 1652-1795', unpublished M.A. dissertation, University of Stellenbosch (1966).

3   Carl Peter Thunberg, *Travels at the Cape of Good Hope 1772-1775*, edited by V. S. Forbes (van Riebeeck Society, Cape Town, 1986), p. 320.

4   G. Barbera, 'History, Economic and Agro-Ecological Importance' in G. Barbera, P. Inglese and E. Pimienta-Barrios (eds.), *Agro-ecology, Cultivation and Uses of Cactus Pear* (FAO, Rome, 1995) Plant Production and Protection Paper, 132, 1.

5   Greenfield, *A Perfect Red*, p. 63.

6   Greenfield, *A Perfect Red*, pp. 110ff.

7   Personal observation, William Beinart.

8   Donkin, *Spanish Red*, p. 40.

9   M.J. Wells, R.J. Poynton, A.A. Balsinhas, K.J. Musil, H. Joffe, E. van Hoepen and S.K. Abbott, 'The History of Invasive Alien Plants to Southern Africa', in Macdonald, Kruger and Ferrar (eds.), *Biological Invasions in Southern Africa*, pp. 21-35.

10   Richard H. Grove, *Green Imperialism: Colonial Expansion, Tropical Island Edens and the Origins of Environmentalism* (Cambridge: Cambridge University Press, 1995).

11   Interviews, Gerhard de Kock, Middelburg, 31 March 2006 and 3 April 2006.

12   Peter Kolbe, *The Present State of the Cape of Good-Hope* (W. Innys, London, 1731), first published in German in 1719. The French edition of 1743 is a little more detailed.

13   Kolbe, *The Present State of the Cape of Good-Hope*, vol. 2, p. 260.

14   Robert Percival, *An Account of the Cape of Good Hope* (C. and B. Baldwin, London, 1804), pp. 62, 142-3.

15   A.9-1891, pp. 20ff., A.C. MacDonald, 'Prickly Pear in South Africa'. Carl Peter Thunberg, *Flora Capensis* (Gerhardum Bonnierum, Hafniae, 1818), p. 26. This has a list of cultivated plants at the Cape which draws on sources additional to his travels; Thunberg, *Travels at the Cape of Good Hope 1772-1775*.

16   Percival, *An Account of the Cape of Good Hope*, pp. 62, 142-3.

17   Lucie Duff Gordon, *Letters from the Cape*, (Project Gutenberg ebook, on web). She visited the Cape from 1860-1862.

18   Elinor G.K. Mellville, *A Plague of Sheep: Environmental Consequences of the Conquest of Mexico* (New York: Cambridge University Press, 1994).

19   Nobel, *Environmental Biology*, p. 35.

20   Nobel, *Remarkable Agaves and Cacti*, p. 58.

21   Smith, *From Frontier to Midlands;* Susan Newton-King, *Masters and Servants on the Cape Eastern Frontier* (Cambridge University Press, Cambridge, 1999).

22   Sparrman, *A Voyage to the Cape of Good Hope Voyage*, vol. 2, p. 260.

23   James Backhouse, *Narrative of a Visit to the Mauritius and South Africa* (Hamilton, Adams, London, 1844), pp. 123, 226, 489. Thanks to Marco Brutsch for the reference.

24   Gibson and Nobel, *The Cactus Primer*, pp. 18ff.

25   MacDonald, 'Prickly Pear in South Africa'. He was given the reference by the botanist Peter MacOwan (see below).

26   Pettey, 'The Biological Control of Prickly Pears'; Department of Agriculture and Forestry, Weeds Section, '*Opuntias* in South Africa', *Farming in South Africa*, March 1940, pp. 119-25 and E.B. Phillips, 'Some Species of *Opuntia* Cultivated or Naturalized in South Africa', Ibid., pp. 125-8. The latter suggested that *O. Megacantha* may have been a parent of *O. ficus-indica*.

27   Backhouse, Narrative of a Visit.

28   Cape of Good Hope, 'Appendix of the Report of the Geological Surveyor presented to Parliament

in June, 1859', by Andrew Wylie.

29   Greenfield, *A Perfect Red*, pp. 241ff.

30   G.23-1864, *Report of the Colonial Botanist for the Year 1863*, pp. 26-8: letter from John C. Brown to Mr. Titterton, Kracha Kama, on the cultivation of the Prickly Pear, with a view to the preparation of Cochineal, 12 January1864.

31   A sketch by Baines of Cradock in 1844 seems to show a few prickly pear plants on the left but they are a little indistinct. See Joan Collett, *A Time to Plant* (Katkop, Fish River, South Africa, 1990), p. 83; Thomas Baines, *Journal of a Residence in South Africa, 1842-1853*, edited by R.F. Kennedy (van Riebeeck Society, Cape Town, 1961-4), vol. 1, p. 37 and vol. 2, p. 190.

32   MacDonald *et al*. (eds.), p. 143.

33   W.A. Maxwell and R.T. McGeogh (eds.), *The Reminiscences of Thomas Stubbs* (A.A. Balkema, Cape Town, 1977), p. 166.

34   A.29-1898, *Report of the Select Committee on Eradication of Prickly Pear*, evidence R.P. Botha, 19.

35   Information from 1:250,000 topocadastral map. Introduced as well as indigenous plant names were used for farms. Poplar Grove, after the tree planted by many English-speaking farmers to hold stream banks, is another example.

36   A.9-1891, 13: evidence B.J.Keyter, MLA Oudtshoorn.

37   A.9-1891, 2.

38   A.9-1891, 14: evidence, B.J. Keyter. G.3-1890, 23: evidence, J.O. Norton MLA.

39   C.3-1890, *Eradication of Prickly Pear and Poisonous Melkbosch*, Select Committee of the Legislative Council, evidence, G.M. Palmer.

40   Interview, P.W. Roux, Middelburg, 2003.

41   C.J. Skead, 'A Study of Black Crow, *Corvus capensis*', *Ibis*, 94, 3 (1952), pp. 434-51.

42   W.R.J. Dean and S.J. Milton, 'Directed dispersal of Opuntia species in the Karoo, South Africa: Are Crows the Responsible Agents?', *Journal of Arid Environments*, 45 (2000), pp. 305-14.

43   Interview, Gladman Tilasi, Mvubu Lodge, Great Fish River Conservation Area, 6 March 2005.

44   Jane M. Meiring, *Sundays River Valley: Its History and Settlement* (A.A. Balkema, Cape Town, 1959), p. 88; M.T. Hoffman, 'Major P.J. Pretorius and the Decimation of the Addo Elephant Herd in 1919-20: Important Reassessments', *Koedoe*, 36, 2 (1993), pp. 23-44.

45   S. Zuckerman, *The Social Life of Monkeys and Apes* (Routledge and Kegan Paul, London, 1981), pp. 195-6. First edition with same text published in 1932.

46   Interview, Roux.

47   Eve Palmer, *The Plains of the Camdeboo* (Fontana, London, 1974), p. 151.

48   George P. Foley, 'The "Baboon Boy" of South Africa', *Science*, 91, 2360 (1940), pp. 291-2 and extended version 'The "Baboon Boy" of South Africa', *American Journal of Psychology*, 53, 1 (1940), p. 128. He later cast doubt on the idea that the boy had been captured from baboons in *Science*, 91, 2374 (1940), pp. 618-9.

49   Interview Tony Jones, The Grange, Rooidraai, Hankey South-East, 13 April 2002.

50   Mary Elizabeth Barber, 'Wanderings in South Africa by Sea and Land, 1879', *Quarterly Bulletin of the South African Public Library*, 17, 2 (1962), pp. 45-6; William Beinart, 'Men, Travel, Science and Nature in the Eighteenth and Nineteenth Century Cape', *Journal of South African Studies*, 24, 4 (1998), pp. 775-99.

51   Pretoria Archives, TAB, Accession A1570, J.F.D. Winter, 'True Stories of Life and Hunting in Sekukuniland in the Old Days'. Reference and information from Peter Delius.

52   Peter Delius, *The Land Belongs to Us* (Heinemann, London, 1983), pp. 68-9.

53   P.J. Quin, *Foods and Feeding Habits of the Pedi* (Witwatersrand University Press, Johannesburg, 1959), p. 91.

54   Joseph Burtt-Davy, 'The Prickly Pear in the Transvaal', *Transvaal Agricultural Journal*, January (1907), pp. 450-2. This article also mentions the story of the Swazi invasion and may be its source.

55   National Archives, Pretoria, Department of Agriculture, PTA LDB 1712 R2846, vol. IV, Pole-Evans – notes.

56   Marie Coetzee, 'Flight for Freedom: Kotie Steenkamp's Story of the South African War', (University of South Africa, Pretoria, UNISA online).

57   Alfred de Jager Jackson, *Manna in the Desert: A Revelation of the Great Karroo* (Christian Literature Depot, Johannesburg, no date, c.1920?), p. 298. On p. 103 he mentions, 'As I write this June month of 1919'. He was a child in the Great Karroo in the 1860s. Thanks to Hugh Macmillan for the reference.

58   Jackson, *Manna in the Desert*, pp. 144-5. He misidentifies the 'Gaap' or 'Ghaap', an indigenous species of Hoodia eaten by the Khoikhoi, as a type of cactus. It is still sometimes referred to as a cactus.

59   Jackson, *Manna in the Desert*, p. 145.

60   Mrs Carey Hobson, *The Farm in the Karoo* (Juta, Heelis, 1883), p. 269.

61   C. Louis Leipoldt, *Gallows Gecko* in *The Valley: A Trilogy* (Stormberg, Cape Town, 2001), pp. 48, 112, written but not published in the early 1930s.

62   C. Louis Leipoldt, *Leipoldt's Cape Cookery* (W.J. Flesch, Cape Town, 1983), p. 146.

63   *Imvo Zabantsundu*, 16 May 1888. Reference from Helen Bradford.

64   Helen Bradford to William Beinart, 10 May 2007, enclosing poem Tolofiya Melit[a]fa transcribed from W.B. Rubusana, Zemk'inkomo Magwaladini (Butler and Tanner, London, 1911), p. 467.

65   *Umteteli wa Bantu*, 21 June 1924. Reference from Jeff Opland.

66   Smith, *Frontier to Midlands*, p. 188.

67   A.9-1891, 13: evidence B.J. Keyter MLA; C.3-1890, evidence, P.H. du Plessis, MLC, an Oudtshoorn farmer. His use of blacks is interesting, and unusual at the time, although it may have been a translation.

68   Norah Massey Pitman, 'The Peoples of Graaff-Reinet and District', *Lantern: Journal of Knowledge and Culture*, 35, 2 (1986), p. 29.

69   A.29-1898, 41-2.

70   National Library of South Africa, Cape Town, photographic collections, 182, Cradock Place Album, 22342.

71   Nerina Mathie, *Atherstone W. G., Man of Many Facets*, vol. 3 (Personal publication, Grahamstown, 1997), photos following page 984, number v. 212.

72   E.L. and R.J. van Reenen, *Op Trek* (Het Volksblad, Bloemfontein, 1917).

73   John L. Comaroff, Jean Comaroff and Deborah James (eds.), *Picturing a Colonial Past: The African Photographs of Isaac Schapera* (University of Chicago Press, Chicago, 2007), pp. 108, 158.

CHAPTER 3

1   Ernst Mayer, 'On the Geographical Distribution of Plants in South Africa' based on notes by J.F. Drege and translated with notes by H. Bolus, *Cape Monthly Magazine*, vol. 8 (1874), p. 57.

2   *Kew Bulletin*, 1888, p. 166.

3   John Noble, *Descriptive Handbook of the Cape Colony: Its Conditions and Resources* (J.C. Juta,

Cape Town, 1875), p. 153. For details of this network of botanists and writers see Beinart, *Rise of Conservation*, Chapter 3.

4   A.8-1906, 6: evidence, Duncan Hutcheon, Acting Director of Agriculture.

5   Kenneth Wyndham Smith, *From Frontier to Midlands: A History of the Graaff-Reinet District, 1786-1910*, Occasional Paper, no. 20, Institute of Social and Economic Research, Rhodes University (Grahamstown, 1976), p. 188.

6   Smith, *From Frontier to Midlands*, p. 243.

7   Smith, *From Frontier to Midlands*, p. 230.

8   A.29-1898, 8, 13: evidence, M.J. du Plessis, MLA, Cradock.

9   Annie Martin, *Home Life on an Ostrich Farm* (George Philip, London, 1890), pp. 54-5.

10   C.3-1890, *Eradication of Prickly Pear and Poisonous Melkbosch*, Select Committee of the Legislative Council, viii.

11   C.3-1890, 7, evidence, George Palmer, President of the Zwart Ruggens Farmers Association.

12   C.3-1890, viii.

13   Chas. F. Juritz, *The Prickly Pear (Opuntia): Possibilities of its Utilization* (Government Printer, Pretoria, 1920), p. 5.

14   C.3-1890, 7, evidence, George Palmer.

15   Cape of Good Hope, G.1-1890, *Report of the Liquor Laws Commission*, 1889-90, pp. 291, 297.

16   These concerns are extensively recorded in the Cape of Good Hope, G.1-1890, *Report of the Liquor Laws Commission, 1889-90;* G.3-1894, *Labour Commission*. See also, P.A. McAllister, 'Indigenous Beer in Southern Africa', *African Studies* , 52, 1 (1993), pp. 72-88; Bertram Hutchinson, 'Alcohol as a Contributing Factor in Social Disorganization: the South African Bantu in the Nineteenth Century' in Mac Marshall (ed.), *Beliefs, Behaviors and Alcoholic Beverages: A Cross-cultural Survey* (University of Michigan Press, Ann Arbor, 1979), pp. 328-40; Wallace G. Mills. 'The Roots of African Nationalism in the Cape Colony: Temperance, 1866-1898', *The International Journal of African Historical Studies*, 13, 2 (1980), pp. 197-213.

17   Interview Gerhard de Kock, Middelburg, 31 March 2006.

18   G.3-1894, 576, 20805.

19   Charles van Onselen, 'Randlords and Rotgut, 1886-1903' in *Studies in the Social and Economic History of the Witwatersrand 1886-1914*, vol. 1, *New Babylon* (Longman, Harlow, 1982).

20   C.3-1890, 25, evidence, J.O. Norton, MLA, who farmed near the Fish.

21   MacDonald, 'Prickly Pear'.

22   A.29-1898, iv.

23   A.29-1898, 39, evidence, Charles Lee.

24   Colin Bundy, 'Vagabond Hollanders and Runaway Englishmen: White Poverty in the Cape before Poor Whiteism' in William Beinart, Peter Delius and Stanley Trapido (eds.), *Putting a Plough to the Ground* (Ravan Press, Johannesburg, 1986), pp. 101-28, see p.111.

25   A.8-1906, 56, evidence, J.J. Vosloo.

26   *Agricultural Journal of the Cape of Good Hope*, 2.7.1891, p. 246: 'Resume of Paper on the Prickly Pear (Opuntia Vulgaris) and its Eradication, read by Mr. A.L. Grobbelaar before "The Cradock Farmers' Association"' , June 6, 1891.

27   A.9-1891, *Report of the Select Committee on the Prickly Pear*, 5.

28   Mayer, 'On the Geographical Distribution of Plants'.

29   A.8-1906, *Report of the Select Committee on the Prickly Pear*, 16: evidence, Dr. Rupert Marloth.

30   C.3-1890, p. 4.

31   *Kew Bulletin*, 1888, p. 168.

32   W. Beinart, 'Transhumance, Animal Diseases and Environment in the Cape, South Africa', *South African Historical Journal*, 58 (2007), pp. 17-41.

33   *Agricultural Journal*, XI, 4, 19.8.1897, P. MacOwan, 'A Plea for the Pricklies', pp. 158-62.

34   *Agricultural Journal*, 14, 12, 8.6.1899, G.M., 'The Much Abused Prickly Pear', p. 817.

35   *Kew Bulletin*, 1888, p. 167.

36   *The New York Times*, 5 January 1879.

37   Mathie, *Atherstone*, p. 1055.

38   *Agricultural Journal*, XIV, 12, 8 June 1899.

39   A.8-1906, p. 41.

40   A.29-1898, 14: evidence, G. Wilhelm.

41   *Agricultural Journal*, XVI, 1, 4 January 1900, p. 52.

42   A.9-1891, p. 18.

43   A.9-1891, 16: evidence P.J. du Toit, MLA, Richmond and 18, A.S. le Roux, MLA for Victoria West.

44   A.9-1891, 7, evidence, E.R. Hobson.

45   PTA LDB 1263, R1688, vol. VIII, Sidney Rubidge, Wellwood, to Minister of Agriculture, 8.11.1947 enclosing memo on 'Spineless Cactus on Wellwood'.

46   A.9-1891, 15, evidence P.J. du Toit, quoting a letter in Dutch from 'Mr Vosloo'.

47   A.29-1898, 41, evidence, Charles George Lee, MLA and secretary of the Zwart Ruggens Farmers Association.

48   PTA LDB 1250, R1592, Prickly Pear Commercial Value of: Mrs. Hannah L. Brown, 'The Prickly Pear: A Source of Wealth for the Union'.

49   PTA LDB 1250, R1592, E. Cawood, Bulawayo, to R.W. Thornton, 29 June 1926.

50   PTA LDB 1250 R1592, cutting from *Die Burger*, 13 August 1923.

51   A.8-1906, 51, evidence J.J. Vosloo, Somerset East.

52   Grobbelaar, 'The Prickly Pear', 246; C.3-1890, 5, evidence R.P. Botha MLC.

53   C.3-1890, 25: evidence P.H. du Plessis MLC.

54   Cape Archives, Department of Agriculture (CA AGR) 74, F244 ff. cutting including House of Assembly debate, 27 July 1893.

55   C.3-1890, 13, evidence George Palmer; Davenport, *Afrikaner Bond*, pp. 6-7.

56   CA AGR 74, F244, cutting including Legislative Council and House of Assembly debates, 27 July 1893.

57   P. Lewsen, *Selections from the Correspondence of John X. Merriman, 1890-1898*, vol. 2 (van Riebeeck Society, Cape Town, 1963), pp. 114-5.

58   A.8-1906, 21ff.: evidence Dr. Rupert Marloth.

59   A.9-1891, 16: evidence P.J. du Toit, MLA, Richmond.

60   Felicity Wood and Michael Lewis, *The Extraordinary Khotso: Millionaire Medicine Man from Lusikisiki* (Jacana, Auckland Park, 2007). The book does not mention the hedge.

61   Dr. Eric A. Nobbs, 'Notes on the Prickly Pear', *Agricultural Journal*, November (1906), p. 637.

62   A.29-1898, 18ff.: evidence R.P. Botha.

63   A.9-1891, 42: evidence A. Fischer, Secretary of Agriculture.

64   CA AGR 74, F244 and following, report by A.C. MacDonald, 18 July 1891.

65   E.A. Nobbs, 'Experiments upon the Destruction of Prickly Pear, 1907, Final Report', *Agricultural Journal*, December, (1907), pp. 676-82.

66   C.3-1890, 12.

67   *Agricultural Journal*, 14 June 1894, 285, extract from A.C. MacDonald's report to the Secretary for Agriculture.

68   A.29-1898, appendix, i, memo by W. Hammond Tooke, 25 November 1898.

69   A29-1898, iv.

70   *Agricultural Journal*, 15, 8, 12.10.1899, 548: Eustace Pillans, Agricultural Assistant, 'Extirpation of Prickly Pear'.

71   A.8-1906, 10: evidence Dr Eric A. Nobbs, Agricultural Assistant.

72   A.8-1906, iv.

73   Nobbs, 'Notes on the Prickly Pear', p. 637.

74   V.C. Moran, 'Critical Reviews of Biological Pest Control in South Africa. 3. The Jointed Cactus, *Opuntia aurantiaca* Lindley', *Journal of the Entomological Society of South Africa*, 42, 2 (1979), pp. 299-329.

75   Dr. S. Schonland, 'The Jointed Cactus', *Journal of the Department of Agriculture*, IX, September (1924), p. 218.

76   *Agricultural Journal*, V, 7, 28.7.1892: A. Fischer (editor), 'New Cactus. (Prickly Pear.)', pp. 93-4; *Agricultural Journal*, 23 August 1894: John B. Bowker, 'Jointed Cactus' (Opuntia aurantiaca), p. 405. Here the Xhosa word is given as *injubalinie*. The meaning of the word is given in Kropf and Godfrey, *Kafir-English Dictionary*, p. 174 although there is no direct reference to jointed cactus here.

77   Eric Nobbs, 'Notes on the Jointed Cactus', *Agricultural Journal*, December, (1906) and 'Experiments upon the Destruction of the Prickly Pear, 1907', *Agricultural Journal*, December, (1907).

78   E.A. Nobbs. 'Experiments upon the Destruction of the Jointed Cactus, 1907', *Agricultural Journal*, March, (1908), pp. 341-6.

79   Cape Archives, Provincial Secretary, (CA PAS), 3/151 N42/2, Noel Janisch, Office of the Adminstrator to Acting Secretary of Agriculture, 29 April 1912.

80   CA PAS 3/151, N36, cutting, *Alice Times*, 19 February 1914: speech by 'Mr Coetzee', Cradock.

81   CA PAS 3/151, N42/2, O. Evans and P.M. Michau to Administrator, 3 November 1916.

82   CA PAS 3/124, N14/6.

83   CA PAS 3/150, N26, Government Chemical Laboratory to Provincial Secretary, 8 June 1918.

84   PTA LDB 1260, R1688, vol. 1, O.C. Roberts to Minister of Lands, 30 September 1919.

85   PTA LDB 1260, R1688, vol. 1, J.B. Grewar to Sec. Ag., 8 May 1925.

CHAPTER 4

1   William MacDonald, 'Agriculture in America', *Transvaal Agricultural Journal*, V, 18 January, (1907).

2   Joseph Burtt-Davy, *Utilizing Prickly Pear and Spineless Cactus: Their Value as Fodder for Live Stock* (Government Printer, Pretoria, 1921), Industrial Bulletin Series, 70, reprinted from the *South African Journal of Industries*, November, 1920; J. Burtt-Davy, 'The Prickly Pear in the Transvaal', *Transvaal Agricultural Journal*, 1907, pp. 450-52.

3   The Luther Burbank Company, *Luther Burbank's Spineless Cactus* (San Francisco, 1913), advertising catalogue on web.

4   John Whitson, Robert John and Henry Smith Williams (eds.), *Luther Burbank: His Methods and Discoveries and their Practical Application*, Volume VIII (1914), p. 173. On web, University

of Wisconsin Digital Collections http://digital.library.wisc.edu/1711.dl/HistSciTech. LutherBurbank.

5   Whitson, John and Williams, *Luther Burbank: His Methods*, p. 207.

6   Whitson, John and Williams, *Luther Burbank: His Methods*, p. 194.

7   William MacDonald, 'Agriculture in America', *Transvaal Agricultural Journal*, V, 18, January, (1907), p. 309

8   Whitson, John and Williams, *Luther Burbank: His Methods*, p. 249.

9   William MacDonald, 'Agriculture in America'.

10   Beinart, *Rise of Conservation*, Chapter 7.

11   *Transvaal Agricultural Journal*, VI (1907-8), p. 649.

12   *Agricultural Journal of the Union of South Africa*, III, 2 February 1912, p. 227: J. Lewis, 'Note on Burbank's Spineless Prickly Pear'.

13   PTA LDB 1713, R2846, vol. VI, F.W. Pettey to T.J. Naude, 26 January 1938.

14   PTA LDB 1713, R2846, vol. IV, F.W. Pettey, Uitenhage to Chief Entomologist, Pretoria, 26 January 1938.

15   PTA LDB 1040, R1194, Spineless Cactus.

16   *Journal of the Department of Agriculture*, II, 5 (May, 1921), 387-89; H.A. Melle, 'Spineless Cactus as a Fodder for Stock', *Journal of the Department of Agriculture*, III, 1 (July, 1921), pp. 68-79.

17   PTA LDB 1260, R1688, vol. 1, Department of Agriculture Weekly Advice service, 3 August 1925.

18   Chas. F. Juritz, *The Prickly Pear (Opuntia). Possibilities of its Utilization* (Government Printer, Pretoria, 1920), Industrial Bulletin Series, 65, reprinted from the *South African Journal of Industries* (August and September, 1920); Chas. F. Juritz, *Prickly Pear as a Fodder for Stock* (Government Printer, Pretoria, 1920), Union of South Africa, Department of Agriculture, Science Bulletin, 16 (1920).

19   Juritz, *The Prickly Pear (Opuntia)*; Juritz, *Prickly Pear as a Fodder*; Burtt-Davy, *Utilizing Prickly Pear*; A. Stead and E.N.S. Warren, *Prickly Pear: Its Value as a Fodder for Sheep in Droughts and in Ordinary Times* (Government Printer, Pretoria, 1922), Union of South Africa, Department of Agriculture, Bulletin no. 4 (1922).

20   Juritz, *The Prickly Pear*, p. 5.

21   Chas. F. Juritz, *Prickly Pear as a Fodder for Stock* (Government Printer, Pretoria, 1920), Union of South Africa, Department of Agriculture, Science Bulletin, 16, p. 7.

22   Beinart, *Rise of Conservation*, Chapter 7.

23   Stead and Warren, *Prickly Pear*.

24   Stead and Warren, *Prickly Pear*, p. 8.

25   A. Stead, 'Succulent Fodders, Vitamins, Prickly Pear', *Journal of the Department of Agriculture*, vol. VII, 2, (August, 1923), 122-30.

26   See also Nobel, *Remarkable Agaves and Cacti*.

27   PTA LDB 1554, R2457/1a, F.C. Smith and G.S. Mare, 'Prickly Pear as a Sheep Feed', 1930.

28   PTA LDB 1554, R2457/1a, F.C. Smith, Officer in Charge, 'Review of Graaff-Reinet Prickly Pear Experiments, March 1927-March 1928'.

29   PTA LDB 91, R40/84, 'Grootfontein Experiments'.

30   David Griffiths, 'Prickly Pear as a Stock Feed', *Farmers Bulletin* 1072, United States Department of Agriculture (Government Printing Office, Washington, 1928), 3.

31   PTA LDB 1250, R1592, copies of advertisements.

32   Karen Middleton, 'Who Killed "Malagasy Cactus"? Science, Environment and Colonialism in Southern Madagascar (1924-1930)', *Journal of Southern African Studies*, 25, 2 (1999), pp. 215-48; Middleton, 'The Ironies of Plant Transfer'.

33   Beinart, *Rise of Conservation*; Richard Rubidge, *The Merino on Wellwood: Four Generations* (Private Publication, Graaff-Reinet, 1979).

34   Rubidge papers, Colin Desmond Hobson, 'Environmental and Socio-Economic Effects associated with the Planting of *Atriplex mummularia Lindl.* (Oldman Saltbush) in the Karoo', unpublished M.Sc., Rhodes University (1990) – research done partly on Wellwood. Richard Rubidge, *The Merino*, 22.

35   Rubidge files, 'Spineless cactus' file, sheet on 'List of camps on Wellwood and carrying capacity', 12 August 1933.

36   *Agricultural Journal of the Cape of Good Hope*, 2 July 1891, p. 246 and 30 July 1891, p. 21.

37   Rubidge Diary, note pinned to diary page, 21 April 1927.

38   Rubidge files, 'Spineless cactus' file, memo 28 December 1946.

39   Rubidge Diary, 6 May 1911.

40   Rubidge Diary, 2 September 1946.

41   Rubidge files, 'Clearing Irrigation Dams' file, cutting of article in *Graaff-Reinet Advertiser*, 11 December 1935 by Sidney Rubidge under pseudonym, 'The Roamer'.

42   Rubidge Diary, 29 October 1938.

43   Rubidge Diary, 2 September 1938.

44   It is difficult to report cattle numbers without making reference to the major cattle diseases that decimated herds in 1897 and 1912-1915. In 1899, two years after Rinderpest, 740,000 cattle were recorded at the Cape but in 1891, before the disease, the census recorded 1.4 million. The latter figure is more indicative of the average between 1891 and 1911.

45   Rubidge files, 'Spineless cactus' file, Sidney Rubidge to W.J.J. van Heerden, 12 September 1946.

46   Rubidge Diary, 3 September 1946. Not all of the sheep necessarily died. At one point in 1947, there were only 870 sheep on the farm, but others were sent away to hired grazing.

CHAPTER 5

1   W. Beinart, *Twentieth-Century South Africa* (Oxford University Press, Oxford, 2001), Chapter 5.

2   P. Palladino, *Entomology, Ecology and Agriculture: the Making of Scientific Careers in North America 1885-1985* (Harwood Academic, Amsterdam, 1996).

3   *Journal of the Entomological Society of Southern Africa*, 48, 2 (1985), pp. 345-6: Obituary, Theunis Johannes Naude (1897-1983).

4   Karen Brown, 'Political Entomology: the Insectile Challenge to Agricultural Development in the Cape Colony, 1895-1910', *JSAS*, 29, 2 (2003), pp. 529-49.

5   *Agricultural Journal of the Cape of Good Hope*, I, 15, 11.10.1888; A.8-1906, 41.

6   M.O. Brutsch and H.G. Zimmermann, 'Control and Utilization of Wild Opuntias' in G. Barbera, P. Inglese and E. Pimienta-Barrios, *Agro-ecology, cultivation and uses of cactus pear* (FAO, Rome, 1995); Plant Production and Protection Paper, 132, pp. 155-66; Greenfield, *A Perfect Red*.

7   *Queensland Prickly Pear Travelling Commission* (Government Printer, Brisbane, 1914).

8   C.P. Lounsbury, 'Plant Killing Insects: The Indian Cochineal', *Agricultural Journal of the Union of South Africa*, I, 5, (May 1915), p. 540.

9   Ernest Warren, 'The Prickly Pear Pest', *Agricultural Journal*, VII, 3, (March 1914), pp. 387-91;
        Lounsbury, 'Plant Killing Insects'.
10   National Archives, Pretoria (PTA), Department of Agriculture paper (LDB) Box 1711 File
        R2846, vol.1, Claude Fuller, Division of Entomology to Sec. Ag, 5.2.1921.
11   Pettey, 'Biological Control of Prickly Pears', p. 3.
12   Alfred C. Harmsworth, Norval's Pont, 'The Prickly Pear Pest', *Agricultural Journal,* VIII,
        1 (July 1914), p. 114.
13   PTA LDB 1711, R2846, vol. 1, I.P. van Heerden to General Kemp, Minister of Agriculture,
        21.11.1925. van Heerden was a former Minister of Agriculture.
14   PTA LDB 1711, R2846, vol. 1, Chief Entomologist to Principal, Grootfontein, 5 December
        1924.
15   PTA LDB R1688, Lounsbury, 'Prickly Pears: Utilization of Natural Checks'.
16   PTA LDB 1711, R2846, vol. 1, R.W.E. Tucker to Sec. Ag., 12 June 1925.
17   PTA LDB 1711, R2846, vol. 1, Sec. Ag. to Senior Entomologist,
        19 May 1925.
18   PTA LDB 1711, R2846, vol. 1, Chief Entomologist to Sec. Ag., 22 August 1925.
19   Brutsch and Zimmermann, 'Control and Utilization of Wild Opuntias'.
20   PTA LDB 1260, R1688, vol. 1, 7 August 1926; PTA LDB 1711 R2846, Lounsbury to Sec. Ag.,
        16 July 1926.
21   PTA LDB 1711, R2846, vol. 1, Thornton to Sec. Ag., 8 October 1926.
22   PTA LDB 1711, R2846, vol. 1, Thornton to Chief, Division of Botany and Entomology,
        28 February 1927.
23   PTA LDB 1711, R2846, Chief Entomologist to Chief, Division of Botany, 7 March 1927.
24   PTA, Department of Native Affairs (NTS), 8194, 4/345, 'Cactoblastis cactorum for Eradication
        of Prickly Pear', 9 July 1930.
25   PTA NTS, 8194, 4/345. Native Commissioner, Fort Beaufort, to Chief Native Commissioner
        (CNC), King William's Town, 20 February 1930.
26   PTA NTS, 8194, 4/345. Secretary, King William's Town Divisional Council to Major R.
        Ballantine, MLA, Cape Town, 18 February 1921.
27   PTA NTS, 8194, 4/345, Native Commissioner, Peddie to CNC, King William's Town,
        21 November 1929.
28   PTA NTS, 8194, 4/345, Resident Magistrate, Middledrift to CNC, King William's Town,
        17 November 1927.
29   PTA NTS, 8194, 4/345, RM, Fort Beaufort to CNC, 2 June 1930 and CNC to SNA,
        4 June 1930.
30   PTA NTS, 8194 4/345, RM, Fort Beaufort to CNC, 26 September 1932.
31   PTA NTS, 8194 4/345, Jointed Cactus: Records of Conference in Grahamstown,
        6 December 1929.
32   Dr S. Schonland, 'The Jointed Cactus', *Journal of the Department of Agriculture*, IX,
        (September 1924), pp. 216-25.
33   Farieda Khan, 'Rewriting South Africa's Conservation History – the Role of the Native
        Farmers Association', *JSAS*, 20, 4 (1994), pp. 499-516.
34   Interview, Nduwe Dwanya (b.1926), and others interviewed, Thornpark (sub-village of
        Annshaw), Middledrift, 15 August 2009.
35   C.R. van der Merwe, 'The Eradication of the Cactus Pest', *Farming in South Africa*, V,
        49 (1930), p. 37.

36   National Archives, Pretoria, Department of Agriculture, Division of Entomology, PTA CEN
      947, SF15/2, Prickly pear survey, responses to circular, 13 February 1931.

37   PTA LDB 1711, R2846, vol.II, F.W. Pettey to Chief: Division of Plant Industry, 4 August 1932,
      'Report of Tour of Inspection of Jointed Cactus and Prickly Pear Areas in the Cape Province
      Eastern Districts, June 5-19, 1932'.

38   Pettey, *Biological Control*, p. 8.

39   PTA CEN 1004, 65/1, vol. II, responses to 1931 survey.

40   PTA LDB 1711, R2846, vol. II, Pettey, 'Report of Tour of Inspection', p. 7, Albany district.

41   To our knowledge, there are no systematic studies of farm sizes during the first few decades
      of the twentieth century.

42   PTA LDB 1711, R2846, vol. 1, Editor, *Midland News*, Cradock to Sec. Ag., 23 January 1931.

43   PTA LDB 1711, R2846, vol. II, Pettey to Chief: Division of Plant Industry, 4 July 1932.

44   PTA LDB 1711, R2846, vol. II, Pettey, 'Report of Tour of Inspection', p. 8.

45   PTA LDB 1711, R2846, vol. 1, Minister of Agriculture to Minister of Lands, 19 June 1930.

46   PTA LDB 1711, R2846, vol. II, J.A. Engelbrecht, Worcester, to Minister of Agriculture,
      21 December 1931.

47   PTA NTS 8194, 4/345, Cutting from *Farmers' Weekly*, 20 August 1930, 'Cape Wants
      Cactoblasitis'.

48   PTA LDB 1711, R2846, vol. II, Willowmore Farmers Union to Minister of Agriculture,
      24 October 1932.

49   PTA LDB 1712, R2846 vol. III, C. Steyn, MP for Willowmore, to Sec. Ag, 15 September 1933.

50   PTA LDB 1712, R2846 vol. III, Cutting from *Farmers' Weekly*, no date, 1933.

51   Eve Palmer, *The Plains of the Camdeboo* (Fontana, London, 1974), p. 266.

52   PTA LDB 1711, R2846, vol. II, Thornton to Sec. Ag., 17 November 1931 and 9 December
      1931.

53   PTA NTS, 8194, 4/345, P. Germond to Thornton, 24 August 1931.

54   Pettey, 'Report of Tour'.

55   PTA LDB 1263, R1688, vol. VIII, cutting from *Farmers' Weekly*, 1 October 1947.

56   PTA LDB 1711, R2846, vol. 1, telegram Williams to Department of Agriculture, 22 June 1931.

57   PTA LDB 1711, R2846, R.J. Tillyard, 'Memorandum re Introduction of Insect Enemies of
      Prickly Pear into South Africa', 19 July 1931.

58   Karen Middleton, 'Who Killed "Malagasy Cactus"? Science, Environment and Colonialism in
      Southern Madagascar (1924-1930)', *JSAS*, 25, 2 (1999), pp. 215-248.

59   PTA LDB 1711, R2846, vol. 1, Secretary of Agriculture to Editor, *Eastern Province Herald*, Port
      Elizabeth, 8 August 1930.

60   PTA LDB 1711, R2846, vol. II, Report by F.W. Pettey in Chief Entomologist to Chief Division
      of Plant Industry, 24 November 1932.

61   PTA LDB 1711, R2846, vol. II, T. J. Naude to Pole-Evans, 23 January 1933, 30 January 1933
      and 1 February 1933.

62   PTA LDB 1711, R2846, vol. III, Pettey to Pole-Evans, 15 May 1934.

63   PTA LDB 1711, R2846, vol. III, Chief Entomologist to Chief Division of Plant Industries,
      15 March 1935.

64   PTA LDB 1712, R2846, vol. IV, Asst. Chief, Plant Industry memo, 7 June 1935.

65   PTA CEN 1004, 65/2, Pettey to Chief Entomologist, 10 September 1934.

66   PTA LDB 1712, R2846, vol. IV, to Asst. Chief to Chief Division of Plant Industry, 7 June 1935.

67   PTA CEN 1004, 65/2, Pettey to E. du Toit, 15 April 1935.

68   PTA LDB 1712, R2846, vol. IV, T.J. Naude to Chief Division of Plant Industry, 23 March 1936.

69   PTA CEN 1004, 65/2, E. du Toit, Officer Controlling Jointed Cactus Eradication to Sec. Ag. and Forestry, 24 December 1936.

70   Jeff Peires, 'The Legend of Fenner-Solomon' in Belinda Bozzoli (ed.), *Class, Community and Conflict: South African Perspectives* (Ravan Press, Johannesburg, 1987), pp. 65-92.

71   PTA LDB 1260, R1688, vol. III, Chief, Division of Entomology to Chief, Division of Soil and Veld Conservation, 4 September 1940 enclosing J.W. Geyer, 'Report on the Progress of *Dactylopius Confusus* as a Biological Control Method of Jointed Cactus, *Opuntia Aurantiaca*'.

72   PTA CEN 1004, SF65/2, vol. I, 26 July 1937.

73   PTA LDB 1712, R2846, vol. IV, Pettey to Chief, Division of Plant Industry, 15 November 1935.

74   P.R. Viljoen, 'Annual Report of the Secretary for Agriculture and Forestry for the Year ended 31 August 1937', *Farming in South Africa*, (December 1937), p. 484.

75   PTA LDB 1713, R2846, vol. VI, cutting 25 June 1937.

76   PTA LDB 1713, R2846, Naude to Sec. Ag., 21 January 1938.

77   PTA LDB 1712, R2846, vol. IV, Pettey to Chief, DPI, 19.8.1935 and E. du Toit to Chief, DPI, August, 1935.

78   L.B. Ripley, 'Nosema Disease of Cactoblastis', *Farming in South Africa*, (August,1937), p. 325.

79   Pettey, 'Biological Control', p. 27.

80   Pettey, 'Biological Control', p. 32.

81   PTA CEN 1004, 65/2, E. du Toit to Chief, Division of Soil and Veld Conservation, 11 September 1940; PTA LDB 1260, R1688, vol. III, J.C. Ross, Chief: Division of Soil and Veld Conservation to Sec. Ag. and Forestry, 31 August 1940; PTA LDB 1260, R1688, Geyer, 'Report on the Progress of *Dactylopius Confusus*'.

82   Pettey, 'Biological Control', p. 69.

83   Pettey, 'Biological Control', p. 105.

84   PTA LDB 1261, R1688, vol. III, T.J. Naude, Chief, Division of Entomology to P.R. Viljoen, Sec. Ag. and For., 1 August 1941, 'Biological Control of Prickly Pear'.

85   Pettey, 'Biological Control', p. 115.

86   PTA LDB 1261, R1688, vol. V, E. du Toit to Chief, Division of Soil and Veld Conservation, 23 May 1944.

87   R. du Toit, Professional Officer (Weed Control), Division of Soil and Veld Conservation, 'The Spread of Prickly Pear in the Union', *Farming in South Africa*, (May 1942), pp. 300-4.

88   PTA LDB 1260, R1688, Pettey to Chief, Division of Entomology, 1 August 1941.

89   R. du Toit, 'The Spread of Prickly Pear in the Union'.

90   PTA LDB 1260, R1688, vol. III, J.S. Taylor, Entomologist, Graaff-Reinet to Chief, Division of Entomology, 19 September 1940 and following correspondence.

91   PTA LDB 1260, R1688, vol. III, Ross to Sec. Ag., 6 November 1940 and following correspondence.

92   PTA LDB 1260, R1688, vol. III, Ross to Sec. Ag., 13 May 1941.

93   PTA LDB 1261, R1688, vol. IV, Naude to Sec. Ag., 3 September 1942; PTA LDB 1261, R1688, vol. IV, Sec. Ag. to Minister, 8 January 1943.

94   PTA LDB 1261, R1688, vol. V, Chief Division of Soil and Veld Conservation to Sec. Ag., 26 January 1944.

95   PTA LDB 1261, R1688, vol. IV, Sec. Ag. to Secretary of Finance, 6 March 1943.

96 PTA LDB 1261, R1688, vol. IV, Chief, Division of Soil and Veld Conservation to Sec. Ag., 28 July 1943.
97 PTA LDB 1261, R1688, vol. V, Chief Division of Soil and Veld Conservation to Sec. Ag., 26 January 1944.
98 PTA LDB 1261, R1688, vol. V, Report by E. du Toit in Ross to Sec. Ag., 6 April 1944.
99 PTA LDB 1261, R1688, vol. V, E. du Toit to Sec. Ag., 31 March 1944.
100 PTA LDB 1261, R1688, vol. V, E. du Toit to Sec. Ag., 31 March 1944.
101 PTA LDB 1261, R1688, vol. IV, Geyer to Chief Entomologist, 19 April 1943.
102 PTA LDB 1260, R1688, Sec. Ag. to P.J. Theron MP, 11 March 1941.
103 PTA LDB 1260, R1688, memo by J.S. Taylor, September 1940.
104 Photographs from Helmuth Zimmermann.
105 PTA LDB 1261, R1688, vol. V, S.H. Elliot, Grootdam, Hofmeyr to Minister of Agriculture.
106 PTA LDB 1262, R1688, vol. VI, E. du Toit to Ross in Ross to Sec. Ag., 7 July 1945.
107 Pettey, 'Biological Control'; D.P. Annecke and V.C. Moran, 'Critical Reviews of Biological Pest Control in South Africa: 2. The Prickly Pear, *Opuntia ficus-indica* (L.) Miller', *Journal of the Entomological Society of South Africa*, 41, 2 (1978), pp. 161-88.
108 Pettey, 'Biological Control', p. 160.
109 PTA LDB 1264, R1688, vol. V, memorandum by R. du Toit, 1953.
110 Lance van Sittert, 'Making the Cape Floral Kingdom: the Discovery and Defence of Indigenous Flora at the Cape *ca*. 1890-1939', *Landscape Research*, 28, 1 (2003), pp. 113-29; Simon Pooley, 'Pressed Flowers: Notions of Indigenous and Alien Vegetation in South Africa's Western Cape, c.1902-1945', forthcoming, *JSAS*, 2010.

CHAPTER 6

1   William Beinart and Rosalie Kingwill, 'Eastern Cape Land Reform Pilot Project Pre-Planning Report', (Working Paper no. 25, Land and Agriculture Policy Centre, Johannesburg and Border Rural Committee, East London, 1995).
2   Luvuyo Wotshela, 'Homeland Consolidation, Resettlement and Local Politics in the Border and Ciskei Region of the Eastern Cape, South Africa, 1960 to 1996', unpublished D.Phil. thesis, University of Oxford (2001).
3   Interview, Mrs Fezeka Mpendukana, Kamastone, 24 June 2003, 21 November 2008.
4   Interview, Fezeka Mpendukana.
5   Interview, Mrs N. Xhaphe and Mrs N. Joko, Ngwenya village, Middledrift, 28 and 29 January 2003.
6   H.G. Zimmermann, V.C. Moran and J.H. Hoffman, 'Insect Herbivores as Determinants of the Present Distribution and Abundance of Invasive Cacti in South Africa' in Macdonald *et al.* (eds.), *Biological Invasions*, pp. 269-74.
7   F.W. Pettey, 'The Biological Control of Prickly Pears in South Africa', *Union of South Africa, Department of Agriculture and Forestry, Scientific Bulletin*, 271 (Government Printer, Pretoria, 1948); D.P. Annecke and V.C. Moran, 'Critical reviews of biological pest control in South Africa: 2. The Prickly Pear, *Opuntia ficus-indica* (L.) Miller', *Journal of the Entomological Society of South Africa*, 41, 2 (1978), pp. 161-88.
8   Zimmermann, Moran and Hoffman, 'Insect Herbivores'.
9   Brutsch and Zimmermann, 'The Prickly Pear'.
10 M. Henderson, D.M.C. Fourie, M.J. Wells and L. Henderson, *Declared Weeds and Alien Invader Plants in South Africa* (Department of Agriculture and Water Supply, Pretoria, 1987).

11 H.G. Zimmermann and V.C. Moran, 'Ecology and Management of Cactus Weeds in South Africa', *South African Journal of Science*, 78 (1982), pp. 314-20.

12 Marc O. Brutsch and Helmuth G. Zimmermann, 'The Prickly Pear (Opuntia Ficus-Indica [Cactaceae]) in South Africa: Utilization of the Naturalized Weed, and of the Cultivated Plant', *Economic Botany*, 47, 2 (1993), pp. 154-62.

13 Interview, N. Muwezi and M. Mtunzi, Mhlambiso village, Amatola basin, Middledrift, 12 November 2002.

14 D. McGarry, C.M. Shackleton, S. Fourie, J. Gambiza, S.E. Shackleton, C.F. Fabricius, 'A Rapid Assessment of the Effects of Invasive Species on Human Livelihoods, Especially of the Rural Poor', unpublished report, Department of Environmental Science, Rhodes University (June, 2005), p. 12.

15 Interview, R. Sokhaba, 27 October 2001, Kamastone, Hewu.

16 Interview, A.D. Sishuba, Lower Hukuwa, Hewu.

17 Interview, T. Jones, The Grange, Hankey South, 13 April 2002.

18 Interview, Muwezi and Mtunzi.

19 Henderson, *et al.*, *Declared Weeds and Alien Invader Plants in South Africa*, pp. 74, 80.

20 Interview, Sokhaba.

21 Interview, Alexander Mpendukana, Kamastone, 7 October 2001; interview, S.M. Matshoba, Bulhoek, 18 October 2001.

22 Interview, Gerhard de Kock, Middelburg, 3 April 2006.

23 Nobel, *Remarkable Agaves and Cacti*, p. 66.

24 Correspondence, Helmuth Zimmermann to Dave Richardson and William Beinart, 15 October 2002.

25 Interview, Welsh Mxiki, former extension officer in the Shiloh Irrigation Scheme, Whittlesea, 23 April 2002.

26 Nobel, *Remarkable Agaves and Cacti*; for a recent survey in North Africa, A. Nefzaoui and H. Ben Salem, 'Opuntiae: A Strategic Fodder and Efficient Tool to Combat Desertification in the Wana Region', published on the Web, Institut National de la Recherche Agronomique de Tunisie, n.d.

27 For a survey of projects Paul Kerkhof, *Agroforestry in Africa: A Survey of Project Experience* (Panos, London, 1990). *Calliandra calothyrsus*, which has met with some success in Kenya, also produces fodder.

28 Interview, Muwezi and Mtunzi.

29 Interview, Sishuba.

30 Interview, Matshoba.

31 Interview, Muwezi and Mtunzi.

32 Diana Wylie, *Starving on a Full Stomach: Hunger and the Triumph of Cultural Racism in Modern South Africa* (University of Virginia Press, Charlottesville, 2001); Trudi Thomas, *Their Doctor Speaks: Aspects of African Social Life in Part of the Ciskei* (Mary Wheeldon, Cape Town, 1973).

33 Robin Palmer, 'Rural Adaptations in the Eastern Cape, South Africa' presented at conference on Gender, Households and Environmental Changes, ISAS, Roma, National University of Lesotho, 1997.

34 Douglas Hey, *A Nature Conservationist Looks Back* (Cape Nature Conservation, Cape Town, 1995), pp. 144-5.

35 Palmer, 'Rural Adaptations'.

36   *ANC Daily News Briefing*, 13 October 1995, quoting Vuyelwa Vika, Development News Agency, East London, 12 October 1995.

37   McGarry, *et al.*,'A Rapid Assessment of the Effects of Invasive Species', p. 12.

38   Interview, M. Gege, Middledrift extension officer, 8 October 2002.

39   Interview, Sishuba.

40   McGarry, *et al.*,'A Rapid Assessment of the Effects of Invasive Species', p. 15.

41   Interview, Xhaphe and Joko.

42   Interview, Mxiki.

43   Interview, Mxiki.

44   Interview, Nofezile Gcweka, Haytor (Sibonile), Zweledinga, November 2001.

45   Interview, Christine Malan, Uitenhage, 26 February 2005.

46   G.F. Malan, *Die Brullende Leeu Getem: Die Geskiedenis van die Mense en die Ontwikkeling van Besproeingsboerdery in die Gamtoosvallei* (Private publication, Patensie, 1970).

47   Interview, D. Schellingerhout, Thorndale farm, Hankey, 1 May 2002.

48   Interview, Danie Malan, Tierhok farm, Patensie, 1 March 2005.

49   Interview, Mrs N. Ferreira, Phillipsville, Hankey, 1 May 2002.

50   Interview, Muwezi and Mtunzi.

51   M.T. Hoffman and R.M. Cowling, 'Vegetation Change in the Semi-arid Eastern Karoo over the Last 200 Years: An Expanding Karoo – Fact or Fiction?', *South African Journal of Science*, 86 (1990), pp. 286-94; A.R. Palmer, C.G. Hobson and M.T. Hoffman, 'Vegetation Change in a Semi-arid Succulent Dwarf Shrubland in the Eastern Cape, South Africa', *South African Journal of Science*, 86 (1990), pp. 392-5; Beinart, *Rise of Conservation*.

52   Nobel, *Remarkable Agaves and Cacti*.

53   A.P. Dold and M.L. Cocks, 'The Medicinal Use of Some Weeds, Problem and Alien Plants in the Grahamstown and Peddie Districts of the Eastern Cape, South Africa', *South African Journal of Science*, 96 (2000), pp. 467-73.

54   Interview, N. Ngudle, Mceula, Zulukama, 23 November 2001.

55   Interview, Daphne le Roux, Spes Bona farm, Rooivlakte, Hankey West, 13 April 2002.

56   Interview, Ngudle.

57   Interview, Danie Malan; Interview Alta Malan, Patensie, 1 March 2005.

58   Interview, Christine Malan.

59   O. Kleiner, Z. Cohen and A.J.Mares, 'Low Colonic Obstruction Due to *Opuntia ficus-indica* seeds: the aftermath of enjoying delicious cactus fruits', *Acta Paediatr*, 91, 5 (2002), pp. 606-7.

60   Interview, Ferguson Miles, Roslin, Cathcart, 24 June 2002.

61   Interview, le Roux.

62   Interview, Zimmermann, 17 March 2008.

63   Interview, Christine Malan.

64   Interview, Matshoba.

65   Interview, S. Kata, member of the Shiloh Farmers Association, Lower Shiloh, 14 June 2002.

66   Tony Dold and Michelle Cocks, '*Turksvy stroop* – a successful home industry in the Eastern Cape', unpublished paper.

67   Interview, Fezeka Mpendukana.

68   Interview, Alta Malan.

69   Interview, A. Mpendukana.

70   Interview, Nofezile Gcweka, Haytor (Sibonile), Zweledinga, November 2001.

71   Interview, August Wenaar and Isak Abels, Grootfontein, September 2003.

72   Palmer, 'Rural Adaptations'.

73   Henderson *et al.*, *Declared Weeds*, 27; T. Olckers, 'Introduction' in T. Olckers and M.P. Hill, *Biological Control of Weeds in South Africa (1990-1998)*, The Entomological Society of South Africa, African Entomology Memoir no. 1 (Pretoria, 1999), p. 6. This has other common names, and is sometimes confused with euphorbia (*isihlehle*). Informants suggest that it can be used for fodder in an emergency, but its sharp spines require very thorough burning and treatment before it is fed to animals.

74   Interview, A. Mpendukana.

75   Interview, M. Mrubatha, Bulhoek, Hewu, 26 October 2001.

76   Interview, J. Ngoma, former Ciskei agricultural officer, Whittlesea, 22 April 2002.

77   Monica Hunter, *Reaction to Conquest: The Effects of Contact with Europeans on the Pondo of South Africa* (Oxford University Press, London, 1964), p. 514, first published 1936.

78   Godfrey and Monica Hunter papers, University of Cape Town manuscripts, BC880, additions, box 3/3, Farms, notes on de Klerk farm.

79   Interview, Matshoba.

80   Interview, Fezeka Mpendukana.

81   Interview, Fezeka Mpendukana.

82   Interview, Matshoba.

83   Interview, Kata.

84   Palmer, 'Rural Adaptations'.

85   No author, *Ouma en Oupa se Boererate* (Tafelberg, Cape Town, 1962), p. 80.

86   Interview, Fezeka Mpendukana.

87   Interview, A. Mpendukana.

88   Dold and Cocks, 'Medicinal Use of Some Weeds'.

89   Interview, Sokhaba.

90   Interview, Ngudle.

91   www.proactol.com/ClinicalStudy 2006.

92   Interview, Riena du Preez, Wisteria farm, Patensie, 1 March 2005.

93   Interview, Mr. Funde, Mgwali, 2004.

94   Interview, Mxiki.

95   Interview, Ferreira.

96   Interview, le Roux.

97   Interview, Miles.

98   Interview, Miles.

99   Interview, Xhaphe and Joko.

CHAPTER 7

1   Interviews, Gerhard de Kock, Middelburg, 31 March 2006 and 3 April 2006.

2   M.O. Brutsch, 'The Role of the Prickly Pear in Less Developed Agriculture', *Ciskei Journal of Agriculture,* 7 (1988), pp. 2-8, quoting Monjauze and Le Houerou.

3   Interview, de Kock.

4   William Beinart, Karen Brown and Daniel Gilfoyle, 'Experts and Expertise in Colonial Africa Reconsidered: Science and the Interpenetration of Knowledge', *African Affairs*, 108, 432 (2009), pp. 413-33.

5   Interview, P.W. Roux, Middelburg, September 2003.

6   Interview, August Wenaar and Isak Abels, Grootfontein, September 2003.

7   Interview, Roux.

8   Interview, Roux.

9   For example, J. Aucamp, 'Spineless Cactus as a Provision against Drought', *Farming in South
        Africa*, January 1970; I. Terblanche, 'Spineless Cactus – the Inexpensive Drought Feed',
        Farming in South Africa, February 1970.

10   Gerhard de Kock, 'Turksvy kan doring van 'n inkomste lever', *Landbouweekblad*, 17 (1974),
        pp. 18-21.

11   Gerhard de Kock, 'Lucerne, King of the Fodder Crops', *Karoo Agriculture*, 1 (1978), pp. 29-31.
        Only 6 of his publications were on prickly pear.

12   Interview, de Kock.

13   Winnie Louw, *Prickly Pear: Don't Abuse It, Use It* (*Turksvy: Die Doring in Ons Vlees*), (Personal
        Publication, Despatch, 1989), printed in Port Elizabeth.

14   Anneke and Moran, 'The Jointed Cactus'.

15   D.P. Annecke, W.A. Burger and H. Coetzee, 'Pest Status of *Cactoblastis cactorum* (Berg)
        (Lepidoptera: Phycitidae) and *Dactolopius opuntiae* (Cockerell) (Coccoidea: Dactylopiidae) in
        Spineless Opuntia plantations in South Africa', *Journal of the Entomological Society of South Africa*,
        39 (1976).

16   Marc O. Brutsch and Helmuth G. Zimmermann, 'The Prickly Pear (Opuntia Ficus-Indica
        [Cactaceae]) in South Africa: Utilization of the Naturalized Weed, and of the Cultivated
        Plant', *Economic Botany*, 47, 2 (1993), p. 158.

17   Anneke and Moran, 'The Jointed Cactus', p. 316.

18   Interview, Helmuth Zimmermann, Rietondale Research Station, 17 March 2008.

19   Interview, Zimmermann.

20   Anneke and Moran, 'The Jointed Cactus', p. 310.

21   Interview, Zimmermann.

22   H.G. Zimmermann, 'Herbicidal Control in Relation to Distribution of *Opuntia Aurantiaca*
        Lindley and Effects on Cochineal Populations', *Weed Research*, 19 (1979), pp. 89-93. Anneke
        and Moran, 'The Jointed Cactus', noted that the Department had not taken into account the
        destructive effects of the particular weed-killers used when choosing them.

23   Zimmermann, 'Herbicidal Control', p. 93.

24   Annecke and Moran, 'Biological Control of Prickly Pear', p. 185.

25   Annecke and Moran, 'Biological Control of Prickly Pear', p. 185.

26   H.G. Zimmermann and Hildegard Zimmermann, 'A Novel Use of a Declared Weed: Young
        Prickly Pear Leaves for Human Consumption', pamphlet published by the Plant Protection
        Research Institute, Uitenhage, Weeds B. 1 February 1987, reprinted from *Farming in South
        Africa*, 1987, reprinted 1989.

27   Beinart, *Rise of Conservation*, Chapter 11; P.W. Roux and M. Vorster, 'Vegetation Change in
        the Karoo', *Proceedings of the Grassland Society of Southern Africa*, 18 (1983), pp. 25-9; M.T.
        Hoffman and R. Cowling, 'Vegetation Change in the Semi-arid Eastern Karoo over the Last
        200 Years – Fact or Fiction', *South African Journal of Science*, 86 (1990), pp. 392-5.

28   Interview, Roux.

29   Interview, Zimmermann.

30   Zimmermann and Zimmermann, 'A Novel Use of a Declared Weed'.

31   Zimmermann and Zimmermann, 'A Novel Use of a Declared Weed'

32   Marc O. Brutsch and Helmuth G. Zimmermann, 'The Prickly Pear (Opuntia Ficus-Indica [Cactaceae]) in South Africa: Utilization of the Naturalized Weed, and of the Cultivated Plant', *Economic Botany*, 47, 2 (1993), pp 154-62.

33   Interview, Zimmermann.

34   Greenfield, *A Perfect Red*.

35   Peter Wiemeler, 'Nutzungsmoglichkeiten von *Opuntia ficus-indica* [L.] MILLER in Raum Uitenhage/Sudafrika', Diplomaarbeit, Giessen, 1988, English summary (from Helmuth Zimmermann).

36   Interview, Zimmermann.

37   Wiemeler, 'Nutzungsmoglichkeiten von *Opuntia ficus-indica*', p. 167.

38   M.O. Brutsch, 'The Prickly Pear (*Opuntia Ficus-indica*) as a Potential Fruit Crop for the Drier Regions of the Ciskei', *Crop Production*, VIII (1979), pp. 131-7.

39   Brutsch, 'The Prickly Pear'.

40   Brutsch, 'The Prickly Pear', p. 136.

41   Brutsch, 'The Prickly Pear', p. 136.

42   Brutsch, personal communication.

43   M.O. Brutsch and M.B. Scott, 'Extending the Fruiting Season of Spineless Prickly Pear (*Opuntia ficus-indica*)', *Journal of the South African Horticulture Society*, 1, 2 (1991), pp. 73-6.

44   Interview, Zimmermann.

45   Brutsch and Zimmermann, 'Prickly Pear', p. 160.

46   M.O. Brutsch and H.G. Zimmermann, 'Control and Utilization of Wild Opuntias' in G. Barbera, P. Inglese and E. Pimienta-Barrios, *Agro-ecology, cultivation and uses of cactus pear* (FAO, Rome, 1995) Plant Production and Protection Paper, 132, pp. 155-66.

47   Interview, Ngoma.

48   Wotshela, 'Homeland Consolidation'; Platzky and Walker, *The Surplus People*.

49   I.P. van Heerden, 'The Establishment of Drought Resistant Fodder Crops in Ciskei', *Ciskei Agricultural Journal*, 6, 1st quarter (1987), pp. 15-7.

50   Interview Mike Colman, Fort Beaufort, 2 April 2006.

51   Brutsch and Zimmermann, 'Prickly Pear'.

52   Interview, Coleman.

53   Interview, J. Ngoma, Whittlesea, 22 April 2002.

54   Interview, Ngoma.

55   Interview, Coleman.

56   Interview, Ngoma.

57   Interview, Sishuba.

58   Interview, Matshoba.

59   Interview, Ngudle.

60   Bhisho, Eastern Cape Department of Agriculture, 8th floor, Land Use Planning unit back files, 6/8/3, R. Norman to N.S. Majiza, joint head of Fort Cox.

61   Ibid., CEAP Committee minutes, 19 November 1987.

62   Ibid., 11 December 1990.

63   Cecil Manona, 'The Collapse of the "Tribal Authority" system and the Rise of Civic Associations' in C. de Wet and M. Whisson (eds.), *From Reserve to Region: Apartheid and Social Change in the Keiskammahoek District of (former) Ciskei: 1950-1990* (Occasional Paper no. 35,

ISER, Rhodes University, Grahamstown, 1997), pp. 49-68.

64   Interview, Coleman and observation, 1994.

65   Interview, Gege.

66   Brutsch, 'The Role of the Prickly Pear in Less Developed Agriculture'.

67   Brutsch and Zimmermann, 'The Prickly Pear: Utilization of the Naturalized Weed', p. 159.

68   Interview, Marco Brutsch and questionnaires from 1996.

69   Interview questionnaire: Marco Brutsch with Mavis Fulani, 7 March 1996.

70   Interview questionnaire: Marco Brutsch with Nozukile Mbalashwa, 7 March 1996.

71   A.P. Mnkeni and M.O. Brutsch, 'A Simple Solar Drier and Fruit-processing Procedure for
      Producing an Edible, Dried Product of High Quality from the Peel of *Opuntia ficus-indica* fruit
      in the Eastern Cape Province, South Africa', paper presented at Fourth International Congress
      on Cactus Pear and Cochineal, Tunisia, 22-28 October 2000; A.P. Mnkeni, P. Soundy and
      M.O. Brutsch, *Solar Drying of Fruit and Vegetables*, (Department of Agriculture, Pretoria, 2001).

72   Interview, Strydom Schoonraad, Grootfontein, September 2003.

73   Interview, August Wenaar and Isak Abels, Grootfontein, September 2003.

74   Discussion, Marina Jordaan, Bloemfontein, 29 March 2006.

CHAPTER 8

1   Esther van Heerden, 'Liminality, Transformation and *Communitas*: Afrikaans Identities as
      Viewed through the Lens of South African Arts Festivals, 1995-2006', unpublished PhD,
      University of Stellenbosch (2009).

2   Danelle van Zyl, '"O Boereplaas, Geboortegrond?": Afrikaner Nostalgia and the
      Romanticisation of the Platteland in post-1994 South Africa', *South African Journal of Cultural
      History*, 22, 2 (2008), pp. 126-48.

3   Grootfontein, G. de Kock files.

4   *Rooi Rose*, 18 February 1987 – cutting in G. de Kock files, Grootfontein.

5   Otto Terblanche (ed.), *Uitenhage 200, 1804-2004: The Garden Town* (Uitenhage Bicentenary
      Committee, 2004); *The Lions Souvenir Book of Uitenhage* (Lions International Club, Uitenhage,
      1973)

6   Interview, Jean van Onselen, 26 February 2006.

7   Terblanche (ed.), *Uitenhage 200*, p. 223.

8   Interview Christine Malan, Uitenhage, 26 February 2005.

9   *UD News*, 26 February 1987 (the local newspaper serving Uitenhage and Despatch).

10   Interview, Malan.

11   *UD News*, 26 February 1987.

12   Interview, Malan.

13   Winnie Louw, *Prickly Pear: Don't Abuse It, Use It*.

14   *UD News*, 4 February 1988; Interview, J. Kleynhans, 25 February 2005.

15   Numbers taken from *UD News* and interviews.

16   *Sunday Times*, February 2000 on web.

17   Van Heerden, 'Liminality'.

18   Interview, Hester Blumenthal, Uitenhage, 26 February 2005.

19   Inteview, Des, Uitenhage, 26 March 2005.

20   Terblanche (ed.), *Uitenhage 200*.

21   Interview, Vasie de Kock, 25 and 26 February 2005.

22   Interview, Jan Blumenthal and others, 25 February 2005.

23   Spanish settlers in the sixteenth century used the indigenous pulque beer, made from agave, as the basis for tequila spirit. Mezcal is made from other types of agave.

24   Interview, Sannie Carelse, 25 February 2005, 2 March 2005.

25   Interview, Rosie Rula, 26 Februaury 2006.

26   International Cactus Pear Conference, (ICPC), Bloemfontein, presentation, J. Parau, 30 March 2006.

27   ICPC, Speech, C. Mondragon-Jacobo, 29 March 2006.

28   ICPC, Bloemfontein, discussion with Bill Stiekema, 30 March 2006.

29   ICPC, Bloemfontein, 30 March 2006.

30   ICPC, Bloemfontein, presentation, W. Swart, 29 March 2006.

31   ICPC, Bloemfontein, discussion with Douglas Reed.

32   Johannes Petrus Potgieter, 'The Influence of Environmental Factors on Spineless Cactus Pear (Opuntia spp.) Fruit Yield in Limpopo Province, South Africa', unpublished MSc., University of the Free State (2007), available on the web.

33   ICPC, Bloemfontein, presentation, J. Potgieter, 29 March 2006.

34   Research subsequently completed as Barbara Keitumetse Mashope, 'Characterisation of Cactus Pear Germplasm in South Africa', unpublished PhD. University of the Free State (2007), available on the web.

35   ICPC, Bloemfontein, presentation, A. Alemseged, 30 March 2006.

36   L. Habtu and M. Fetene, 'Cactus in Southern Tigray: Current Status, Utilization, and Threat'; the spiny cactus has become invasive.

37   ICPC, Bloemfontein, presentation, A. Alemseged.

38   ICPC, Bloemfontein, presentation, H. Zimmermann; interview, Zimmermann, 17 March 2008.

39   H. Zimmermann and H. Klein, 'The Use of Biological Control Agents for the Control of Plant Invaders and the Importance of Partnerships', paper on web (no date, 1998?)

40   International Cactus Pear Conference, Bloemfontein, presentation, H. Zimmermann, 30 March 2006.

41   H.G. Zimmermann, V.C. Moran and J.H. Hoffmann, 'The renowned cactus moth, Cactoblastis cactorum (Lepidoptera: Pyralidae): its natural history and threat to native Opuntia floras in Mexico and the United States of America', *Florida Entomologist*, 84, 4 (2001), p. 543; H. Zimmermann, S. Bloem and H. Klein, *Biology, History, Threat, Surveillance and Control of the Cactus Moth, Cactoblastis cactorum* (FAO/IAEA, Austria, 2004).

42   McGarry, *et al*.,'A Rapid Assessment of the Effects of Invasive Species'; Kirby, 'Invasive Alien Plants'.

43   Bernadette le Roux and Marianne Palmer, *Prickly Pears and Pomegranates: Local, Organic and Seasonal Foods from the Plains of the Camdeboo* (Quiver Tree, Cape Town, 2008). The title appears to have been borrowed from an American book published in Phoenix.

CHAPER 9

1   Conversations, Nowinile Ngcengele, Nositile Lungisa and others, 25 March 2006, 1 April 2006, 2 April 2006.

2   Conversation, Nowinile Ngcengele, Bhofolo, 13 May 2009.

3   Republic of South Africa, Conservation of Agricultural Resources Act 43 of 1983, clauses 5, 1a and 1b.

4   Henderson *et al.*, *Declared Weeds*.

5   Visit to Uitenhage Plant Protection Research Institute and Interview, Francois Dorfling, Rietfontien farm, Uitenhage, 4 April 2006.

6   C. Marais, B.W. van Wilgen and D. Stevens, 'The Clearing of Invasive Alien Plants in South Africa: a Preliminary Assessment of Costs and Progress', *South African Journal of Science*, 100, (2004), pp. 97-103; Paddy Woodworth, 'Working for Water in South Africa: Saving the World on a Single Budget', *World Policy Journal*, summer 2006, pp. 31-43.

7   CSIR Environmentek and Institute for Plant Conservation, UCT, *An Assessment of Invasion Potential of Invasive Alien Plant Species in South Africa* (Final Report, Stellenbosch, 2004). Thanks to Ahmed Khan for this multi-authored report which included some of the key specialists on invasive plants.

8   Interview, Guy Preston and Ahmed Khan, Kirstenbosch, Cape Town, 2 April 2009.

9   Interview, Brian van Wilgen, CSIR, Stellenbosch, 2 April 2009.

10   De Wit *et al.*, 'Conflicts of interest in environmental management'; De Neergaard *et al.*, 'Australian wattle species in the Drakensberg'.

11   Interview, Phumla Mzazi-Geja, Queenstown, 18 March 2009.

12   Interview, Gwen Sgwabe, 7 May 2009.

13   Inteview, Ndumiso Nongwe, Grahamstown, 9 May 2009.

14   Pavan Sukhdev, 'Costing the Earth', *Nature* , 462, 277 (2009).

15   Michael E. Soule, 'The Onslaught of Alien Species, and Other Challenges in the Coming Decades', *Conservation Biology*, Vol. 4, No. 3 (1990), pp. 233-9.

16   Cocks, *Wild Resources*, p. 9.

17   J.H. Hoffman, V.C. Moran and D.A. Zeller, 'Evaluation of Cactoblastis cactorum (Lepidoptera: Phycitidae) as a Biological Control Agent of *Opuntia Stricta* (cactaceae) in the Kruger National Park, South Africa', *Biological Control*, 12, 1 (1998), pp. 20-4.

18   Tracy Cumming, 'Conservation Incentives for Private Commercial Farmers in the Thicket Biome, Eastern Cape, South Africa', unpublished MSc thesis, Rhodes University (2007).

19   www.justice.gov.za, Truth and Reconciliation Commission, Amnesty Hearings, Phokeng, 20 May 1996, paragraph 17.

20   News24.com 'Cope is like a prickly pear', 10 January 2009, 18:05 – (SA)

21   Interview, Mxiki.

22   Interview, Garth Cambray, 6 April 2006; Garth Cambray, 'Science has Never Tasted This Good! *IQhilika* – a Product with a Golden Future', *Science in Africa*, 31.5.2004.

INDEX

Printed and bound by CPI Group (UK) Ltd, Croydon, CR0 4YY

09/06/2025

14685834-0001